Practical
File System
Design

with the Be File System

Practical File System Design

with the Be File System

Dominic Giampaolo

Be, Inc.

MK®

MORGAN KAUFMANN PUBLISHERS, INC.
San Francisco, California

Editor   Tim Cox
Director of Production and Manufacturing   Yonie Overton
Assistant Production Manager   Julie Pabst
Editorial Assistant   Sarah Luger
Cover Design   Ross Carron Design
Cover Image   William Thompson/Photonica
Copyeditor   Ken DellaPenta
Proofreader   Jennifer McClain
Text Design   Side by Side Studios
Illustration   Cherie Plumlee
Composition   Ed Sznyter, Babel Press
Indexer   Ty Koontz
Printer   Edwards Brothers

Designations used by companies to distinguish their products are often claimed as trademarks or registered trademarks. In all instances where Morgan Kaufmann Publishers, Inc. is aware of a claim, the product names appear in initial capital or all capital letters. Readers, however, should contact the appropriate companies for more complete information regarding trademarks and registration.

Morgan Kaufmann Publishers, Inc.
Editorial and Sales Office
340 Pine Street, Sixth Floor
San Francisco, CA 94104-3205
USA
Telephone   415/392-2665
Facsimile   415/982-2665
Email   mkp@mkp.com
WWW   http://www.mkp.com
Order toll free   800/745-7323

03   02   01   00   99   5   4   3   2   1

Library of Congress Cataloging-in-Publication Data is available for this book.
ISBN 1-55860-497-9

Contents

Preface

Although many operating system textbooks offer high-level descriptions of file systems, few go into sufficient detail for an implementor, and none go into details about advanced topics such as journaling. I wrote this book to address that lack of information. This book covers the details of file systems, from low-level to high-level, as well as related topics such as the disk cache, the file system interface to the kernel, and the user-level APIs that use the features of the file system. Reading this book should give you a thorough understanding of how a file system works in general, how the Be File System (BFS) works in particular, and the issues involved in designing and implementing a file system.

The Be operating system (BeOS) uses BFS as its native file system. BFS is a modern 64-bit journaled file system. BFS also supports extended file attributes (name/value pairs) and can index the extended attributes, which allows it to offer a query interface for locating files in addition to the normal name-based hierarchical interface. The attribute, indexing, and query features of BFS set it apart from other file systems and make it an interesting example to discuss.

Throughout this book there are discussions of different approaches to solving file system design problems and the benefits and drawbacks of different techniques. These discussions are all based on the problems that arose when implementing BFS. I hope that understanding the problems BFS faced and the changes it underwent will help others avoid mistakes I made, or perhaps spur them on to solve the problems in different or more innovative ways.

Now that I have discussed what this book is about, I will also mention what it is not about. Although there is considerable information about the details of BFS, this book does not contain exhaustive bit-level information about every BFS data structure. I know this will disappoint some people, but it is the difference between a reference manual and a work that is intended to educate and inform.

My only regret about this book is that I would have liked for there to be more information about other file systems and much more extensive performance analyses of a wider variety of file systems. However, just like software, a book has to ship, and it can't stay in development forever.

You do not need to be a file system engineer, a kernel architect, or have a PhD to understand this book. A basic knowledge of the C programming language is assumed but little else. Wherever possible I try to start from first principles to explain the topics involved and build on that knowledge throughout the chapters. You also do not need to be a BeOS developer or even use the BeOS to understand this book. Although familiarity with the BeOS may help, it is not a requirement.

It is my hope that if you would like to improve your knowledge of file systems, learn about how the Be File System works, or implement a file system, you will find this book useful.

Acknowledgments

I'd like to thank everyone that lent a hand during the development of BFS and during the writing of this book. Above all, the BeOS QA team (led by Baron Arnold) is responsible for BFS being where it is today. Thanks, guys! The rest of the folks who helped me out are almost too numerous to mention: my fiancée, Maria, for helping me through many long weekends of writing; Mani Varadarajan, for taking the first crack at making BFS write data to double-indirect blocks; Cyril Meurillon, for being stoic throughout the whole project, as well as for keeping the fsil layer remarkably bug-free; Hiroshi Lockheimer, for keeping me entertained; Mike Mackovitch, for letting me run tests on SGI's machines; the whole BeOS team, for putting up with all those buggy versions of the file system before the first release; Mark Stone, for approaching me about writing this book; the people who make the cool music that gets me through the 24-, 48-, and 72-hour programming sessions; and of course Be, Inc., for taking the chance on such a risky project. Thanks!

1

Introduction to the BeOS and BFS

1.1 History Leading Up to BFS

In late 1990 Jean Louis Gassée founded Be, Inc., to address the shortcomings he saw in operating systems of the time. He perceived that the problem most operating systems shared was that they were weighed down with the baggage of many years of legacy. The cost of this legacy was of course performance: the speed of the underlying hardware was not being fully exploited.

To solve that problem, Be, Inc., began developing, from scratch, the BeOS and the BeBox. The original BeBox used two AT&T Hobbit CPUs and three DSP chips. A variety of plug-in cards for the box provided telephony, MIDI, and audio support. The box was moderately low cost and offered impressive performance for the time (1992). During the same time period, the BeOS evolved into a symmetric multiprocessing (SMP) OS that supported virtual memory, preemptive multitasking, and lightweight threading. User-level servers provided most of the functionality of the system, and the kernel remained quite small. The primary interface to the BeOS was through a graphical user interface reminiscent of the Macintosh. Figure 1-1 shows the BeOS GUI.

The intent for the Hobbit BeBox was that it would be an information device that would be connected to a network, could answer your phone, and worked well with MIDI and other multimedia devices. In retrospect the original design was a mix of what we now call a "network computer" (NC) and a set-top box of sorts.

The hardware design of the original BeBox met an unfortunate end when AT&T canceled the Hobbit processor in March 1994. Reworking the design to use more common parts, Be modified the BeBox to use the PowerPC chip, which, at the time (1994), had the most promising future. The redesigned box

Figure 1-1   A BeOS screenshot.

had dual PowerPC 603 chips, a PCI bus, an ISA bus, and a SCSI controller. It used off-the-shelf components and sported a fancy front bezel with dual LED meters displaying the processor activity. It was a geek magnet.

In addition to modifying the BeBox hardware, the BeOS also underwent changes to support the new hardware and to exploit the performance offered by the PowerPC processor. The advent of the PowerPC BeBox brought the BeOS into a realm where it was almost usable as a regular operating system. The original design goals changed slightly, and the BeOS began to grow into a full-fledged desktop operating system. The transformation from the original design goals left the system with a few warts here and there, but nothing that was unmanageable.

The Shift

Be, Inc., announced the BeOS and the BeBox to the world in October 1995, and later that year the BeBox became available to developers. The increased exposure brought the system under very close scrutiny. Several problems became apparent. At the time, the BeOS managed extra information about files (e.g., header fields from an email message) in a separate database that existed independently of the underlying hierarchical file system (the old file system, or OFS for short). The original design of the separate database and file system was done partially out of a desire to keep as much code in user space as possible. However, with the database separate from the file system, keeping the two in sync proved problematic. Moreover, moving into the realm of general-purpose computing brought with it the desire to support other file systems (such as ISO-9660, the CD-ROM file system), but there was no provision for that in the original I/O architecture.

In the spring of 1996, Be came to the realization that porting the BeOS to run on other PowerPC machines could greatly increase the number of people able to run the BeOS. The Apple Macintosh Power Mac line of computers were quite similar to the BeBox, and it seemed that a port would help everyone. By August 1996 the BeOS ran on a variety of Power Mac hardware. The system ran very fast and attracted a lot of attention because it was now possible to do an apples-to-apples comparison of the BeOS against the Mac OS on the same hardware. In almost all tests the BeOS won hands down, which of course generated considerable interest in the BeOS.

Running on the Power Mac brought additional issues to light. The need to support HFS (the file system of the Mac OS) became very important, and we found that the POSIX support we offered was getting heavy use, which kept exposing numerous difficulties in keeping the database and file system in sync.

The Solution

Starting in September 1996, Cyril Meurillon and I set about to define a new I/O architecture and file system for BeOS. We knew that the existing split of file system and database would no longer work. We wanted a new, high-performance file system that supported the database functionality the BeOS was known for as well as a mechanism to support multiple file systems. We also took the opportunity to clean out some of the accumulated cruft that had worked its way into the system over the course of the previous five years of development.

The task we had to solve had two very clear components. First there was the higher-level file system and device interface. This half of the project involved defining an API for file systems and device drivers, managing the name space, connecting program requests for files into file descriptors, and managing all the associated state. The second half of the project involved writing a file system that would provide the functionality required by the rest of the BeOS. Cyril, being the primary kernel architect at Be, took on the first portion of the task. The most difficult portion of Cyril's project involved defining the file system API in such a way that it was as multithreaded as possible, correct, deadlock-free, and efficient. That task involved many major iterations as we battled over what a file system had to do and what the kernel layer would manage. There is some discussion of this level of the file system in Chapter 10, but it is not the primary focus of this book.

My half of the project involved defining the on-disk data structures, managing all the nitty-gritty physical details of the raw disk blocks, and performing the I/O requests made by programs. Because the disk block cache is intimately intertwined with the file system (especially a journaled file system), I also took on the task of rewriting the block cache.

1.2 Design Goals

Before any work could begin on the file system, we had to define what our goals were and what features we wanted to support. Some features were not optional, such as the database that the OFS supported. Other features, such as journaling (for added file system integrity and quick boot times), were extremely attractive because they offered several benefits at a presumably small cost. Still other features, such as 64-bit file sizes, were required for the target audiences of the BeOS.

The primary feature that a new Be File System had to support was the database concept of the old Be File System. The OFS supported a notion of *records* containing named *fields*. Records existed in the database for every file in the underlying file system as well. Records could also exist purely in the database. The database had a query interface that could find records matching various criteria about their fields. The OFS also supported *live queries*—persistent queries that would receive updates as new records entered or left the set of matching records. All these features were mandatory.

There were several motivating factors that prompted us to include journaling in BFS. First, journaled file systems do not need a consistency check at boot time. As we will explain later, by their very nature, journaled file systems are always consistent. This has several implications: boot time is very fast because the entire disk does not need checking, and it avoids any problems with forcing potentially naive users to run a file system consistency check program. Next, since the file system needed to support sophisticated indexing data structures for the database functionality, journaling made the task of recovery from failures much simpler. The small development cost to implement journaling sealed our decision to support it.

Our decision to support 64-bit volume and file sizes was simple. The target audiences of the BeOS are people who manipulate large audio, video, and still-image files. It is not uncommon for these files to grow to several gigabytes in size (a mere 2 minutes of uncompressed CCIR-601 video is greater than 2^{32} bytes). Further, with disk sizes regularly in the multigigabyte range today, it is unreasonable to expect users to have to create multiple partitions on a

9 GB drive because of file system limits. All these factors pointed to the need for a 64-bit-capable file system.

In addition to the above design goals, we had the long-standing goals of making the system as multithreaded and as efficient as possible, which meant fine-grained locking everywhere and paying close attention to the overhead introduced by the file system. Memory usage was also a big concern. We did not have the luxury of assuming large amounts of memory for buffers because the primary development system for BFS was a BeBox with 8 MB of memory.

1.3   Design Constraints

There were also several design constraints that the project had to contend with. The first and foremost was the lack of engineering resources. The Be engineering staff is quite small, at the time only 13 engineers. Cyril and I had to work alone because everyone else was busy with other projects. We also did not have very much time to complete the project. Be, Inc., tries to have regular software releases, once every four to six months. The initial target was for the project to take six months. The short amount of time to complete the project and the lack of engineering resources meant that there was little time to explore different designs and to experiment with completely untested ideas. In the end it took nine months for the first beta release of BFS. The final version of BFS shipped the following month.

1.4   Summary

This background information provides a canvas upon which we will paint the details of the Be File System. Understanding what the BeOS is and what requirements BFS had to fill should help to make it more clear why certain paths were chosen when there were multiple options available.

2

What Is a File System?

2.1 The Fundamentals

This chapter is an introduction to the concepts of what a file system is, what it manages, and what abstractions it provides to the rest of the operating system. Reading this chapter will provide a thorough grounding in the terminology, the concepts, and the standard techniques used to implement file systems.

Most users of computers are roughly familiar with what a file system does, what a file is, what a directory is, and so on. This knowledge is gained from direct experience with computers. Instead of basing our discussion on prior experiences, which will vary from user to user, we will start over again and think about the problem of storing information on a computer, and then move forward from there.

The main purpose of computers is to create, manipulate, store, and retrieve data. A file system provides the machinery to support these tasks. At the highest level a file system is a way to organize, store, retrieve, and manage information on a permanent storage medium such as a disk. File systems manage permanent storage and form an integral part of all operating systems.

There are many different approaches to the task of managing permanent storage. At one end of the spectrum are simple file systems that impose enough restrictions to inconvenience users and make using the file system difficult. At the other end of the spectrum are persistent object stores and object-oriented databases that abstract the whole notion of permanent storage so that the user and programmer never even need to be aware of it. The problem of storing, retrieving, and manipulating information on a computer is of a general-enough nature that there are many solutions to the problem.

There is no "correct" way to write a file system. In deciding what type of filing system is appropriate for a particular operating system, we must weigh the needs of the problem with the other constraints of the project. For example, a flash-ROM card as used in some game consoles has little need for an advanced query interface or support for attributes. Reliability of data writes to the medium, however, are critical, and so a file system that supports journaling may be a requirement. Likewise, a file system for a high-end mainframe computer needs extremely fast throughput in many areas but little in the way of user-friendly features, and so techniques that enable more transactions per second would gain favor over those that make it easier for a user to locate obscure files.

It is important to keep in mind the abstract goal of what a file system must achieve: to store, retrieve, locate, and manipulate information. Keeping the goal stated in general terms frees us to think of alternative implementations and possibilities that might not otherwise occur if we were to only think of a file system as a typical, strictly hierarchical, disk-based structure.

2.2   The Terminology

When discussing file systems there are many terms for referring to certain concepts, and so it is necessary to define how we will refer to the specific concepts that make up a file system. We list the terms from the ground up, each definition building on the previous.

■ *Disk:* A permanent storage medium of a certain size. A disk also has a sector or block size, which is the minimum unit that the disk can read or write. The block size of most modern hard disks is 512 bytes.

■ *Block:* The smallest unit writable by a disk or file system. Everything a file system does is composed of operations done on blocks. A file system block is always the same size as or larger (in integer multiples) than the disk block size.

■ *Partition:* A subset of all the blocks on a disk. A disk can have several partitions.

■ *Volume:* The name we give to a collection of blocks on some storage medium (i.e., a disk). That is, a volume may be all of the blocks on a single disk, some portion of the total number of blocks on a disk, or it may even span multiple disks and be all the blocks on several disks. The term "volume" is used to refer to a disk or partition that has been initialized with a file system.

■ *Superblock:* The area of a volume where a file system stores its critical volumewide information. A superblock usually contains information such as how large a volume is, the name of a volume, and so on.

- *Metadata:* A general term referring to information that is about something but not directly part of it. For example, the size of a file is very important information about a file, but it is not part of the data in the file.
- *Journaling:* A method of insuring the correctness of file system metadata even in the presence of power failures or unexpected reboots.
- *I-node:* The place where a file system stores all the necessary metadata about a file. The i-node also provides the connection to the contents of the file and any other data associated with the file. The term "i-node" (which we will use in this book) is historical and originated in Unix. An i-node is also known as a *file control block* (FCB) or *file record*.
- *Extent:* A starting block number and a length of successive blocks on a disk. For example an extent might start at block 1000 and continue for 150 blocks. Extents are always contiguous. Extents are also known as *block runs*.
- *Attribute:* A name (as a text string) and value associated with the name. The value may have a defined type (string, integer, etc.), or it may just be arbitrary data.

2.3   The Abstractions

The two fundamental concepts of any file system are files and directories.

Files

The primary functionality that all file systems must provide is a way to store a named piece of data and to later retrieve that data using the name given to it. We often refer to a named piece of data as a *file*. A file provides only the most basic level of functionality in a file system.

A file is where a program stores data permanently. In its simplest form a file stores a single piece of information. A piece of information can be a bit of text (e.g., a letter, program source code, etc.), a graphic image, a database, or any collection of bytes a user wishes to store permanently. The size of data stored may range from only a few bytes to the entire capacity of a volume. A file system should be able to hold a large number of files, where "large" ranges from tens of thousands to millions.

The Structure of a File

Given the concept of a file, a file system may impose no structure on the file, or it may enforce a considerable amount of structure on the contents of the file. An unstructured, "raw" file, often referred to as a "stream of bytes," literally has no structure. The file system simply records the size of the file and allows programs to read the bytes in any order or fashion that they desire.

An unstructured file can be read 1 byte at a time, 17 bytes at a time, or whatever the programmer needs. Further, the same file may be read differently by different programs; the file system does not care about the alignments of or sizes of the I/O requests it gets. Treating files as unstructured streams is the most common approach that file systems use today.

If a file system chooses to enforce a formal structure on files, it usually does so in the form of *records*. With the concept of records, a programmer specifies the size and format of the record, and then all I/O to that file must happen on record boundaries and be a multiple of the record length. Other systems allow programs to create VSAM (virtual sequential access method) and ISAM (indexed sequential access method) files, which are essentially databases in a file. These concepts do not usually make their way into general-purpose desktop operating systems. We will not consider structured files in our discussion of file systems. If you are interested in this topic, you may wish to look at the literature about mainframe operating systems such as MVS, CICS, CMS, and VMS.

A file system also must allow the user to name the file in a meaningful way. Retrieval of files (i.e., information) is key to the successful use of a file system. The way in which a file system allows users to name files is one factor in how easy or difficult it is to later find the file. Names of at least 32 characters in length are mandatory for any system that regular users will interact with. Embedded systems or those with little or no user interface may find it economical and/or efficient to limit the length of names.

File Metadata

The name of a file is metadata because it is a piece of information about the file that is not in the stream of bytes that make up the file. There are several other pieces of metadata about a file as well—for example, the owner, security access controls, date of last modification, creation time, and size.

The file system needs a place to store this metadata in addition to storing the file contents. Generally the file system stores file metadata in an i-node. Figure 2-1 diagrams the relationship between an i-node, what it contains, and its data.

The types of information that a file system stores in an i-node vary depending on the file system. Examples of information stored in i-nodes are the last access time of the file, the type, the creator, a version number, and a reference to the directory that contains the file. The choice of what types of metadata information make it into the i-node depends on the needs of the rest of the system.

The Data of a File

The most important information stored in an i-node is the connection to the data in the file (i.e., where it is on disk). An i-node refers to the contents of the file by keeping track of the list of blocks on the disk that belong to this

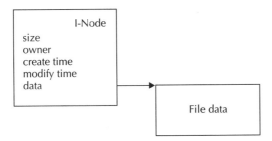

Figure 2-1   A simplified diagram of an i-node and the data it refers to.

file. A file appears as a continuous stream of bytes at higher levels, but the blocks that contain the file data may not be contiguous on disk. An i-node contains the information the file system uses to map from a logical position in a file (for example, byte offset 11,239) to a physical position on disk.

Figure 2-2 helps illustrate (we assume a file system block size of 1024 bytes). If we would like to read from position 4096 of a file, we need to find the fourth block of the file because the file position, 4096, divided by the file system block size, is 4. The i-node contains a list of blocks that make up the file. As we'll see shortly, the i-node can tell us the disk address of the fourth block of the file. Then the file system must ask the disk to read that block. Finally, having retrieved the data, the file system can pass the data back to the user.

We simplified this example quite a bit, but the basic idea is always the same. Given a request for data at some position in a file, the file system must translate that logical position to a physical disk location, request that block from the disk, and then pass the data back to the user.

When a request is made to read (or write) data that is not on a file system block boundary, the file system must round down the file position to the beginning of a block. Then when the file system copies data to/from the block, it must add in the offset from the start of the block of the original position. For example, if we used the file offset 4732 instead of 4096, we would still need to read the fourth block of the file. But after getting the fourth block, we would use the data at byte offset 636 (4732 − 4096) within the fourth block.

When a request for I/O spans multiple blocks (such as a read for 8192 bytes), the file system must find the location for many blocks. If the file system has done a good job, the blocks will be contiguous on disk. Requests for contiguous blocks on disk improve the efficiency of doing I/O to disk. The fastest thing a disk drive can do is to read or write large contiguous regions of disk blocks, and so file systems always strive to arrange file data as contiguously as possible.

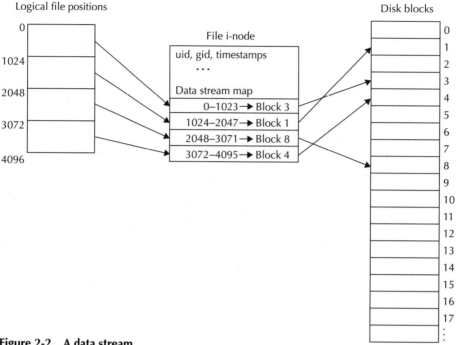

Figure 2-2   A data stream.

File position	Disk block address
0–1023	329922
1024–2047	493294
2048–3071	102349
3072–4095	374255

Table 2-1   An example of mapping file data with direct blocks.

The Block Map

There are many ways in which an i-node can store references to file data. The simplest method is a list of blocks, one for each of the blocks of the file. For example, if a file was 4096 bytes long, it would require four disk blocks. Using fictitious disk block numbers, the i-node might look like Table 2-1.

Generally an i-node will store between 4 and 16 block references directly in the i-node. Storing a few block addresses directly in the i-node simplifies finding file data since most files tend to weigh in under 8K. Providing enough space in the i-node to map the data in most files simplifies the task of the file system. The trade-off that a file system designer must make is between the size of the i-node and how much data the i-node can map. The size of the

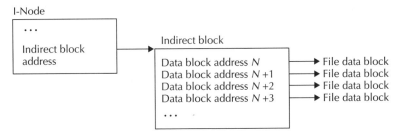

Figure 2-3   Relationship of an i-node and an indirect block.

i-node usually works best when it is an even divisor of the block size, which therefore implies a size that is a power of two.

The i-node can only store a limited number of block addresses, which therefore limits the amount of data the file can contain. Storing all the pointers to data blocks is not practical for even modest-sized files. To overcome the space constraints for storing block addresses in the i-node, an i-node can use *indirect blocks*. When using an indirect block, the i-node stores the block address of (i.e., a pointer to) the indirect block instead of the block addresses of the data blocks. The indirect block contains pointers to the blocks that make up the data of the file. Indirect blocks do not contain user data, only pointers to the blocks that do have user data in them. Thus with one disk block address the i-node can access a much larger number of data blocks. Figure 2-3 demonstrates the relationship of an i-node and an indirect block.

The data block addresses contained in the indirect block refer to blocks on the disk that contain file data. An indirect block extends the amount of data that a file can address. The number of data blocks an indirect block can refer to is equal to the file system block size divided by the size of disk block addresses. In a 32-bit file system, disk block addresses are 4 bytes (32 bits); in a 64-bit file system, they are 8 bytes (64 bits). Thus, given a file system block size of 1024 bytes and a block address size of 64 bits, an indirect block can refer to 128 blocks.

Indirect blocks increase the maximum amount of data a file can access but are not enough to allow an i-node to locate the data blocks of a file much more than a few hundred kilobytes in size (if even that much). To allow files of even larger size, file systems apply the indirect block technique a second time, yielding *double-indirect blocks*.

Double-indirect blocks use the same principle as indirect blocks. The i-node contains the address of the double-indirect block, and the double-indirect block contains pointers to indirect blocks, which in turn contain pointers to the data blocks of the file. The amount of data double-indirect blocks allow an i-node to map is slightly more complicated to calculate. A double-indirect block refers to indirect blocks much as indirect blocks refer to data blocks. The number of indirect blocks a double-indirect block can refer to is the same as the number of data blocks an indirect block can refer to. That is, the number of block addresses in a double-indirect block is the file system block size divided by the disk block address size. In the example we gave above, a 1024-byte block file system with 8-byte (64-bit) block addresses, a double-indirect block could contain references to 128 indirect blocks. Each of the indirect blocks referred to can, of course, refer to the same number of data blocks. Thus, using the numbers we've given, the amount of data that a double-indirect block allows us to map is

128 indirect blocks × 128 data blocks per indirect block = 16,384 data blocks

that is, 16 MB with 1K file system blocks.

This is a more reasonable amount of data to map but may still not be sufficient. In that case *triple-indirect blocks* may be necessary, but this is quite rare. In many existing systems the block size is usually larger, and the size of a block address smaller, which enables mapping considerably larger amounts of data. For example, a 4096-byte block file system with 4-byte (32-bit) block addresses could map 4 GB of disk space (4096/4 = 1024 block addresses per block; one double-indirect block maps 1024 indirect blocks, which each map 1024 data blocks of 4096 bytes each). The double- (or triple-) indirect blocks generally map the most significant amount of data in a file.

In the list-of-blocks approach, mapping from a file position to a disk block address is simple. The file position is taken as an index into the file block list. Since the amount of space that direct, indirect, double-indirect, and even triple-indirect blocks can map is fixed, the file system always knows exactly where to look to find the address of the data block that corresponds to a file position.

The pseudocode for mapping from a file position that is in the double-indirect range to the address of a data block is shown in Listing 2-1.

Using the dbl_indirect_index and indirect_index values, the file system can load the appropriate double-indirect and indirect blocks to find the address of the data block that corresponds to the file position. After loading the data block, the block_offset value would let us index to the exact byte offset that corresponds to the original file position. If the file position is only in the indirect or direct range of a file, the algorithm is similar but much simpler.

As a concrete example, let us consider a file system that has eight direct blocks, a 1K file system block size, and 4-byte disk addresses. These parameters imply that an indirect or double-indirect block can map 256 blocks. If we want to locate the data block associated with file position 786769, the pseudocode in Listing 2-1 would look like it does in Listing 2-2.

With the above calculations completed, the file system would retrieve the double-indirect block and use the double-indirect index to get the address of the indirect block. Next the file system would use that address to load the indirect block. Then, using the indirect index, it would get the address of the

```
blksize = size of the file system block size
dsize   = amount of file data mapped by direct blocks
indsize = amount of file data mapped by an indirect block

if (filepos >= (dsize + indsize)) {          /* double-indirect blocks */
    filepos -= (dsize + indsize);
    dbl_indirect_index = filepos / indsize;

    if (filepos >= indsize) {                /* indirect blocks */
        filepos -= (dbl_indirect_index * indsize);
        indirect_index = filepos / blksize;
    }

    filepos -= (indirect_index * blksize); /* offset in data block */
    block_offset = filepos;
}
```

Listing 2-1   Mapping from a file position to a data block with double-indirect blocks.

```
blksize = 1024;
dsize   = 8192;
indsize = 256 * 1024;
filepos = 786769;

if (filepos >= (dsize+indsize)) {            /* 786769 >= (8192+262144) */
    filepos -= (dsize+indsize);              /* 516433 */
    dbl_indirect_index = filepos / indsize; /* 1 */

    /* at this point filepos == 516433 */

    if (filepos >= indsize) {                        /* 516433 > 262144 */
        filepos -= (dbl_indirect_index * indsize); /* 254289 */
        indirect_index = filepos / blksize;        /* 248 */
    }

    /* at this point filepos == 254289 */

    filepos -= (indirect_index * blksize);    /* 337 */
    block_offset = filepos;                   /* 337 */
}
```

Listing 2-2   Mapping from a specific file position to a particular disk block.

last block (a data block) to load. After loading the data block, the file system would use the block offset to begin the I/O at the exact position requested.

Extents

Another technique to manage mapping from logical positions in a byte stream to data blocks on disk is to use extent lists. An extent list is similar to the simple block list described previously except that each block address is not just for a single block but rather for a range of blocks. That is, every block address is given as a starting block and a length (expressed as the number of successive blocks following the starting block). The size of an extent is usually larger than a simple block address but is potentially able to map a much larger region of disk space.

For example, if a file system used 8-byte block addresses, an extent might have a length field of 2 bytes, allowing the extent to map up to 65,536 contiguous file system blocks. An extent size of 10 bytes is suboptimal, however, because it does not evenly divide any file system block size that is a power of two in size. To maximize the number of extents that can fit in a single block, it is possible to compress the extent. Different approaches exist, but a simple method of compression is to truncate the block address and squeeze in the length field. For example, with 64-bit block addresses, the block address can be shaved down to 48 bits, leaving enough room for a 16-bit length field. The downside to this approach is that it decreases the maximum amount of data that a file system can address. However, if we take into account that a typical block size is 1024 bytes or larger, then we see that in fact the file system will be able to address up to 2^{58} bytes of data (or more if the block size is larger). This is because the block address must be multiplied by the block size to calculate a byte offset on the disk. Depending on the needs of the rest of the system, this may be acceptable.

Although extent lists are a more compact way to refer to large amounts of data, they may still require use of indirect or double-indirect blocks. If a file system becomes highly fragmented and each extent can only map a few blocks of data, then the use of indirect and double-indirect blocks becomes a necessity. One disadvantage to using extent lists is that locating a specific file position may require scanning a large number of extents. Because the length of an extent is variable, when locating a specific position the file system must start at the first extent and scan through all of them until it finds the extent that covers the position of interest. In the case of a large file that uses double-indirect blocks, this may be prohibitive. One way to alleviate the problem is to fix the size of extents in the double-indirect range of a file.

File Summary

In this section we discussed the basic concept of a file as a unit of storage for user data. We touched upon the metadata a file system needs to keep track of for a file (the i-node), structured vs. unstructured files, and ways to

name:	foo
i-node:	525
name:	bar
i-node:	237
name:	blah
i-node:	346

Figure 2-4   Example directory entries with a name and i-node number.

store user data (simple lists and extents). The basic abstraction of a "file" is the core of any file system.

Directories

Beyond a single file stored as a stream of bytes, a file system must provide a way to name and organize multiple files. File systems use the term *directory* or *folder* to describe a container that organizes files by name. The primary purpose of a directory is to manage a list of files and to connect the name in the directory with the associated file (i.e., i-node).

As we will see, there are several ways to implement a directory, but the basic concept is the same for each. A directory contains a list of names. Associated with each name is a handle that refers to the contents of that name (which may be a file or a directory). Although all file systems differ on exactly what constitutes a file name, a directory needs to store both the name and the i-node number of this file.

The name is the key that the directory searches on when looking for a file, and the i-node number is a reference that allows the file system to access the contents of the file and other metadata about the file. For example, if a directory contains three entries named foo (i-node 525), bar (i-node 237), and blah (i-node 346), then conceptually the contents of the directory can be thought of as in Figure 2-4.

When a user wishes to open a particular file, the file system must search the directory to find the requested name. If the name is not present, the file system can return an error such as Name not found. If the file does exist, the file system uses the i-node number to locate the metadata about the file, load that information, and then allow access to the contents of the file.

Storing Directory Entries

There are several techniques a directory may use to maintain the list of names in a directory. The simplest method is to store each name linearly in an array, as in Figure 2-4. Keeping a directory as an unsorted linear list is a popular method of storing directory information despite the obvious disadvantages. An unsorted list of directory entries becomes inefficient for lookups when there are a large number of names because the search must scan the entire directory. When a directory starts to contain thousands of files, the amount of time it takes to do a lookup can be significant.

Another method of organizing directory entries is to use a sorted data structure suitable for on-disk storage. One such data structure is a B-tree (or its variants, B+tree and B*tree). A B-tree keeps the keys sorted by their name and is efficient at looking up whether a key exists in the directory. B-trees also scale well and are able to deal efficiently with directories that contain many tens of thousands of files.

Directories can also use other data structures, such as hash tables or radix sorting schemes. The primary requirements on a data structure for storing directory entries are that it perform efficient lookups and have reasonable cost for insertions/deletions. This is a common enough problem that there are many readily adaptable solutions. In practice, if the file system does anything other than a simple linear list, it is almost always a B-tree keyed on file names.

As previously mentioned, every file system has its own restrictions on file names. The maximum file name length, the set of allowable characters in a file name, and the encoding of the character set are all policy decisions that a file system designer must make. For systems intended for interactive use, the bare minimum for file name length is 32 characters. Many systems allow for file names of up to 255 characters, which is adequate headroom. Anecdotal evidence suggests that file names longer than 150 characters are extremely uncommon.

The set of allowable characters in a file name is also an important consideration. Some file systems, such as the CD-ROM file system ISO-9660, allow an extremely restricted set of characters (essentially only alphanumeric characters and the underscore). More commonly, the only restriction necessary is that some character must be chosen as a separator for path hierarchies. In Unix this is the forward slash (/), in MS-DOS it is the backslash (\), and under the Macintosh OS it is the colon (:). The directory separator can never appear in a file name because if it did, the rest of the operating system would not be able to parse the file name: there would be no way to tell which part of the file name was a directory component and which part was the actual file name.

Finally, the character set encoding chosen by the file system affects how the system deals with internationalization issues that arise with multibyte character languages such as Japanese, Korean, and Chinese. Most Unix systems make no policy decision and simply store the file name as a sequence of non-null bytes. Other systems, such as the Windows NT file system, explicitly store all file names as 2-byte Unicode characters. HFS on the Macintosh stores only single-byte characters and assumes the Macintosh character set encoding. The BeOS uses UTF-8 character encoding for multibyte characters;

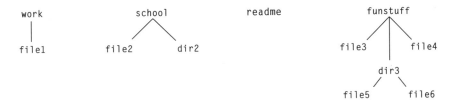

Figure 2-5   An example file system hierarchy.

thus, BFS does not have to worry about multibyte characters because UTF-8 encodes multibyte characters as strings of nonnull bytes.

Hierarchies

Storing all files in a single directory is not sufficient except for the smallest of embedded or stand-alone systems. A file system must allow users to organize their files and arrange them in the way they find most natural. The traditional approach is a hierarchical organization. A hierarchy is a familiar concept to most people and adapts readily to the computer world. The simplest implementation is to allow an entry in a directory to refer to another directory. By allowing a directory to contain a name that refers to a different directory, it is possible to build hierarchical structures.

Figure 2-5 shows what a sample hierarchy might look like. In this example, there are three directories (work, school, and funstuff) and a single file (readme) at the top level. Each of the directories contain additional files and directories. The directory work contains a single file (file1). The directory school has a file (file2) and a directory (dir2). The directory dir2 is empty in this case. The directory funstuff contains two files (file3 and file4) as well as a directory (dir3) that also contains two files (file5 and file6).

Since a directory may contain other directories, it is possible to build arbitrarily complex hierarchies. Implementation details may put limits on the depth of the hierarchy, but in theory there is nothing that limits the size or depth of a directory hierarchy.

Hierarchies are a useful, well-understood abstraction that work well for organizing information. Directory hierarchies tend to remain fixed though and are not generally thought of as malleable. That is, once a user creates a directory hierarchy, they are unlikely to modify the structure significantly over the course of time. Although it is an area of research, alternative ways to view a hierarchy exist. We can think of a hierarchy as merely one representation of the relationships between a set of files, and even allow programs to modify their view of a hierarchy.

Other Approaches

A more flexible architecture that allows for different views of a set of information allows users to view data based on their current needs, not on how they organized it previously. For example, a programmer may have several projects, each organized into subdirectories by project name. Inside of each project there will likely be further subdirectories that organize source code, documentation, test cases, and so on. This is a very useful way to organize several projects. However, if there is a need to view all documentation or all source code, the task is somewhat difficult because of the rigidity of the existing directory hierarchy. It is possible to imagine a system that would allow the user to request all documentation files or all source code, regardless of their location in the hierarchy. This is more than a simple "find file" utility that only produces a static list of results. A file system can provide much more support for these sorts of operations, making them into true first-class file system operations.

Directory Summary

This section discussed the concept of a directory as a mechanism for storing multiple files and as a way to organize information into a hierarchy. The contents of a directory may be stored as a simple linear list, B-trees, or even other data structures such as hash tables. We also discussed the potential for more flexible organizations of data other than just fixed hierarchies.

2.4   Basic File System Operations

The two basic abstractions of files and directories form the basis of what a file system can operate on. There are many operations that a file system can perform on files and directories. All file systems must provide some basic level of support. Beyond the most basic file system primitives lie other features, extensions, and more sophisticated operations.

In this discussion of file system operations, we focus on what a file system must implement, not necessarily what the corresponding user-level operations look like. For example, opening a file in the context of a file system requires a reference to a directory and a name, but at the user level all that is needed is a string representing the file name. There is a close correlation between the user-level API of a file system and what a file system implements, but they are not the same.

Initialization

Clearly the first operation a file system must provide is a way to create an empty file system on a given volume. A file system uses the size of the volume to be initialized and any user-specified options to determine the size and placement of its internal data structures. Careful attention to the placement of these initial data structures can improve or degrade performance significantly. Experimenting with different locations is useful.

Generally the host operating system provides a way to find out the size of a volume expressed in terms of a number of device blocks. This information is then used to calculate the size of various data structures such as the free/used block map (usually a bitmap), the number of i-nodes (if they are preallocated), and the size of the journal area (if there is one). Upon calculating the sizes of these data structures, the file system can then decide where to place them within the volume. The file system places the locations of these structures, along with the size of the volume, the state of the volume (clean or dirty), and other file system global information, into the superblock data structure. File systems generally write the superblock to a known location in the volume.

File system initialization must also create an empty top-level directory. Without a top-level directory there is no container to create anything in when the file system is mounted for normal use. The top-level directory is generally known as the *root directory* (or simply *root*) of a file system. The expression "root directory" comes from the notion of a file system directory hierarchy as an inverted tree, and the top-level directory is the root of this tree. Unless the root directory is always at a fixed location on a volume, the i-node number (or address) of the root directory must also be stored in the superblock.

The task of initializing a file system may be done as a separate user program, or it may be part of the core file system code. However it is done, initializing a file system simply prepares a volume as an empty container ready to accept the creation of files and directories. Once a file system is initialized it can then be "mounted."

Mounting

Mounting a file system is the task of accessing a raw device, reading the superblock and other file system metadata, and then preparing the system for access to the volume. Mounting a file system requires some care because the state of the file system being mounted is unknown and may be damaged. The superblock of a file system often contains the state of the file system. If the file system was properly shut down, the superblock will indicate that the volume is clean and needs no consistency check. An improperly shut-down file system should indicate that the volume is dirty and must be checked.

The validation phase for a dirty file system is extremely important. Were a corrupted file system mounted, the corrupted data could potentially cause further damage to user data or even crash the system if it causes the file system to perform illegal operations. The importance of verifying that a file system is valid before mounting cannot be overstated. The task of verifying and possibly repairing a damaged file system is usually a very complex task. A journaled file system can replay its log to guarantee that the file system is consistent, but it should still verify other data structures before proceeding. Because of the complexity of a full file system check, the task is usually relegated to a separate program, a file system check program. Full verification of a file system can take considerable time, especially when confronted with a multigigabyte volume that contains hundreds of thousands of files. Fortunately such lengthy check and repair operations are only necessary when the superblock indicates that the volume is dirty.

Once a file system determines that a given volume is valid, it must then use the on-disk data structures to construct in-memory data structures that will allow it to access the volume. Generally a file system will build an internal version of the superblock along with references to the root directory and the free/used block map structure. Journaled file systems must also load information regarding the log. The in-memory state that a file system maintains allows the rest of the operating system access to the contents of the volume.

The details of how a file system connects with the rest of the operating system tend to be very operating system specific. Generally speaking, however, the operating system asks a file system to mount a volume at the request of a user or program. The file system is given a handle or reference to a volume and then initiates access to the volume, which allows it to read in and verify file system data structures. When the file system determines that the volume is accessible, it returns to the operating system and hooks in its operations so that the operating system can call on the file system to perform operations that refer to files on the volume.

Unmounting

Corresponding to mounting a file system, there is also an unmount operation. Unmounting a file system involves flushing out to disk all in-memory state associated with the volume. Once all the in-memory data is written to the volume, the volume is said to be "clean." The last operation of unmounting a disk is to mark the superblock to indicate that a normal shutdown occurred. By marking the superblock in this way, the file system guarantees that to the best of its knowledge the disk is not corrupted, which allows the next mount operation to assume a certain level of sanity. Since a file system not marked clean may potentially be corrupt, it is important that a file system cleanly unmount all volumes. After marking the superblock, the system should not access the volume unless it mounts the volume again.

Creating Files

After mounting a freshly initialized volume, there is nothing on the volume. Thus, the first major operation a file system must support is the ability to create files. There are two basic pieces of information needed to create a file: the directory to create the file in and the name of the file. With these two pieces of information a file system can create an i-node to represent the file and then can add an entry to the directory for the file name/i-node pair. Additional arguments may specify file access permissions, file modes, or other flags specific to a given file system.

After allocating an i-node for a file, the file system must fill in whatever information is relevant. File systems that store the creation time must record that, and the size of the file must be initialized to zero. The file system must also record ownership and security information in the i-node if that is required.

Creating a file does not reserve storage space for the contents of the file. Space is allocated to hold data when data is written to the file. The creation of a file only allocates the i-node and enters the file into the directory that contains it. It may seem counterintuitive, but creating a file is a simple operation.

Creating Directories

Creating a directory is similar to creating a file, only slightly more complex. Just as with a file, the file system must allocate an i-node to record metadata about the directory as well as enter the name of the directory into its parent directory.

Unlike a file, however, the contents of a directory must be initialized. Initializing a directory may be simple, such as when a directory is stored as a simple list, or it may be more complex, such as when a B-tree is used to store the contents of a directory. A directory must also contain a reference back to its parent directory. The reference back is simply the i-node number of the parent directory. Storing a link to the parent directory makes navigation of the file system hierarchy much simpler. A program may traverse down through a directory hierarchy and at any point ask for the parent directory to work its way back up. If the parent directory were not easily accessible in any given directory, programs would have to maintain state about where they are in the hierarchy—an error-prone duplication of state. Most POSIX-style file systems store a link to the parent directory as the name "`..`" (dot-dot) in a directory. The name "`.`" (dot) is always present and refers to the directory itself. These two standardized names allow programs to easily navigate from one location in a hierarchy to another without having to know the full path of their current location.

Creating a directory is the fundamental operation that allows users to build hierarchical structures to represent the organization of their information. A directory must maintain a reference to its parent directory to enable navigation of the hierarchy. Directory creation is central to the concept of a hierarchical file system.

Opening Files

Opening existing files is probably the most used operation of a file system. The task of opening a file can be somewhat complex. Opening a file is composed of two operations. The first operation, lookup, takes a reference to a directory and a name and looks up the name in that directory. Looking up a name involves traversing the directory data structure looking to see if a name exists and, if it does, returning the associated i-node. The efficiency of the lookup operation is important. Many directories have only a few files, and so the choice of data structure may not be as important, but large servers routinely have directories with thousands of entries in them. In those situations the choice of directory data structure may be of critical importance.

Given an i-node number, the second half of an open operation involves verifying that the user can access the file. In systems that have no permission checking, this is a no-op. For systems that care about security, this involves checking permissions to verify that the program wishing to access the file is allowed to do so. If the security check is successful, the file system then allocates an in-memory structure to maintain state about access to the file (such as whether the file was opened read-only, for appending, etc.).

The result of an open operation is a handle that the requesting program can use to make requests for I/O operations on the file. The handle returned by the file system is used by the higher-level portions of the operating system. The operating system has additional structures that it uses to store this handle. The handle used by a user-level program is related indirectly to the internal handle returned by the open operation. The operating system generally maps a user-level file descriptor through several tables before it reaches the file system handle.

Writing to Files

The write operation of a file system allows programs to store data in files. The arguments needed to write data to a file are a reference to the file, the position in the file to begin writing the data at, a memory buffer, and the length of the data to write. A write to a file is equivalent to asking the file system to copy a chunk of data to a permanent location within the file.

The write operation takes the memory buffer and writes that data to the file at the position specified. If the position given is already at the end of the file, the file needs to grow before the write can take place. Growing the size of a file involves allocating enough disk blocks to hold the data and adding those blocks to the list of blocks "owned" by the file.

Growing a file causes updates to happen to the free/used block list, the file i-node, and any indirect or double-indirect blocks involved in the transaction. Potentially the superblock of the file system may also be modified.

Once there is enough space for the data, the file system must map from the logical position in the file to the disk block address of where the data should be written to. With the physical block address the file system can then write the data to the underlying device, thus making it permanent.

After the write completes, the file offset maintained by the kernel is incremented by the number of bytes written.

Reading Files

The read operation allows programs to access the contents of a file. The arguments to a read are the same as a write: a handle to refer to the file, a position, a memory buffer, and a length.

A read operation is simpler than a write because a read operation does not modify the disk at all. All a read operation needs to do is to map from the logical position in the file to the corresponding disk address. With the physical disk address in hand, the file system can retrieve the data from the underlying device and place that data into the user's buffer.

The read operation also increments the file position by the amount of data read.

Deleting Files

Deleting a file is the next logical operation that a file system needs to support. The most common way to delete a file is to pass the name of the file. If the name exists, there are two phases to the deletion of the file. The first phase is to remove the name of the file from the directory it exists in. Removing the name prevents other programs from opening the file after it is deleted. After removing the name, the file is marked for deletion.

The second phase of deleting a file only happens when there are no more programs with open file handles to the file. With no one else referencing the file, it is then possible to release the resources used by the file. It is during this phase that the file system can return the data blocks used by the file to the free block pool and the i-node of the file to the free i-node list.

Splitting file deletion into two phases is necessary because a file may be open for reading or writing when a delete is requested. If the file system were to perform both phases immediately, the next I/O request on the file would be invalid (because the data blocks would no longer belong to the file). Having the delete operation immediately delete a file complicates the semantics of performing I/O to a file. By waiting until the reference count of a file goes to zero before deleting the resources associated with a file, the system can guarantee to user programs that once they open a file it will remain valid for reading and writing until they close the file descriptor.

Another additional benefit of the two-phase approach is that a program can open a temporary file for I/O, immediately delete it, and then continue normal I/O processing. When the program exits and all of its resources are closed, the file will be properly deleted. This frees the program from having to worry about cleanup in the presence of error conditions.

Renaming Files

The rename operation is by far the most complex operation a file system has to support. The arguments needed for a rename operation are the source directory handle, the source file name, the destination directory handle, and the destination file name.

Before the rename operation can take place, a great deal of validation of the arguments must take place. If the file system is at all multithreaded, the entire file system must be locked to prevent other operations from affecting the state of this operation.

The first validation needed is to verify that the source and destination file names are different if the source and destination directory handles are the same. If the source and destination directories are different, then it is acceptable for the source and destination names to be the same.

The next step in validation is to check if the source name refers to a directory. If so, the destination directory cannot be a subdirectory of the source (since that would imply moving a directory into one of its own children). Checking this requires traversing the hierarchy from the destination directory all the way to the root directory, making sure that the source name is not a parent directory of the destination. This operation is the most complicated and requires that the entire file system be locked; otherwise, it would be possible for the destination directory to move at the same time that this operation took place. Such race conditions could be disastrous, potentially leaving large branches of the directory hierarchy unattached.

Only if the above complicated set of criteria are met can the rename operation begin. The first step of the rename is to delete the destination name if it refers to a file or an empty directory.

The rename operation itself involves deleting the source name from the source directory and then inserting the destination name into the destination directory. Additionally if the source name refers to a directory, the file system must update the reference to the source directory's parent directory. Failing to do this would lead to a mutated directory hierarchy with unpredictable results when navigating through it.

Reading Metadata

The read metadata operation is a housekeeping function that allows programs to access information about a file. The argument to this function is simply a reference to a file. The information returned varies from system to system but is essentially a copy of some of the fields in the i-node structure (last modification time, owner, security info, etc.). This operation is known as stat() in the POSIX world.

Writing Metadata

If there is the ability to read the metadata of a file, it is also likely that it will be necessary to modify it. The write metadata operation allows a program to modify fields of a file's i-node. At the user level there may be potentially many different functions to modify each of the fields (chown(), chmod(), utimes(), etc.), but internally there need only be one function to do this. Of course, not all fields of an i-node may be modifiable.

Opening Directories

Just as access to the contents of a file is initiated with open(), there is an analog for directories, usually called opendir(). The notion of "opening" a directory is simple. A directory needs to provide a mechanism to access the list of files stored in the directory, and the opendir operation is the operation used to grant access to a directory. The argument to opendir is simply a reference to a directory. The requesting program must have its permissions checked; if nothing prevents the operation, a handle is returned that the requesting program may use to call the readdir operation.

Internally the opendir function may need to allocate a state structure so that successive calls to readdir to iterate through the contents of the directory can maintain their position in the directory.

Reading Directories

The readdir operation enumerates the contents of a directory. There is no corresponding WriteDir (strictly speaking, create and makedir both "write" to a directory). The readdir operation must iterate through the directory, returning successive name/i-node pairs stored in the directory (and potentially any other information also stored in the directory). The order in which entries are returned depends on the underlying data structure.

If a file system has a complex data structure for storing the directory entries, then there is also some associated state (allocated in opendir) that the file system preserves between calls to readdir. Each call to readdir updates the state information so that on the next call to readdir, the successive element in the directory can be read and returned.

Without readdir it would be impossible for programs to navigate the file system hierarchy.

Basic File System Operation Summary

The file system operations discussed in this section delineate a baseline of functionality for any file system. The first operation any file system must provide is a way to initialize a volume. Mounting a file system so that the rest of an operating system can access it is the next most basic operation needed. Creating files and directories form the backbone of a file system's functionality. Writing and reading data allows users to store and retrieve information from permanent storage. The delete and rename operations provide mechanisms to manage and manipulate files and directories. The read metadata and write metadata functions allow users to read and modify the information that the file system maintains about files. Finally, the `opendir` and `readdir` calls allow users to iterate through and enumerate the files in the directory hierarchy. This basic set of operations provides the minimal amount of functionality needed in a file system.

2.5   Extended File System Operations

A file system that provided only the most basic features of plain files and directories would hardly be worth talking about. There are many features that can enhance the capabilities of a file system. This section discusses some extensions to a basic file system as well as some of the more advanced features that modern file systems support.

We will only briefly introduce each of the topics here and defer in-depth discussion until later chapters.

Symbolic Links

One feature that many file systems implement is *symbolic links*. A symbolic link is a way to create a named entity in the file system that simply refers to another file; that is, a symbolic link is a named entity in a directory, but instead of the associated i-node referring to a file, the symbolic link contains the name of another file that should be opened. For example, if a directory contains a symbolic link named Feeder and the symbolic link refers to a file called Breeder, then whenever a program opens Feeder, the file system transparently turns that into an open of Breeder. Because the connection between the two files is a simple text string of the file being referred to, the connection is tenuous. That is, if the file Breeder were renamed to Breeder.old, the symbolic link Feeder would be left dangling (it still refers to Breeder) and would thus no longer work. Despite this issue, symbolic links are extremely handy.

Hard Links

Another form of link is known as a *hard link*. A hard link is also known as an *alias*. A hard link is a much stronger connection to a file. With a hard link, a named entity in a directory simply contains the i-node number of some other file instead of its own i-node (in fact, a hard link does not have an i-node at all). This connection is very strong for several reasons: Even if the original file were moved or renamed, its i-node address remains the same, and so a connection to a file cannot ever be destroyed. Even if the original file were deleted, the file system maintains a reference count and only deletes the file when the reference count is zero (meaning no one refers to the file). Hard links are preferable in situations where a connection to a file must not be broken.

Dynamic Links

A third form of link, a *dynamic link*, is really just a symbolic link with special properties. As previously mentioned, a symbolic link contains a reference to another file, and the reference is stored as a text string. Dynamic links add another level of indirection by interpreting the string of text. There are several ways the file system can interpret the text of the link. One method is to treat the string as an environment variable and replace the text of the link with the contents of the matching environment variable. Other more sophisticated interpretations are possible. Dynamic links make it possible to create a symbolic link that points to a number of different files depending on the person examining the link. While powerful, dynamic links can also cause confusion because what the link resolves to can change without any apparent action by the user.

Memory Mapping of Files

Another feature that some operating systems support is the ability to memory map a file. Memory mapping a file creates a region of virtual memory in the address space of the program, and each byte in that region of memory corresponds to the bytes of the file. If the program maps a file beginning at address 0x10000, then memory address 0x10000 is equivalent to byte offset 0 in the file. Likewise address 0x10400 is equivalent to offset 0x400 (1024) in the file.

The Unix-style `mmap()` call can optionally sync the in-memory copy of a file to disk so that the data written in memory gets flushed to disk. There are also flags to share the mapped file across several processes (a powerful feature for sharing information).

Memory mapping of files requires close cooperation between the virtual memory system of the OS and the file system. The main requirement is that the virtual memory system must be able to map from a file offset to the corresponding block on disk. The file system may also face other constraints about what it may do when performing operations on behalf of the virtual memory (VM) system. For example, the VM system may not be able to tolerate a page fault or memory allocation request from the file system during an operation related to a memory-mapped file (since the VM system is already locked). These types of constraints and requirements can make implementing memory-mapped files tricky.

Attributes

Several recent file systems (OS/2's HPFS, NT's NTFS, SGI's XFS and BFS) support extended file attributes. An *attribute* is simply a name (much like a file name) and some value (a chunk of data of arbitrary size). Often it is desirable to store additional information about a file with the file, but it is not feasible (or possible) to modify the contents of the file. For example, when a Web browser downloads an image, it could store, as an attribute, the URL from which the image originated. This would be useful when several months later you want to return to the site where you got the image. Attributes provide a way to associate additional information about a file with the file. Ideally the file system should allow any number of additional attributes and allow the attributes to be of any size. Where a file system chooses to store attribute information depends on the file system. For example, HPFS reserves a fixed 64K area for the attributes of a file. BFS and NTFS offer more flexibility and can store attributes anywhere on the disk.

Indexing

File attributes allow users to associate additional information with files, but there is even more that a file system can do with extended file attributes to aid users in managing and locating their information. If the file system also indexes the attributes, it becomes possible to issue queries about the contents of the attributes. For example, if we added a `Keyword` attribute to a set of files and the `Keyword` attribute was indexed, the user could then issue queries asking which files contained various keywords regardless of their location in the hierarchy.

When coupled with a good query language, indexing offers a powerful alternative interface to the file system. With queries, users are not restricted to navigating a fixed hierarchy of files; instead they can issue queries to find the working set of files they would like to see, regardless of the location of the files.

Journaling/Logging

Avoiding corruption in a file system is a difficult task. Some file systems go to great lengths to avoid corruption problems. They may attempt to order disk writes in such a way that corruption is recoverable, or they may force operations that can cause corruption to be synchronous so that the file system is always in a known state. Still other systems simply avoid the issue and depend on a very sophisticated file system check program to recover in the event of failures. All of these approaches must check the disk at boot time, a potentially lengthy operation (especially as disk sizes increase). Further, should a crash happen at an inopportune time, the file system may still be corrupt.

A more modern approach to avoiding corruption is *journaling*. Journaling, a technique borrowed from the database world, avoids corruption by batching groups of changes and committing them all at once to a transaction log. The batched changes guarantee the atomicity of multiple changes. That atomicity guarantee allows the file system to guarantee that operations either happen completely or not at all. Further, if a crash does happen, the system need only replay the transaction log to recover the system to a known state. Replaying the log is an operation that takes at most a few seconds, which is considerably faster than the file system check that nonjournaled file systems must make.

Guaranteed Bandwidth/Bandwidth Reservation

The desire to guarantee high-bandwidth I/O for multimedia applications drives some file system designers to provide special hooks that allow applications to guarantee that they will receive a certain amount of I/O bandwidth (within the limits of the hardware). To accomplish this the file system needs a great deal of knowledge about the capabilities of the underlying hardware it uses and must schedule I/O requests. This problem is nontrivial and still an area of research.

Access Control Lists

Access control lists (ACLs) provide an extended mechanism for specifying who may access a file and how they may access it. The traditional POSIX approach of three sets of permissions—for the owner of a file, the group that the owner is in, and everyone else—is not sufficient in some settings. An access control list specifies the exact level of access that any person may have to a file. This allows for fine-grained control over the access to a file in comparison to the broad divisions defined in the POSIX security model.

2.6   Summary

This chapter introduced and explained the basics of what a file system is, what it does, and what additional features a file system may choose to implement. At the simplest level a file system provides a way to store and retrieve data in a hierarchical organization. The two fundamental concepts of any file system are files and directories.

In addition to the basics, a file system may choose to implement a variety of additional features that enable users to more easily manage, navigate, and manipulate their information. Attributes and indexing are two features that provide a great deal of additional functionality. Journaling is a technique for keeping a file system consistent, and guaranteeing file I/O bandwidth is an option for systems that wish to support real-time multimedia applications.

A file system designer must make many choices when implementing a file system. Not all features are appropriate or even necessary for all systems. System constraints may dictate some choices, while available time and resources may dictate others.

3

Other File Systems

The Be File System is just one example of a file system. Every operating system has its own native file system, each providing some interesting mix of features. This section provides background detail on historically interesting file systems (BSD FFS), traditional modern file systems (Linux ext2), Macintosh HFS, and other more advanced current file systems (Windows NT's NTFS and XFS from SGI Irix).

Historically, file systems provided a simple method of storage management. The most basic file systems support a simple hierarchical structure of directories and files. This design has seen many implementations. Perhaps the quintessential implementation of this design is the Berkeley Software Distribution Fast File System (BSD FFS, or just FFS).

3.1 BSD FFS

Most current file systems can trace their lineage back, at least partly, to FFS, and thus no discussion of file systems would be complete without at least touching on it. The BSD FFS improved on performance and reliability of previous Unix file systems and set the standard for nearly a decade in terms of robustness and speed. In its essence, FFS consists of a superblock, a block bitmap, an i-node bitmap, and an array of preallocated i-nodes. This design still forms the underlying basis of many file systems.

The first (and easiest) technique FFS used to improve performance over previous Unix file systems was to use much larger file system block sizes. FFS uses block sizes that are any power of two greater than or equal to 4096 bytes. This technique alone accounted for a doubling in performance over previous file systems (McKusick, p. 196). The lesson is clear: contiguous disk reads

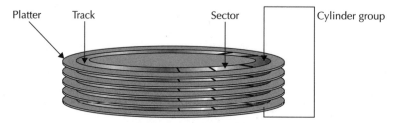

Platter   Track   Sector   Cylinder group

Figure 3-1   Simplified diagram of a disk.

provide much higher bandwidth than having to seek to read different blocks of a file. It is impossible to overstate the importance of this. Reading or writing contiguous blocks from a disk is without a doubt the fastest possible way of accessing disks and will likely remain so for the foreseeable future.

Larger block sizes come at a cost: wasted disk space. A 1-byte file still consumes an entire file system block. In fact, McKusick reports that with a 4096-byte block file system and a set of files of about 775 MB in size, there is 45.6% overhead to store the files (i.e., the file system uses 353 MB of extra space to hold the files). FFS overcomes this limitation by also managing fragments within a block. Fragments can be as small as 512 bytes, although more typically they are 1024 bytes. FFS manages fragments through the block bitmap, which records the state of all fragments, not just all blocks. The use of fragments in FFS allows it to use a large block size for larger files while not wasting excessive amounts of space for small files.

The next technique FFS uses to improve performance is to minimize disk head movement. Another truism with disk drives is that the seek time to move the disk heads from one part of a disk to another is considerable. Through careful organization of the layout of data on the disk, the file system can minimize seek times. To accomplish this, FFS introduced the concept of *cylinder groups*. A cylinder group attempts to exploit the geometry of a disk (i.e., the number of heads, tracks, cylinders, and sectors per track) to improve performance. Physically a cylinder group is the collection of all the blocks in the same track on all the different heads of a disk (Figure 3-1).

In essence a cylinder group is a vertical slice of the disk. The performance benefit of this organization is that reading successive blocks in a cylinder group only involves switching heads. Switching disk heads is an electrical operation and thus significantly faster than a mechanical operation such as moving the heads.

FFS uses the locality offered by cylinder groups in its placement of data on the disk. For example, instead of the file system storing one large contiguous bitmap at the beginning of the disk, each cylinder group contains a small portion of the bitmap. The same is true for the i-node bitmap and the pre-allocated i-nodes. FFS also attempts to allocate file data close to the i-node, which avoids long seeks between reading file metadata and accessing the file contents. To help spread data around the disk in an even fashion, FFS puts new directories in different cylinder groups.

Organizing data into cylinder groups made sense for the disk drives available at the time of the design of FFS. Modern disks, however, hide much of their physical geometry, which makes it difficult for a file system like FFS to do its job properly. All modern disk drives do much of what FFS did in the drive controller itself. The disk drive can do this more effectively and more accurately since the drive controller has intimate knowledge of the disk drive. Cylinder groups were a good idea at the time, but managing them has now migrated from the file system into the disk drive itself.

The other main goal of FFS was to improve file system reliability through careful ordering of writes to file system metadata. Careful ordering of file system metadata updates allows the file system consistency check program (fsck) to more easily recover in the event of a crash. If fsck discovers inconsistent data, it can deduce what the file system tried to do when the crash occurred based on what it finds. In most cases the fsck program for FFS could recover the file system back to a sane state. The recovery process is not cheap and requires as many as five passes through the file system to repair a disk. This can require a considerable amount of time depending on the size of the file system and the number of files it contains.

In addition to careful ordering of writes to file system metadata, FFS also forces all metadata writes to be done synchronously. For example, when deleting a file, the corresponding update to the directory will be written through to disk immediately and not buffered in memory. Writing metadata synchronously allows the file system to guarantee that if a call that modifies metadata completes, the data really has been changed on disk. Unfortunately file system metadata updates tend to be a few single-block writes with reasonable locality, although they are almost never contiguous. Writing metadata synchronously ties the limit of the maximum number of I/O operations the file system can support to the speed at which the disk can write multiple individual blocks, almost always the slowest way to operate a disk drive.

For its time FFS offered new levels of performance and reliability that were uncommon in Unix file systems. The notion of exploiting cylinder group locality enabled large gains in performance on the hardware of the mid-1980s. Modern disk drives hide most of a drive's geometry, thus eroding the performance advantage FFS gained from cylinder groups. Carefully ordering metadata writes and writing them synchronously allows FFS to more easily recover from failures, but it costs considerably in terms of performance. FFS set the standard for Unix file systems although it has since been surpassed in terms of performance and reliability.

3.2 Linux ext2

The Linux ext2 file system is a blindingly fast implementation of a classic Unix file system. The only nonstandard feature supported by ext2 is access control lists. The ext2 file system offers superior speed by relaxing its consistency model and depending on a very sophisticated file system check program to repair any damage that results from a crash.

Linux ext2 is quite similar to FFS, although it does not use cylinder groups as a mechanism for dividing up allocation on the disk. Instead ext2 relies on the drive to do the appropriate remapping. The ext2 file system simply divides the disk into fixed-size block groups, each of which appears as a miniature file system. Each block group has a complete superblock, bitmap, i-node map, and i-node table. This allows the file system consistency checker to recover files even if large portions of the disk are inaccessible.

The main difference between ext2 and FFS is that ext2 makes no guarantees about consistency of the file system or whether an operation is permanently on the disk when a file system call completes. Essentially ext2 performs almost all operations in memory until it needs to flush the buffer cache to disk. This enables outstanding performance numbers, especially on benchmarks that fit in memory. In fact, on some benchmarks nothing may ever need to actually be written to disk, so in certain situations the ext2 file system is limited only by the speed at which the kernel can `memcpy()` data.

This consistency model is in stark contrast to the very strict synchronous writes of FFS. The trade-off made by ext2 is clear: under Linux, reboots are infrequent enough that having the system be fast 99.99% of the rest of time is preferable to having the system be slower because of synchronous writes.

If this were the only trade-off, all file systems would do this. This consistency model is not without drawbacks and may not be appropriate at all for some applications. Because ext2 makes no guarantees about the order of operations and when they are flushed to disk, it is conceivable (although unlikely) that later modifications to the file system would be recorded on disk but earlier operations would not be. Although the file system consistency check would ensure that the file system is consistent, the lack of ordering on operations can lead to confused applications or, even worse, crashing applications because of the inconsistencies in the order of modifications to the file system.

As dire as the above sounds, in practice such situations occur rarely. In the normal case ext2 is an order of magnitude faster than traditional FFS-based file systems.

3.3   Macintosh HFS

HFS came to life in 1984 and was unlike any other prior file system. We discuss HFS because it is one of the first file systems designed to support a graphical user interface (which can be seen in the design of some of its data structures).

Almost nothing about HFS resembles a traditional file system. It has no i-node table, it has no explicit directories, and its method of recording which blocks belong to a file is unusual. About the only part of HFS that is similar to existing systems is the block bitmap that records which blocks are allocated or free.

HFS extensively utilizes B*trees to store file system structures. The two main data structures in HFS are the catalog file and the extent overflow file. The catalog file stores four types of entries: directory records, directory threads, file records, and file threads.

A file or directory has two file system structures associated with it: a record and a thread. The thread portion of a file system entity stores the name of the item and which directory it belongs to. The record portion of a file system entity stores the usual information, such as the last modification time, how to access the file data, and so on. In addition to the normal information, the file system also stores information used by the GUI with each file. Both directories and files require additional information to properly display the position of a file's icon when browsing the file system in the GUI. Storing this information directly in the file record was unusual for the time.

The catalog file stores references to all files and directories on a volume in one monolithic structure. The catalog file encodes the hierarchical structure of the file system; it is not explicit as in a traditional file system, where every directory is stored separately. The contents of a directory are threaded together via thread records in the catalog.

The key used to look up items in the catalog file is a combination of the parent directory ID and the name of the item in question. In HFS there is a strong connection between a file and the directory that contains it since each file record contains the parent directory ID.

The catalog file is a complicated structure. Because it keeps all file and directory information, it forces serialization of the file system—not an ideal situation when there are a large number of threads wanting to perform file I/O. In HFS, any operation that creates a file or modifies a file in any way has to lock the catalog file, which prevents other threads from even read-only access to the catalog file. Access to the catalog file must be single-writer/multireader.

At the time of its introduction HFS offered a concept of a *resource fork* and *data fork* both belonging to the same file. This was a most unusual abstraction for the time but provided functionality needed by the GUI system. The notion of two streams of data (i.e., "forks") associated with one file made it possible to cleanly store icons, program resources, and other metadata about a file directly with the file.

Data in either the resource or data forks of an HFS file is accessed through extent maps. HFS stores three extents in the file record contained in the catalog file. The extent overflow file stores additional extents for each file. The key used to do lookups encodes the file ID, the position of the extent, and which fork of the file to look in. As with the catalog file, the extent overflow file stores all extents for all files in the file system. This again forces a single-writer/multireader serialization of access to the extent overflow file. This presents serious limitations when there are many threads vying for access to the file system.

HFS imposes one other serious limitation on volumes: each volume can have at most 65,536 blocks. The master directory block provides only 2 bytes to store the number of blocks on the volume. This limitation forces HFS to use large block sizes to compensate. It is not uncommon for an HFS volume to allocate space in 32K chunks on disks 1 GB or larger. This is extremely wasteful for small files. The lesson here is clear: make sure the size of your data structures will last. In retrospect the master directory block has numerous extraneous fields that could have provided another 2 bytes to increase the size for the "number of blocks" field.

A recent revision to HFS, HFS+, removes some of the original limitations of HFS, such as the maximum number of blocks on a volume, but otherwise makes very few alterations to the basic structure of HFS. HFS+ first shipped with Mac OS 8.1 about 14 years after the first version of HFS.

Despite its serious limitations, HFS broke new ground at the time of its release because it was the first file system to provide direct support for the rest of the graphical environment. The most serious limitations of HFS are that it is highly single threaded and that all file and directory information is in a single file, the catalog file. Storing all file extent information in a single file and limiting the number of blocks to allocate from to 65,536 also imposes serious limitations on HFS. The resource and data forks of HFS offered a new approach to storing files and associated metadata. HFS set the standard for file systems supporting a GUI, but it falls short in many other critical areas of performance and scalability.

3.4 Irix XFS

The Irix operating system, a version of Unix from SGI, offers a very sophisticated file system, XFS. XFS supports journaling, 64-bit files, and highly parallel operation. One of the major forces driving the development of XFS was the support for very large file systems—file systems with tens to hundreds of gigabytes of online storage, millions of files, and very large files spanning many gigabytes. XFS is a file system for "big iron."

While XFS supports all the traditional abstractions of a file system, it departs dramatically in its implementation of those abstractions. XFS differs from the straightforward implementation of a file system in its management of free disk space, i-nodes, file data, and directory contents.

As previously discussed, the most common way to manage free disk blocks in a file system is to use a bitmap with 1 bit per block. XFS instead uses a pair of B+trees to manage free disk space. XFS divides a disk up into large-sized chunks called *allocation groups* (a term with a similar meaning in BFS). Each allocation group maintains a pair of B+trees that record information about free space in the allocation group. One of the B+trees records free space sorted by starting block number. The other B+tree sorts the free blocks by their length. This scheme offers the ability for the file system to find free disk space based on either the proximity to already allocated space or based on the size needed. Clearly this organization offers significant advantages for efficiently finding the right block of disk space for a given file. The only potential drawback to such a scheme is that the B+trees both maintain the same information in different forms. This duplication can cause inconsistencies if, for whatever reason, the two trees get out of sync. Because XFS is journaled, however, this is not generally an issue.

XFS also does not preallocate i-nodes as is done in traditional Unix file systems. In XFS, instead of having a fixed-size table of i-nodes, each allocation group allocates disk blocks for i-nodes on an as-needed basis. XFS stores the locations of the i-nodes in a B+tree in each allocation group—a very unusual organization. The benefits are clear: no wasted disk space for unneeded files and no limits on the number of files after creating the file system. However, this organization is not without its drawbacks: when the list of i-nodes is a table, looking up an i-node is a constant-time index operation, but XFS must do a B+tree lookup to locate the i-node.

XFS uses extent maps to manage the blocks allocated to a file. An extent map is a starting block address and a length (expressed as a number of blocks). Instead of simply maintaining a list of fixed-size blocks with direct, indirect, double-indirect, and triple-indirect blocks, XFS again uses B+trees. The B+tree is indexed by the block offset in the file that the extent maps. That is, the extents that make up a file are stored in a B+tree sorted by which position of the file they correspond to.

The B+trees allow XFS to use variable-sized extents. The cost is that the implementation is considerably more difficult than using fixed-size blocks. The benefit is that a small amount of data in an extent can map very large regions of a file. XFS can map up to two million blocks with one extent map.

Another departure from a traditional file system is that XFS uses B+trees to store the contents of a directory. A traditional file system stores the contents of a directory in a linear list. Storing directory entries linearly does not scale well when there are hundreds or thousands of items. XFS again uses B+trees to store the entries in a directory. The B+tree sorts the entries based on their name, which makes lookups of specific files in a directory very efficient. This use of B+trees allows XFS to efficiently manage directories with several hundred thousand entries.

The final area that XFS excels in is its support for parallel I/O. Much of SGI's high-end hardware is highly parallel, with some machines scaling up to as many as 1024 processors. Supporting fine-grained locking was essential for XFS. Although most file systems allow the same file to be opened multiple times, there is usually a lock around the i-node that prevents true simultaneous access to the file. XFS removes this limitation and allows single-writer/multireader access to files. For files residing in the buffer cache, this allows multiple CPUs to copy the data concurrently. For systems with large disk arrays, allowing multiple readers to access the file allows multiple requests to be queued up to the disk controllers. XFS can also support multiple-writer access to a file, but users can only achieve this using an access mode to the file that bypasses the cache.

XFS offers an interesting implementation of a traditional file system. It departs from the standard techniques, trading implementation complexity for performance gains. The gains offered by XFS make a compelling argument in favor of the approaches it takes.

3.5   Windows NT's NTFS

The Windows NT file system (NTFS) is a journaled 64-bit file system that supports attributes. NTFS also supports file compression built in to the file system and works in conjunction with other Windows NT services to provide high reliability and recoverability. Microsoft developed NTFS to support Windows NT and to overcome the limitations of existing file systems at the time of the development of Windows NT (circa 1990).

The Master File Table and Files

The main data structure in NTFS is the master file table (MFT). The MFT contains the i-nodes ("file records" in NTFS parlance) for all files in the file system. As we will describe later, the MFT is itself a file and can therefore grow as needed. Each entry in the MFT refers to a single file and has all the information needed to access the file. Each file record is 1, 2, or 4 KB in size (determined at file system initialization time).

The NTFS i-node contains all of the information about a file organized as a series of typed attributes. Some attributes, such as the timestamps, are required and always present. Other attributes, such as the file name, are also required, but there may be more than one instance of the attribute (as is the case with the truncated MS-DOS version of an NTFS file name). Still other attributes may have only their header stored in the i-node, and they only contain pointers to their associated data.

If a file has too many attributes to fit in a single i-node, another attribute is added, an attribute list attribute. The attribute list attribute contains the i-node number of another slot in the MFT where the additional attributes can be found. This allows files to have a potentially unbounded list of attributes.

NTFS stores file and attribute data in what it refers to as "attribute streams." NTFS uses extents to record the blocks allocated to a file. Extents compactly refer to large amounts of disk space, although they do suffer the disadvantage that finding a specific position in a file requires searching through the entire list of extents to locate the one that covers the desired position.

Because there is little information available about the details of NTFS, it is not clear whether NTFS uses indirect blocks to access large amounts of file data.

File System Metadata

NTFS takes an elegant approach toward storing and organizing its metadata structures. All file system data structures in NTFS, including the MFT itself, are stored as files, and all have entries in the MFT. The following nine items are always the first nine entries in the MFT:

- MFT
- Partial MFT copy
- Log file
- Volume file
- Attribute definition file
- Root directory
- Bitmap file
- Boot file
- Bad cluster file

NTFS also reserves eight more entries in the MFT for any additional system files that might be needed in the future. Each of these entries is a regular file with all the properties associated with a file.

By storing all file system metadata as a file, NTFS allows file system structures to grow dynamically. This is very powerful because it enables growing items such as the volume bitmap, which implies that a volume could grow simply by adding more storage and increasing the size of the volume bitmap file. Another system capable of this is IBM's JFS.

NTFS stores the name of a volume and sundry other information global to the volume in the volume file. The log is also stored in a file, which again enables the log to increase in size if desired, potentially increasing the throughput of the file system (at the cost of more lost data if there is a crash). The attribute definition file is another small housekeeping file that contains the list of attribute types supported on the volume, whether they can be indexed, and whether they can be recovered during a file system recovery.

Of these reserved system files, only the boot file must be at a fixed location on disk. The boot file must be at a fixed location so that it is easy for any boot ROMs on the computer to load and execute the boot file. When a disk is initialized with NTFS, the formatting utility reserves the fixed location for the boot file and also stores in the boot file the location of the MFT.

By storing all metadata information in files, NTFS can be more dynamic in its management of resources and allow for growth of normally fixed file system data structures.

Directories

Directories in NTFS are stored in B+trees that keep their entries sorted in alphabetic order. Along with the name of a file, NTFS directories also store the file reference number (i-node number) of the file, the size of the file, and the last modification time. NTFS is unusual in that it stores the size and last modification time of a file in the directory as well as in the i-node (file record). The benefit of duplicating the information on file size and last modification time in the directory entry is that listing the contents of a directory using the normal MS-DOS `dir` command is very fast. The downside to this approach is that the data is duplicated (and thus potentially out of sync). Further, the speed benefit is questionable since the Windows NT GUI will probably have to read the file i-node anyway to get other information needed to display the file properly (icon, icon position, etc.).

Journaling and the Log File Service

Journaling in NTFS is a fairly complex task. The file system per se does not implement logging, but rather the log file service implements the logic and provides the mechanisms used by NTFS. Logging involves the file system, the log file service, and the cache manager. All three components must cooperate closely to ensure that file system transactions are properly recorded and able to be played back in the event of a system failure.

NTFS uses *write-ahead logging*—it first writes planned changes to the log, and then it writes the actual file system blocks in the cache. NTFS writes entries to the log whenever one of the following occurs:

■ Creating a file
■ Deleting a file
■ Changing the size of a file
■ Setting file information
■ Renaming a file

■ Changing access permissions of a file

NTFS informs the log file service of planned updates by writing entries to the log file. When a transaction is complete, NTFS writes a checkpoint record indicating that no more updates exist for the transaction in question.

The log file service uses the log file in a circular fashion, providing the appearance of an infinite log to NTFS. To prevent the log from overwriting necessary information, if the log becomes full, the log file service will return a "log file full" error to NTFS. NTFS then raises an exception, reschedules the operation, and asks the cache manager to flush unwritten data to disk. By flushing the cache, NTFS forces blocks belonging to uncompleted transactions to be written to disk, which allows those transactions to complete and thus frees up space in the log. The "log file full" error is never seen by user-level programs and is simply an internal mechanism to indicate that the cache should be flushed so as to free up space in the log.

When it is necessary to flush the log, NTFS first locks all open files (to prevent further I/O) and then calls the cache manager to flush any unwritten blocks. This has the potential to disrupt important I/O at random and unpredictable times. From a user's viewpoint, this behavior would cause the system to appear to freeze momentarily and then continue normally. This may not be acceptable in some situations.

If a crash occurs on a volume, the next time NTFS accesses the volume it will replay the log to repair any damage that may have occurred. To replay the log, NTFS first scans the log to find where the last checkpoint record was written. From there it works backwards, replaying the update records until it reaches the last known good position of the file system. This process takes at most a few seconds and is independent of the size of the disk.

Data Compression

NTFS also offers transparent data compression of files to reduce space. There are two types of data compression available with NTFS. The first method compresses long ranges of empty (zero-filled) data in the file by simply omitting the blocks instead of filling them with zeros. This technique, commonly called *sparse files*, is prevalent in Unix file systems. Sparse files are a big win for scientific applications that require storing large sparse matrices on disk.

The second method is a more traditional, although undocumented, compression technique. In this mode of operation NTFS breaks a file into chunks of 16 file system blocks and performs compression on each of those blocks. If the compressed data does not save at least one block, the data is stored normally and not compressed. Operating on individual chunks of a file opens up the possibility that the compression algorithm can use different techniques for different portions of the file.

In practice, the speed of CPUs so far outstrips the speed of disks that NTFS sees little performance difference in accessing compressed or uncompressed files. Because this result is dependent on the speed of the disk I/O, a fast RAID subsystem would change the picture considerably.

Providing compression in the file system, as opposed to applying it to an entire volume, allows users and programs to selectively compress files based on higher-level knowledge of the file contents. This arrangement requires more programmer or administrator effort but has the added benefits that other file I/O is not impeded by the compression and the files selected for compression will likely benefit from it most.

NTFS Summary

NTFS is an advanced modern file system that supports file attributes, 64-bit file and volume sizes, journaling, and data compression. The only area that NTFS does not excel in is making use of file attributes since they cannot be indexed or queried. NTFS is a sophisticated file system that performs well in the target markets of Windows NT.

3.6 Summary

This chapter touched on five members of the large family of existing file systems. We covered the grandfather of most modern file systems, BSD FFS; the fast and unsafe grandchild, ext2; the odd-ball cousin, HFS; the burly nephew, XFS; and the blue-suited distant relative, NTFS. Each of these file systems has its own characteristics and target audiences. BSD FFS set the standard for file systems for approximately 10 years. Linux ext2 broke all the rules regarding safety and also blew the doors off the performance of its predecessors. HFS addressed the needs of the GUI of the Macintosh although design decisions made in 1984 seem foolhardy in our current enlightened day. The aim of XFS is squarely on large systems offering huge disk arrays. NTFS is a good, solid modern design that offers many interesting and sophisticated features and fits well into the overall structure of Windows NT.

No one file system is the absolute "best." Every file system has certain features that make it more or less appropriate in different situations. Understanding the features and characteristics of a variety of file systems enables us to better understand what choices can be made when designing a file system.

4

The Data Structures of BFS

4.1 What Is a Disk?

BFS views a disk as a linear array of blocks and manages all of its data structures on top of this basic abstraction. At the lowest level a raw device (such as a SCSI or IDE disk) has a notion of a device block size, usually 512 bytes. The concept of a block in BFS rests on top of the blocks of a raw device. The size of file system blocks is only loosely coupled to the raw device block size.

The only restriction on the file system block size is that it must be a multiple of the underlying raw device block size. That is, if the raw device block size is 512 bytes, then the file system can have a block size of 512, 1024, or 2048 bytes. Although it is possible to have a block size of 1536 (3×512), this is a really poor choice because it is not a power of two. Although it is not a strict requirement, creating a file system with a block size that is not a power of two would have significant performance impacts. The file system block size has implications for the virtual memory system if the system supports memory-mapped files. Further, if you wish to unify the VM system and the buffer cache, having a file system block size that is a power of two is a requirement (the ideal situation is when the VM page size and the file system block size are equal).

BFS allows block sizes of 1024, 2048, 4096, or 8192 bytes. We chose not to allow 512-byte block sizes because then certain critical file system data structures would span more than one block. Data structures spanning more than one disk block complicated the cache management because of the requirements of journaling. Structures spanning more than one block also caused noticeable performance problems. We explain the maximum block size (8192 bytes) later because it requires understanding several other structures first.

It is important to realize that the file system block size is independent of the size of the disk (unlike the Macintosh HFS). The choice of file system block size should be made based on the types of files to be stored on the disk: lots of small files would waste considerable space if the block size were 8K; a file system with very large files benefits from larger block sizes instead of very small blocks.

4.2   How to Manage Disk Blocks

There are several different approaches to managing free space on a disk. The most common (and simplest) method is a bitmap scheme. Other methods are extent based and B+trees (XFS). BFS uses a bitmap scheme for simplicity.

The bitmap scheme represents each disk block as 1 bit, and the file system views the entire disk as an array of these bits. If a bit is on (i.e., a one), the corresponding block is allocated. The formula for the amount of space (in bytes) required for a block bitmap is

$$\frac{\text{disk size in bytes}}{\text{file system block size} \times 8}$$

Thus, the bitmap for a 1 GB disk with 1K blocks requires 128K of space.

The main disadvantage to the bitmap allocation scheme is that searching for large contiguous sections of free space requires searching linearly through the entire bitmap. There are also those who think that another disadvantage to the bitmap scheme is that as the disk fills up, searching the bitmap will become more expensive. However, it can be proven mathematically that the cost of finding a free bit in a bitmap stays constant regardless of how full the bitmap is. This fact, coupled with the ease of implementation, is why BFS uses a bitmap allocation scheme (although in retrospect I wish there had been time to experiment with other allocation schemes).

The bitmap data structure is simply stored on disk as a contiguous array of bytes (rounded up to be a multiple of the block size). BFS stores the bitmap starting at block one (the superblock is block zero). When creating the file system, the blocks consumed by the superblock and the bitmap are preallocated.

4.3   Allocation Groups

Allocation groups are purely logical structures. Allocation groups have no real `struct` associated with them. BFS divides the array of blocks that make up a file system into equal-sized chunks, which we call "allocation groups." BFS uses the notion of allocation groups to spread data around the disk.

An allocation group is simply some number of blocks of the entire disk. The number of blocks that make up an allocation group is intimately tied to the file system block size and the size of the bitmap for the disk. For efficiency and convenience BFS forces the number of blocks in an allocation group to be a multiple of the number of blocks mapped by a bitmap block.

Let's consider a 1 GB disk with a file system block size of 1K. Such a disk has a 128K block bitmap and therefore requires 128 blocks on disk. The minimum allocation group size would be 8192 blocks because each bitmap block is 1K and thus maps 8192 blocks. For reasons discussed later, the maximum allocation group size is always 65,536. In choosing the size of an allocation group, BFS balances disk size (and thus the need for large allocation groups) against the desire to have a reasonable number of allocation groups. In practice, this works out to be about 8192 blocks per allocation group per gigabyte of space.

As mentioned earlier, BFS uses allocation groups to help spread data around the disk. BFS tries to put the control information (the i-node) for a file in the same allocation group as its parent directory. It also tries to put new directories in different allocation groups from the directory that contains them. File data is also put into a different allocation group from the file that contains it. This organization policy tends to cluster the file control information together in one allocation group and the data in another. This layout encourages files in the same directory to be close to each other on disk. It is important to note that this is only an advisory policy, and if a disk were so full that the only free space for some data were in the same allocation group as the file control information, it would not prevent the allocation from happening.

To improve performance when trying to allocate blocks, BFS maintains information in memory about each of the allocation groups in the block bitmap. Each allocation group has an index of the last free block in that allocation group. This enables the bitmap allocation routines to quickly jump to a free block instead of always searching from the very beginning of an allocation group. Likewise, if an allocation group is full, it is wasteful to search its bitmap to find this out. Thus we also maintain a "full" indicator for each allocation group in the block bitmap so that we can quickly skip large portions of the disk that are full.

4.4   Block Runs

The block_run data structure is the fundamental way that BFS addresses disk blocks. A block_run is a simple data structure:

```
typedef struct block_run
{
    int32   allocation_group;
```

```
        uint16   start;
        uint16   len;
} block_run;
```

The allocation_group field tells us which allocation group we are in, and the start field tells us which block within that allocation group this block_run begins at. The len field indicates how many blocks long this run is. There are several important issues to notice about this data structure. The maximum block number it can represent is 2^{48} in size, and thus with a 1K block size, the largest disk that BFS can use is 2^{58} bytes in size. This may seem a disadvantage compared to a pure 64-bit block number, but a disk that is 2^{58} bytes in size is large enough to hold over 217 years of continuous uncompressed video (720 × 486, 4 bytes per pixel) at 30 frames per second. We felt that this offered enough headroom for the foreseeable future.

The 16-bit len field allows a block_run to address up to 65,536 blocks. Although it is not the enormous advantage we might imagine, being able to address as much as 64 MB (and potentially more, if the file system block size is larger) with one 8-byte block_run is very useful.

One limitation of the block_run data structure is the 16-bit starting block number. Since it is an unsigned 16-bit number, that limits us to a maximum of 65,536 blocks in any allocation group. That, in turn, places the 8192-byte limit on the block size of the file system. The reasoning is somewhat subtle: each allocation group is at least one block of the bitmap; a block size of 8192 bytes means that each block of the bitmap maps 65,536 blocks (8 bits per byte × 8192 bytes per block), and thus 8192 bytes is the maximum block size a BFS file system can have. Were we to allow larger block sizes, each allocation group could contain more blocks than the start field of a block_run could address, and that would lead to blocks that could never be allocated.

BFS uses the block_run data structure as an i-node address structure. An inode_addr structure is a block_run structure with a len field equal to one.

4.5 The Superblock

The BFS superblock contains many fields that not only describe the physical size of the volume that the file system resides on but additional information about the log area and the indices. Further, BFS stores some redundant information to enable better consistency checking of the superblock, the volume name, and the byte order of the file system.

The BFS superblock data structure is

```
typedef struct disk_super_block
{
        char         name[B_OS_NAME_LENGTH];
        int32        magic1;
```

```
    int32           fs_byte_order;

    uint32          block_size;
    uint32          block_shift;

    off_t           num_blocks;
    off_t           used_blocks;

    int32           inode_size;

    int32           magic2;
    int32           blocks_per_ag;
    int32           ag_shift;
    int32           num_ags;

    int32           flags;

    block_run       log_blocks;
    off_t           log_start;
    off_t           log_end;

    int32           magic3;
    inode_addr      root_dir;
    inode_addr      indices;

    int32           pad[8];
} disk_super_block;
```

You will notice that there are three magic numbers stored in the super-block. When mounting a file system, these magic numbers are the first round of sanity checking that is done to ensure correctness. Note that the magic numbers were spread around throughout the data structure so that if any part of the data structure became corrupt, it is easier to detect the corruption than if there were just one or two magic numbers only at the beginning of the structure.

The values of the magic numbers are completely arbitrary but were chosen to be large, moderately interesting 32-bit values:

```
#define SUPER_BLOCK_MAGIC1    0x42465331    /* BFS1 */
#define SUPER_BLOCK_MAGIC2    0xdd121031
#define SUPER_BLOCK_MAGIC3    0x15b6830e
```

The first real information in the superblock is the block size of the file system. BFS stores the block size in two ways. The first is the block_size field, which is an explicit number of bytes. Because BFS requires the block size to be a power of two, it is also convenient to store the number of bits needed to shift a block number by to get a byte address. We use the block_shift field for this purpose. Storing both forms of the block size allows for an additional level of checking when mounting a file system: the block_size and block_shift fields must agree in a valid file system.

The next two fields, num_blocks and used_blocks, record the number of blocks available on this volume and how many are currently in use. The type of these values is off_t, which on the BeOS is a 64-bit quantity. It is not a requirement that off_t be 64-bit, and in fact the early development versions of BFS were only 32-bit because the compiler did not support a 64-bit data type at the time. The num_blocks and block_size fields tell you exactly how big a disk is. When multiplied together the result is the exact number of bytes that the file system has available. The used_blocks field records how many blocks are currently in use on the file system. This information is not strictly necessary but is much more convenient to maintain than to sum up all the one bits in the bitmap each time we wish to know how full a disk is.

The next field, inode_size, tells us the size of each i-node (i.e., file control block). BFS does not use a preallocated table of i-nodes as most Unix file systems do. Instead, BFS allocates i-nodes on demand, and each i-node is at least one disk block. This may seem excessive, but as we will describe shortly, it turns out not to waste as much space as you would initially think. BFS primarily uses the inode_size field when allocating space for an i-node, but it is also used as a consistency check in a few other situations (the i-node size must be a multiple of the file system block size, and i-nodes themselves store their size so that it can be verified against the inode_size field in the superblock).

Allocation groups have no real data structure associated with them aside from this information recorded here in the superblock. The blocks_per_ag field of the superblock refers to the number of bitmap blocks that are in each allocation group. The number of bitmap blocks per allocation group must never map more than 65,536 blocks for the reasons described above. Similar to the block_shift field, the ag_shift field records the number of bits to shift an allocation group number by when converting a block_run address to a byte offset (and vice versa). The num_ags field is the number of allocation groups in this file system and is used to control and check the allocation_group field of block_run structures.

The flags field records the state of the superblock: Is it clean or dirty? Because BFS is journaled, it always writes the superblock with a value of BFS_CLEAN (0x434c454e). In memory during transactions that modify the disk, the field is set to BFS_DIRTY (0x44495254). At mount time the flags field is checked to verify that the file system is clean.

Information about the journal is the next chunk of information that we find in the superblock. The journal (described in depth in Chapter 7) is the area that records upcoming changes to the file system. As far as the superblock is concerned, the journal is simply a contiguous array of disk blocks. Therefore the superblock primarily needs to record a `block_run` data structure that describes the area of the disk that makes up the journal. To maintain the state of the journal and where we are in it (since the journal is a circular buffer), we also maintain pointers to the start and end of the journal in the variables `log_start` and `log_end`.

The last two members of the superblock structure, `root_dir` and `indices`, connect the superblock with all the data stored on the volume. The address of the i-node of the root directory is the connection from the superblock to the root of the hierarchy of all files and directories on the volume. The address of the i-node of the index directory connects the superblock with the indices stored on a volume.

Without these two pieces of information, BFS would have no way to find any of the files on the disk. As we will see later, having the address of an i-node on disk allows us to get at the contents of that i-node (regardless of whether it is a directory or a file). An i-node address is simply a `block_run` structure whose `len` field is one.

When a file system is in active use, the superblock is loaded into memory. In memory there is a `bfs_info` structure, which holds a copy of the superblock, the file descriptor used to access the underlying device, semaphores, and other state information about the file system. The `bfs_info` structure stores the data necessary to access everything else on the volume.

4.6   The I-Node Structure

When a user opens a file, they open it using a human-readable name. The name is a string of characters and is easy for people to deal with. Associated with that name is an i-node number, which is convenient for the file system to deal with. In BFS, the i-node number of a file is an address of where on disk the i-node data structure lives. The i-node of a file is essential to accessing the contents of that file (i.e., reading or writing the file, etc.).

The i-node data structure maintains the metainformation about entities that live in the file system. An i-node must record information such as the size of a file, who owns it, its creation time, last modification time, and various other bits of information about the file. The most important information in an i-node is the information about where the data belonging to this i-node exists on disk. That is, an i-node is the connection that takes you to the data that is in the file. This basic structure is the fundamental building block of how data is stored in a file on a file system.

The BFS i-node structure is

```
typedef struct bfs_inode
{
```

```
        int32         magic1;
        inode_addr    inode_num;
        int32         uid;
        int32         gid;
        int32         mode;
        int32         flags;
        bigtime_t     create_time;
        bigtime_t     last_modified_time;
        inode_addr    parent;
        inode_addr    attributes;
        uint32        type;

        int32         inode_size;
        binode_etc    *etc;

        data_stream   data;
        int32         pad[4];
        int32         small_data[1];
} bfs_inode;
```

Again we see the use of magic numbers for consistency checking. The magic number for an i-node is 0x3bbe0ad9. If needed, the magic number can also be used to identify different versions of an i-node. For example, if in the future it is necessary to add to or change the i-node, the new format i-nodes can use a different magic number to identify themselves.

We also store the i-node number of this i-node inside of itself so that it is easy to simply maintain a pointer to the disk block in memory and still remember where it came from on disk. Further, the inode_num field provides yet another consistency checkpoint.

The uid/gid fields are a simple method of maintaining ownership information about a file. These fields correspond very closely to POSIX-style uid/gid fields (except that they are 32 bits in size).

The mode field is where file access permission information is stored as well as information about whether a file is a regular file or a directory. The file permission model in BFS follows the POSIX 1003.1 specification very closely. That is, there is a notion of user, group, and "other" access to a file system entity. The three types of permission are read, write, and execute. This is a very simple model of permission checking (and it has a correspondingly simple implementation).

Another method of managing ownership information is through access control lists. ACLs have many nice properties, but it was not deemed reasonable to implement ACLs in the amount of time that was available to complete BFS. ACLs store explicit information about which users may access a file system item. This is much finer-grained than the standard POSIX permission model; in fact, they are required to achieve certain forms of U.S. government security certifications (e.g., C2-level security). It may be possible to implement ACLs using file attributes (discussed later), but that avenue has not yet been explored.

As always, a flags field is very useful for recording various bits of state information about an i-node. BFS needs to know several things about an i-node, some of which it records permanently and some of which are only used while in memory. The flags currently understood by BFS are

```
#define INODE_IN_USE      0x00000001
#define ATTR_INODE        0x00000004
#define INODE_LOGGED      0x00000008
#define INODE_DELETED     0x00000010


#define PERMANENT_FLAGS   0x0000ffff


#define INODE_NO_CACHE    0x00010000
#define INODE_WAS_WRITTEN 0x00020000
#define NO_TRANSACTION    0x00040000
```

All active i-nodes always have the INODE_IN_USE flag set. If an i-node refers to an attribute, the ATTR_INODE flag is set. The ATTR_INODE flag affects how other portions of BFS will deal with the i-node.

The INODE_LOGGED flag implies a great deal about how BFS handles the i-node. When this flag is set, all data written to the data stream referred to by this i-node is journaled. That is, when a modification happens to the data stream of this i-node, the changes are journaled just as with any other journaled transaction (see Chapter 7 for more details).

So far, the only use of the INODE_LOGGED flag is for directories. The contents of a directory constitute file system metadata information—information that is necessary for the correct operation of the system. Because corrupted directories would be a disastrous failure, any changes to the contents of a directory must be logged in the journal to prevent corruption.

The INODE_LOGGED flag has potentially serious implications. Logging all data written to a file potentially could overflow the journal (again, see Chapter 7 for a more complete description). Therefore the only i-nodes for which this flag is set are directories where the amount of I/O done to the data segment can be reasonably bounded and is very tightly controlled.

When a user removes a file, the file system sets the INODE_DELETED flag for the i-node corresponding to the file. The INODE_DELETED flag indicates that access is no longer allowed to the file. Although this flag is set in memory, BFS does not bother to write the i-node to disk, saving an extra disk write during file deletions.

The remaining flags only affect the handling of the i-node while it is loaded in memory. Discussion of how BFS uses these other flags is left to the sections where they are relevant.

Getting back to the remaining fields of the i-node, we find the create_time and last_modified_time fields. Unlike Unix file systems, BFS maintains the creation time of files and does not maintain a last accessed time (often know as atime). The last accessed time is expensive to maintain, and in general the last modified time is sufficient. The performance cost of maintaining the last accessed time (i.e., a disk write every time a file is touched) is simply too great for the small amount of use that it gets.

For efficiency when indexing the time fields, BFS stores them as a bigtime_t, which is a 64-bit quantity. The value stored is a normal POSIX time_t shifted up by 16 bits with a small counter logically ORed in. The purpose of this manipulation is to help create unique time values to avoid unnecessary duplicates in the time indices (see Chapter 5 for more details).

The next field, parent, is a reference back to the directory that contains this file. The presence of this field is a departure from Unix-style file systems. BFS requires the parent field to support reconstructing a full path name from an i-node. Reconstructing a full path name from an i-node is necessary when processing queries (described in Chapter 5).

The next field, attributes, is perhaps the most unconventional part of an i-node in BFS. The field attributes is an i-node address. The i-node it points to is a directory that contains attributes about this file. The entries in the attributes directory are names that correspond to attributes (name/value pairs) of the file. We will discuss attributes and the necessity of this field later because they require a lengthy explanation.

The type field only applies to i-nodes used to store attributes. Indexing of attributes requires that they have a type (integer, string, floating point, etc.), and this field maintains that information. The choice of the name type for this field perhaps carries a bit more semantic baggage than it should: it is most emphatically not meant to store information such as the type and creator fields of the Macintosh HFS. The BeOS stores real type information about a file as a MIME string in an attribute whose name is BEOS:TYPE.

The inode_size field is mainly a sanity check field. Very early development versions of BFS used the field in more meaningful ways, but now it is simply another check done whenever an i-node is loaded from disk.

The etc field is simply a pointer to in-memory information about the i-node. It is part of the i-node structure stored on disk so that, when we load a block of a file system into memory, it is possible to use it in place and there is no need to massage the on-disk representation before it can be used.

4.7 The Core of an I-Node: The Data Stream

The purpose of an i-node is to connect a file with some physical storage. The `data` member of an i-node is the meat of an i-node. The `data` member is a `data_stream` structure that provides the connection between the stream of bytes that a programmer sees when doing I/O to a file and where those bytes live on disk.

The `data_stream` structure provides a way to map from a logical file position, such as byte 5937, to a file system block at some location on the disk. The `data_stream` structure is

```
#define NUM_DIRECT_BLOCKS     12

typedef struct data_stream
{
        block_run direct[NUM_DIRECT_BLOCKS];
        off_t     max_direct_range;
        block_run indirect;
        off_t     max_indirect_range;
        block_run double_indirect;
        off_t     max_double_indirect_range;
        off_t     size;
} data_stream;
```

Looking at a simple example will help to understand the `data_stream` structure. Consider a file with 2048 bytes of data. If the file system has 1024-byte blocks, the file will require two blocks to map all the data. Recalling the `block_run` data structure, we see that it can map a run of 65,536 contiguous blocks. Since we only need two, this is trivial. So a file with 2048 bytes of data could have a `block_run` with a length of two that would map all of the data of the file. On an extremely fragmented disk, it would be possible to need two `block_run` data structures, each with a length of one. In either case, the `block_run` data structures would fit in the space provided for direct blocks (which is 12 `block_run`s).

The direct `block_run` structures can potentially address quite a large amount of data. In the best-case scenario the direct blocks can map 768 MB of space (12 `block_run`s × 65,536 1K blocks per `block_run`). In the worst-case scenario the direct blocks can map only 12K of space (12 blocks × 1 1K block per `block_run`). In practice the average amount of space mapped by the direct blocks is in the range of several hundred kilobytes to several megabytes.

Large files (from the tens of megabytes to multigigabyte monster files) almost certainly require more than the 12 `block_run` data structures that fit in the i-node. The `indirect` and `double_indirect` fields provide access to larger amounts of data than can be addressed by the direct `block_run` structures.

Figure 4-1 illustrates how direct, indirect, and double-indirect blocks map

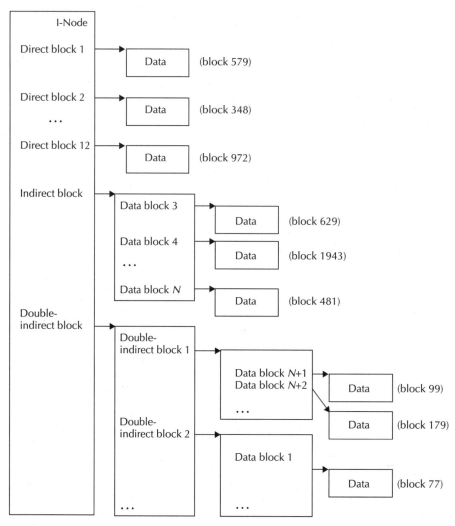

Figure 4-1   The relationship of direct, indirect, and double-indirect blocks.

the stream of data that makes up a file. The rectangles marked "data" are the data blocks that are the contents of the file. The fictitious block numbers beside the data blocks simply demonstrate that contiguous bytes of a file need not be contiguous on disk (although it is preferable when they are). The `indirect` field of the `data_stream` is the address of a block on disk, and the contents of that block are more block addresses that point to real data blocks. The `double_indirect` block address points to a block that contains block addresses of indirect blocks (which contain yet more block addresses of data blocks).

You may wonder, Are so many levels of indirection really necessary? The answer is yes. In fact, most common Unix-style file systems will also have a triple-indirect block. BFS avoids the added complexity of a triple-indirect block through its use of the `block_run` data structure. The BFS `block_run` structure can map up to 65,536 blocks in a single 8-byte structure. This saves considerable space in comparison to a file system such as Linux ext2, which would require 65,536 4-byte entries to map 65,536 blocks.

What then is the maximum file size that BFS can address? The maximum file size is influenced by several factors, but we can compute it for both best- and worst-case scenarios. We will assume a 1K file system block size in the following computations.

Given the above data structures, the worst-case situation is that each `block_run` maps a minimal amount of data. To increase the amount of data mapped in the worst case, BFS imposes two restrictions. The `block_run` referenced by the indirect field is always at least 4K in size and therefore it can contain 512 `block_runs` (4096/8). The data blocks mapped by the double-indirect blocks are also always at least 4K in length. This helps to avoid fragmentation and eases the task of finding a file position (discussed later). With those constraints,

direct blocks =	12K	(12 `block_runs`, 1K each)
indirect blocks =	512K	(4K indirect block maps 512 `block_runs` of 1K each)
double-indirect blocks =	1024 MB	(4K double-indirect page maps 512 indirect pages that map 512 `block_runs` of 4K each)

Thus the maximum file size in the worst case is slightly over 1 GB. We consider this acceptable because of how difficult it is to achieve. The worst-case situation only occurs when every other block on the disk is allocated. Although this is possible, it is extremely unlikely (although it is a test case we routinely use).

The best-case situation is quite different. Again with a 1K file system block size,

direct blocks =	768 MB	(12 `block_runs`, 65,536K each)
indirect blocks =	32,768 MB	(4K indirect block maps 512 `block_runs` of 65,536K each)
double-indirect blocks =	1 GB	(4K double-indirect page maps 512 indirect pages that map 512 `block_runs` of 4K each)

In this case, the maximum file size would be approximately 34 GB, which is adequate for current disks. Increasing the file system block size or the amount of data mapped by each double-indirect block run would significantly increase the maximum file size, providing plenty of headroom for the forseeable future.

Armed with the knowledge of how a data_stream structure maps the blocks of a file, we can now answer the question of how a logical file position like byte 37,934 maps to a specific block on disk. Let's begin with a simple example. Assume that the data_stream of a file has four direct block_run structures that each maps 16K of data. The array would look like this:

```
direct[0] = { 12,  219, 16 }
direct[1] = { 15, 1854, 16 }
direct[2] = { 23,  962, 16 }
direct[3] = { 39,   57, 16 }
direct[4] = {  0,    0,  0 }
```

To find position 37,934 we would iterate over each of the direct blocks until we find the block_run that covers the position we are interested in. In pseudocode this looks like

```
pos = 37934;

for (i=0, sum=0;  i < NUM_DIRECT_BLOCKS;
     sum += direct[i].len * block_size, i++) {
    if (pos >= sum && pos < sum + (direct[i].len * block_size))
        break;
}
```

In prose the algorithm reads as follows: Iterate over each of the block_run structures until the position we want is greater than or equal to the beginning position of this block_run and the position we want is less than the end of this current block_run. After the above loop exits, the index variable i would refer to the block_run that covers the desired position. Using the array of direct block_runs given above and the position 37,934, we would exit the loop with the index equal to two. This would be the block_run { 23, 962, 16 }. That is, starting at block 962 in allocation group 23 there is a run of 16 blocks. The position we want (37,934) is in that block_run at offset 5166 (37,934 − 32,768).

As a file grows and starts to fill indirect blocks, we would continue the above search by loading the indirect blocks and searching through them in a manner similar to how we searched the direct blocks. Because each block_run in the direct and indirect blocks can map a variable amount of the file data, we must always search linearly through them.

The potentially enormous number of double-indirect blocks makes it untenable to search through them linearly as done with direct and indirect blocks. To alleviate this problem, BFS always allocates double-indirect blocks in fixed-length runs of blocks (currently four). By fixing the number of blocks each double-indirect block maps, we eliminate the need to iterate linearly through all the blocks. The problem of finding a file position in the double-indirect blocks simplifies to a series of divisions (shifts) and modulo operations.

4.8 Attributes

A key component of BFS is its ability to store attributes about a file with the file. An attribute is a name/value pair. That is PhoneNum = 415-555-1212 is an attribute whose name is PhoneNum and whose value is 415-555-1212. The ability to add attributes to a file offers a great number of possibilities. Attributes allow users and programmers to store metainformation about a file with the file but not in the file data. Attributes such as Keywords, From, Type, Version, URL, and Icon are examples of the types of information that someone might want to store about a file but not necessarily in the file.

In BFS a file may have any number of attributes associated with it. The value portion of an attribute can have an integral type (int32, int64, float, double, or string) or it can be raw data of any size. If an attribute is of an integral type, then, if desired, BFS can index the attribute value for efficient retrieval through the query interface (described in depth in Chapter 5).

The BeOS takes advantage of attributes to store a variety of information. The email daemon uses attributes to store information about email messages. The email daemon also asks to index these attributes so that using the query interface (e.g., the find panel on the desktop) we can find and display email messages. The text editor supports styled editing (different fonts, colors, etc.), but instead of inventing another file format for text, it stores the style run information as an attribute, and the unblemished text is stored in the regular data stream of the file (thus allowing the ability to edit multifont source code, for example). And of course all files on the system have a type attribute so that it is easy to match programs that manipulate a given MIME type with files of that type.

With that rough sketch of what attributes are and how they are used, we can now look at the implementation. BFS stores the list of attributes associated with a file in an attribute directory (the attributes field of the bfs_inode structure). The directory is not part of the normal directory hierarchy but rather "hangs" on the side of the file. The named entries of the attribute directory point to the corresponding attribute value. Figure 4-2 shows the relationships.

This structure has a nice property. It reuses several data structures: the list of attributes is just a directory, and the individual attributes are really just files. This reuse eased the implementation considerably. The one main deficiency of this design is that it is also rather slow in the common case of having several small attributes.

To understand why storing all attributes in this manner was too slow, we have to understand the environment in which BFS runs. The primary

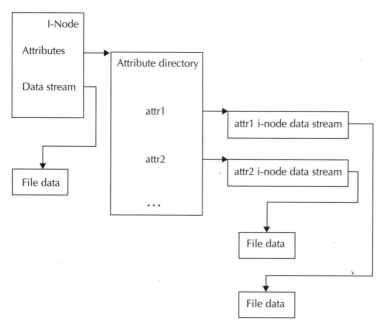

Figure 4-2   The structure of a file and its attributes.

interface of the BeOS is graphical—windows and icons, all of which have positions, sizes, current location, and so on. The user interface agent (the Tracker) stores all of this information as attributes of files and directories. Assuming a user opens a directory with 10 items in it and the Tracker has one attribute per item, that would require as many as 30 different seek operations to load all the information: one for each file to load the i-node, one for each attribute directory of each file, and one for the attribute of each file. The slowest thing a disk can do is to have to seek to a new position, and 30 disk seeks would easily cause a user-visible delay for opening even a small directory of 10 files.

The need to have very efficient access to a reasonable number of small attributes was the primary reason that BFS chose to store each i-node in its own disk block. The i-node `struct` only consumes slightly more than 200 bytes, which leaves considerable space available to store small attributes. BFS uses the spare area of the i-node disk block to store small attributes. This area is known as the `small_data` area and contains a tightly packed array of variable-sized attributes. There are about 760 bytes of space—sufficient to store all the information needed by the Tracker as well as all the information needed by the email daemon (which stores nine different attributes) and still leave about 200 bytes for other additional attributes. The performance gain from doing this is significant. Now with one disk seek and read, we immediately have all the information needed to display an item in a graphical interface.

The `small_data` area has the following structure:

```
typedef struct small_data {
        uint32    type;
        uint16    name_size;
        uint16    data_size;
        char      name[1];
} small_data;
```

BFS puts the first `small_data` structure directly after the end of the `bfs_inode` structure. The bytes of the name begin in the `name` field and continue from there. The attribute value (its data) is stored immediately following the bytes of the name. To maximally conserve space, no padding is done to align the structure (although I will probably regret that decision if the BeOS must ever run on processors with stricter alignment restrictions than the PPC or x86). The `small_data` areas continue until the end of the block that contains the i-node. The last area is always the free space (unless the amount of free space is less than the size of a `small_data` structure).

All files have a hidden attribute that contains the name of the file that this i-node refers to. BFS stores the name of an i-node as a hidden attribute that always lives in the `small_data` area of the i-node. BFS must store the name of a file in the i-node so that it can reconstruct the full path name of a file given just the i-node. As we will see later, the ability to go from an i-node to a full path name is necessary for queries.

The introduction of the `small_data` area complicated the management of attributes considerably. All attribute operations must first check if an attribute exists in the `small_data` area and, failing that, then look in the attribute directory. An attribute can exist in either the `small_data` area or the attribute directory but never both places. Despite the additional complexity of the `small_data` area, the performance benefit made the effort worthwhile.

4.9 Directories

Directories are what give a hierarchical file system its structure: a directory maps names that users see to i-node numbers that the file system manipulates. The i-node number contained in a directory entry may refer to a file or another directory. As we saw when examining the superblock, the superblock must contain the i-node address of the root directory. The root directory i-node allows us to access the contents of the root directory and thus traverse the rest of the file system hierarchy.

The mapping of name to i-node numbers is the primary function of a directory, and there are many schemes for maintaining such a mapping. A traditional Unix-style file system stores the entries of a directory (name/i-node pairs) in a simple linear list as part of the data stream of the directory. This scheme is extremely simple to implement; however, it is not particularly efficient when there are a large number of files in a directory. You have to read, on average, about half the size of the directory to locate a given file. This works fine for small numbers of files (less than a few hundred) but degrades significantly as the number of files increases.

Another approach to maintaining the mapping of name/i-node number is to use a more sophisticated data structure such as a B-tree. B-trees store key/value pairs in a balanced tree structure. For a directory, the key is the name and the value is the i-node address. The most attractive feature of B-trees is that they offer log(n) search time to locate an item. Storing directory entries in a B-tree speeds up the time it takes to look up an item. Because the time to look up an item to locate its i-node can be a significant portion of the total time it takes to open a file, making that process as efficient as possible is important.

Using B+trees to store directories was the most attractive choice for BFS. The speed gain for directory lookups was a nice benefit but not the primary reason for this decision. Even more important was that BFS also needed a data structure for indexing attributes, and reusing the same B+tree data structure for indexing and directories eased the implementation of BFS.

4.10 Indexing

As alluded to previously, BFS also maintains indices of attribute values. Users and programmers can create indices if they wish to run queries about a particular attribute. For example, the mail daemon creates indices named From, To, and Subject corresponding to the fields of an email message. Then for each message that arrives (which are stored in individual files), the mail daemon adds attributes to the file for the From, To, and Subject fields of the message. The file system then ensures that the value for each of the attributes gets indexed.

Continuing with this example, if a piece of email arrives with a From field of pike@research.att.com, the mail daemon adds an attribute whose name is From and whose value is pike@research.att.com to the file that contains the message. BFS sees that the attribute name From is indexed, and so it adds the value of that attribute (pike@research.att.com) and the i-node address of the file to the From index.

The contents of the From index are the values of all From attributes of all files. The index makes it possible to locate all email messages that have a particular From field or to iterate over all the From attributes. In all cases the location of the file is irrelevant: the index stores the i-node address of the file, which is independent of its location.

BFS also maintains indices for the name, size, and last modification time of all files. These indices make it easy to pose queries such as size > 50MB or last modified since yesterday without having to iterate over all files to decide which match.

To maintain these indices, BFS uses B+trees. There are a great deal of similarities between directories and B+trees; in fact, there are so many similarities that they are nearly indistinguishable. The basic requirement of an index is to map attribute values to i-node numbers. In the case that an attribute value is a string, an index is identical to a directory. The B+tree routines in BFS support indexing integers (32- and 64-bit), floats, doubles, and variable-length strings. In all cases the data associated with the key is an i-node address.

BFS allows an arbitrary number of indices, which presents the problem of how to store the list of all indices. The file system already solved this problem for files (a directory can have any number of files), and so we chose to store the list of available indices as a "hidden" directory. In addition to the i-node address of the root directory, the superblock also contains the i-node address of the index directory. Each of the names in the index directory corresponds to an index, and the i-node number stored with each of the names points to the i-node of the index (remember, indices and directories are identical).

4.11   Summary

The structures you saw defined in this chapter were not defined magically, nor are they the same as the structures I began with. The structures evolved over the course of the project as I experimented with different sizes and organizations. Running benchmarks to gain insight about the performance impact of various choices led to the final design you saw in this chapter.

The i-node structure underwent numerous changes over the course of development. The i-node began life as a smallish 256-byte structure, and each file system block contained several i-nodes. Compared to the current i-node size (one file system block), a size of 256 bytes seems miniscule. The original i-node had no notion of a small_data area for storing small attributes (a serious performance impact). Further, the management of free i-nodes became a significant bottleneck in the system. BFS does not preallocate i-nodes; thus, having to allocate i-nodes in chunks meant that there also had to be a free list (since only one i-node out of a disk block might be free). The management of that free i-node list forced many updates to the superblock (which stored the head of the list), and it also required touching additional disk blocks on file deletion. Switching each i-node to be its own disk block provided space for the small data area and simplified the management of free i-nodes (freeing the disk block is all that's needed).

The default file system block size also underwent several changes. Originally I experimented with 512-byte blocks but found that too restrictive. A 512-byte block size did not provide enough space for the small_data area nor did it mesh well with the B+tree routines. The B+tree routines also have a notion of page size (although it is completely independent of the rest of the file system). The B+tree routines have a restriction that the maximum size of a stored item must be less than half the B+tree page size. Since BFS allows 255-character file names, the B+tree page size also had to be at least 1024 bytes. Pushing the minimum file system block size to 1024 bytes ensures that i-nodes have sufficient space to store a reasonable number of attributes and that the B+tree pages correspond nicely to file system blocks so that allocation and I/O done on behalf of the B+trees does not need any additional massaging.

You may ask, If 1024 bytes is a good file system block size, why not jump to 2048 bytes? I did experiment with 2048-byte blocks and 4096-byte blocks. The additional space available for attributes was not often used (an email message uses on average about 500 bytes to store nine attributes). B+trees also presented a problem as their size grew significantly with a 2048-byte page size: a balanced B+tree tends to be half full, so on average each page of a B+tree would have only 1024 bytes of useful data. Some quick experiments showed that directory and index sizes grew much larger than desirable with a 2048-byte page size. The conclusion was that although larger block sizes have desirable properties for very large files, the added cost for normal files was not worthwhile.

The allocation group concept also underwent considerable revision. Originally the intent was that each allocation group would allow operations to take place in parallel in the file system; that is, each allocation group would appear as a mini file system. Although still very attractive (and it turns out quite similar to the way the Linux ext2 file system works), the reality was that journaling forced serialization of all file system modifications. It might have been possible to have multiple logs, one per allocation group; however, that idea was not pursued because of a lack of time.

The original intent of the allocation group concept was for very large allocation groups (about eight per gigabyte). However, this proved unworkable for a number of reasons: first and foremost, the block_run data structure only had a 16-bit starting block number, and further, such a small number of allocation groups didn't carve the disk into enough chunks. Instead the number of allocation groups is a factor of the number of bitmap blocks required to map 65,536 blocks. By sizing the allocation groups this way, we allow maximum use of the block_run data structure.

It is clear that many factors influence design decisions about the size, layout, and organization of file system data structures. Although decisions may be based on intuition, it is important to verify that those decisions make sense by looking at the performance of several alternatives.

This introduction to the raw data structures that make up BFS lays the foundation for understanding the higher-level concepts that go into making a complete file system.

5

Attributes, Indexing, and Queries

This chapter is about three closely related topics: attributes and indexing of attributes. In combination these three features add considerable power to a file system and endow the file system with many of the features normally associated with a database. This chapter aims to show why attributes, indexing, and queries are an important feature of a modern file system. We will discuss the high-level issues as well as the details of the BFS implementation.

5.1 Attributes

What are attributes? In general an attribute is a name (usually a short descriptive string) and a value such as a number, string, or even raw binary data. For example, an attribute could have a name such as Age and a value of 27 or a name of Keywords and a value of Computers File System Journaling. An attribute is information about an entity. In the case of a file system, an attribute is additional information about a file that is not stored in the file itself. The ability to store information about a file with the file but not in it is very important because often modifying the contents of a file to store the information is not feasible—or even possible.

There are many examples of data that programs can store in attributes:

- Icon position and information for a window system
- The URL of the source of a downloaded Web document
- The type of a file
- The last backup date of a file
- The "To," "From," and "Subject" lines of an email message
- Keywords in a document

- Access control lists for a security system
- Style information for a styled text editor (fonts, sizes, etc.)
- Gamma correction, color depth, and dimensions of an image
- A comment about a file
- Contact database information (address, phone/fax numbers, email address, URL)

These are examples of information about an object, but they are not necessarily information we would—or even could—store in the object itself. These examples just begin to touch upon the sorts of information we might store in an attribute. The ability to attach arbitrary name/value pairs to a file opens up many interesting possibilities.

Examples of the Use of Attributes

Consider the need to manage information about people. An email program needs an email address for a person, a contact manager needs a phone number, a fax program needs a fax number, and a mail-merge for a word processor needs a physical address. Each of these programs has specific needs, and generally each program would have its own private copy of the information it needs about a person, although much information winds up duplicated in each application. If some piece of information about a person should change, it requires updating several different programs—not an ideal situation.

Instead, using attributes, the file system can represent the person as a file. The name of the file would be the name of the person or perhaps a more unique identifier. The attributes of this "person file" can maintain the information about the person: the email address, phone number, fax number, URL, and so on. Then each of the programs mentioned above simply accesses the attributes that it needs. All of the programs go to the same place for the information. Further, programs that need to store different pieces of information can add and modify other attributes without disturbing existing programs.

The power of attributes in this example is that many programs can share information easily. Because access to attributes is uniform, the applications must agree on only the names of attributes. This facilitates programs working together, eliminates wasteful duplication of data, and frees programs from all having to implement their own minidatabase. Another benefit is that new applications that require previously unknown attributes can add the new attributes without disrupting other programs that use the older attributes.

In this example, other benefits also accrue by storing the information as attributes. From the user's standpoint a single interface exists to information about people. They can expect that if they select a person in an email program, the email program will use the person's email attribute and allow the user to send them email. Likewise if the user drags and drops the icon of a "person file" onto a fax program, it is natural to expect that the fax program will know that you want to send a fax to that person. In this example, attributes provide an easy way to centralize storage of information about people and to do it in a way that facilitates sharing it between applications.

Other less sophisticated examples abound. A Web browser could store the URL of the source of a downloaded file to allow users to later ask, "Go back to the site where this file came from." An image-scanning program could store color correction information about a scan as an attribute of the file. A text editor that uses fonts and styles could store the style information about the text as an attribute, leaving the original text as plain ASCII (this would enable editing source code with multiple fonts, styles, colors, etc.). A text editor could synthesize the primary keywords contained in a document and store those as attributes of the document so that later files could be searched for a certain type of content.

These examples all illustrate ways to use attributes. Attributes provide a mechanism for programs to store data about a file in a way that makes it easy to later retrieve the information and to share it with other applications.

Attribute API

Many operations on attributes are possible, but the file system interface in the BeOS keeps the list short. A program can perform the following operations on file attributes:

- Write attribute
- Read attribute
- Open attribute directory
- Read attribute directory
- Rewind attribute directory
- Close attribute directory
- Stat attribute
- Remove attribute
- Rename attribute

Not surprisingly, these operations bear close resemblance to the corresponding operations for files, and their behavior is virtually identical. To access the attributes of a file, a program must first open the file and use that file descriptor as a handle to access the attributes. The attributes of a file do not have individual file descriptors. The attribute directory of a file is similar to a regular directory. Programs can open it and iterate through it to enumerate all the attributes of a file.

Notably absent from the list are operations to open and close attributes as we would with a regular file. Because attributes do not use separate file descriptors for access, open and close operations are superfluous. The user-level API calls to read and write data from attributes have the following prototypes:

```
ssize_t fs_read_attr(int fd, const char *attribute, uint32 type,
                     off_t pos, void *buf, size_t count);

ssize_t fs_write_attr(int fd, const char *attribute, uint32 type,
                      off_t pos, const void *buf, size_t count);
```

Each call encapsulates all the state necessary to perform the I/O. The file descriptor indicates which file to operate on, the attribute name indicates which attribute to do the I/O to, the type indicates the type of data being written, and the position specifies the offset into the attribute to do the I/O at. The semantics of the attribute read/write operations are identical to file read/write operations. The write operation has the additional semantics that if the attribute name does not exist, it will create it implicitly. Writing to an attribute that exists will overwrite the attribute (unless the position is nonzero, and then it will extend the attribute if it already exists).

The functions to list the attributes of a file correspond very closely with the standard POSIX functions to list the contents of a directory. The open attribute directory operation initiates access to the list of attributes belonging to a file. The open attribute directory operation returns a file descriptor because the state associated with reading a directory cannot be maintained in user space. The read attribute directory operation returns the next successive entry until there are no more. The rewind operation resets the position in the directory stream to the beginning of the directory. Of course, the close operation simply closes the file descriptor and frees the associated state.

The remaining operations (stat, remove, and rename) are typical housekeeping operations and have no subtleties. The stat operation, given a file descriptor and attribute name, returns information about the size and type of the attribute. The remove operation deletes the named attribute from the list of attributes associated with a file. The rename operation is not currently implemented in BFS.

Attribute Details

As defined previously, an attribute is a string name and some arbitrary chunk of data. In the BeOS, attributes also declare the type of the data stored with the name. The type of the data is either an integral type (string, integer, or floating-point number) or it is simply raw data of arbitrary size. The type field is only strictly necessary to support indexing.

In deciding what data structure to use to store an attribute, our first temptation might be to define a new data structure. But if we resist that temptation and look closer at what an attribute must store, we find that the description is strikingly similar to that of a file. At the most basic level an attribute is a named entity that must store an arbitrary amount of data. Although it is true that most attributes are likely to be small, storing large amounts of data

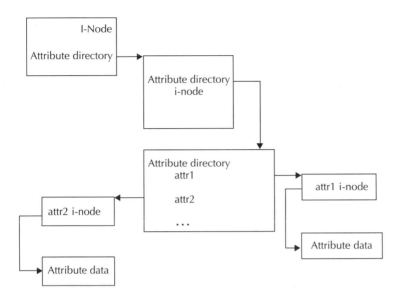

Figure 5-1 **Relationship between an i-node and its attributes.**

in an attribute is quite useful and needs full support. With this in mind it makes good sense to reuse the data structure that underlies files—an i-node. An i-node represents a stream of data on disk and thus can store an arbitrary amount of information. By storing the contents of an attribute in the data stream of an i-node, the file system does not have to manage a separate set of data structures specific to attributes.

The list of attributes associated with a file also needs a data structure and place for storage. Taking our cue from what we observed about the similarity of attributes to files, it is natural to store the list of attributes as a directory. A directory has exactly the properties needed for the task: it maps names to i-nodes. The final glue necessary to bind together all the structures is a reference from the file i-node to the attribute directory i-node. Figure 5-1 diagrams the relationships between these structures. Then it is possible to traverse from a file i-node to the directory that lists all the attributes. From the directory entries it is possible to find the i-node of each of the attributes, and having access to the attribute i-node gives us access to the contents of the attribute.

This implementation is the simplest to understand and implement. The only drawback to this approach is that, although it is elegant in theory, in practice its performance will be abysmal. Performance will suffer because each attribute requires several disk operations to locate and load. The initial design of BFS used this approach. When it was first presented to other engineers, it was quickly shot down (and rightly so) because of the levels of indirection necessary to reach an attribute.

This performance bottleneck is an issue because in the BeOS the window system stores icon positions for files as attributes of the file. Thus, with this design, when displaying all the files in a directory, each file would need at least one disk access to get the file i-node, one access to load the attribute directory i-node, another directory access to look up the attribute name, another access to load the attribute i-node, and finally yet another disk access to load the data of the attribute. Given that current disk drives have access times on the order of milliseconds (and sometimes tens of milliseconds) while CPU speeds reach into the sub-5-nanosecond range, it is clear that forcing the CPU to wait for five disk accesses to display a single file would devastate performance.

We knew that a number of the attributes of a file would be small and that providing quick access to them would benefit many programs. In essence the problem was that at least some of the attributes of a file needed more efficient access. The solution came together as another design issue reared its head at roughly the same time. BFS needed to be able to store an arbitrary number of files on a volume, and it was not considered acceptable to reserve space on a volume for i-nodes up front. Reserving space for i-nodes at file system initialization time is the traditional approach to managing i-nodes, but this can lead to considerable wasted space on large drives with few files and invariably can become a limitation for file systems with lots of files and not enough i-nodes. BFS needed to only consume space for as many or as few files as were stored on the disk—no more, no less. This implied that i-nodes would likely be stored as individual disk blocks. Initially it seemed that storing each i-node in its own disk block would waste too much space because the size of the i-node structure is only 232 bytes. However, when this method of storing i-nodes is combined with the need to store several small attributes for quick access, the solution is clear. The spare space of an i-node block is suitable for storage of small attributes of the file. BFS terms this space at the end of an i-node block as the small_data area. Conceptually a BFS i-node looks like Figure 5-2.

Because not all attributes can fit in the small_data area of an i-node, BFS continues to use the attribute directory and i-nodes to store additional attributes. The cost of accessing nonresident attributes is indeed greater than attributes in the small_data area, but the trade-off is well worth it. The most common case is extremely efficient because one disk read will retrieve the i-node and a number of small attributes that are often the most needed.

The small_data area is purely an implementation detail of BFS and is completely transparent to programmers. In fact, it is not possible to request that an attribute be put in the small_data area. Exposing the details of this performance tweak would mar the otherwise clean attribute API.

small_data Area Detail

The data structure BFS uses to manage space in the small_data area is

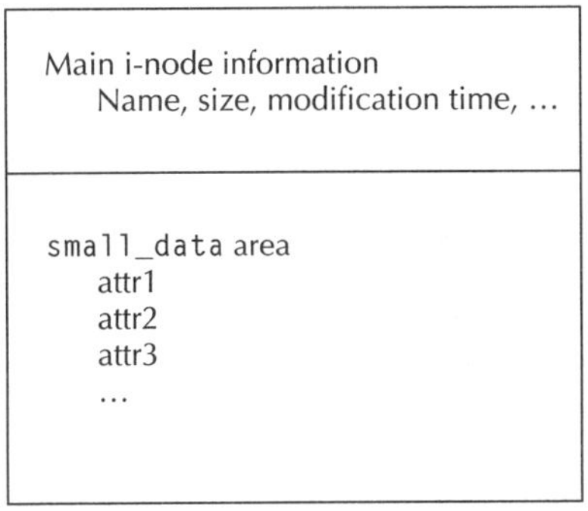

```
Main i-node information
     Name, size, modification time, ...

small_data area
     attr1
     attr2
     attr3
     ...
```

Figure 5-2   A high-level view of a BFS i-node and small_data **area.**

```
typedef struct small_data {
    uint32    type;
    uint16    name_size;
    uint16    data_size;
    char      name[1];
} small_data;
```

This data structure is optimized for size so that as many as possible could be packed into the i-node. The two size fields, name_size and data_size, are limited to 16-bit integers because we know the size of the i-node will never be more than 8K. The type field would also be 16 bits but we must preserve the exact type passed in from higher-level software.

The content of the name field is variable sized and begins in the last field of the small_data structure (the member name in the structure is just an easy way to refer to the beginning of the bytes that constitute the name rather than a fixed-size name of only one character). The data portion of the attribute is stored in the bytes following the name with no padding. A C macro that yields a pointer to the data portion of the small_data structure is

```
#define SD_DATA(sd)            \
    (void *)((char *)sd + sizeof(*sd) + (sd->name_size-sizeof(sd->name)))
```

In typical obfuscated C programming fashion, this macro uses pointer arithmetic to generate a pointer to the bytes following the variable-sized name field. Figure 5-3 shows how the small_data area is used.

All routines that manipulate the small_data structure expect a pointer to an i-node, which in BFS is not just the i-node structure itself but the entire disk block that the i-node resides in. The following routines exist to manipulate the small_data area of an i-node:

▪ Find a small_data structure with a given name
▪ Create a new small_data structure with a name, type, and data

i-node #, size, owner, permissions, ...		bfs_inode structure
type name_size data_size name data	type	small_data area
name_size data_size name data	type name_size	
data_size name data	type name_size data_size	
name data	type name_size data_size name data	
Free space		

Figure 5-3   **A BFS i-node, including the** small_data **area.**

- Update an existing small_data structure
- Get the data portion of a small_data structure
- Delete a small_data structure

Starting from the i-node address, the address of the first small_data structure is easily calculated by adding the size of the i-node structure to its address. The resulting pointer is the base of the small_data area. With the address of the first small_data structure in hand, the routines that operate on the small_data area all expect and maintain a tightly packed array of small_data structures. The free space is always the last item in the array and is managed as a small_data item with a type of zero, a zero-length name, and a data_size equal to the size of the remaining free space (not including the size of the structure itself).

Because BFS packs the small_data structures as tightly as possible, any given instance of the small_data structure is not likely to align itself on a "nice" memory boundary (i.e., "nice" boundaries are addresses that are multiples of four or eight). This can cause an alignment exception on certain RISC processors. Were the BeOS to be ported to an architecture such as MIPS, BFS would have to first copy the small_data structure to a properly aligned temporary variable and dereference it from there, complicating the code considerably. Because the CPUs that the BeOS runs on currently (PowerPC and Intel x86) do not have this limitation, the current BFS code ignores the problem despite the fact that it is nonportable.

The small_data area of an i-node works well for storing a series of tightly packed attributes. The implementation is not perfect though, and there are other techniques BFS could have used to reduce the size of the small_data structure even further. For example, a C union type could have been employed to eliminate the size field for fixed-size attributes such as integers or floating-point numbers. Or the attribute name could have been stored as a hashed value, instead of the explicit string, and the string looked up in a

```
if length of data being written is small
    find the attribute name in the small_data area
    if found
        delete it from small_data and from any indices
    else
        create the attribute name

    write new data
    if it fits in the small_data area
        delete it from the attribute directory if present
    else
        create the attribute in the attribute directory
        write the data to the attribute i-node
        delete name from the small_data area if it exists
else
    create the attribute in the attribute directory
    write the data to the attribute i-node
    delete name from the small_data area if it exists
```

Listing 5-1   Pseudocode for the write attribute operation of BFS.

hash table. Although these techniques would have saved some space, they would have complicated the code further and made it even more difficult to debug. As seemingly simple as it is, the handling of small_data attributes took several iterations to get correct.

The Big Picture: small_data Attributes and More

The previous descriptions provide ample detail of the mechanics of using the small_data structure but do not provide much insight into how this connects with the general attribute mechanisms of BFS. As we discussed earlier, a file can have any number of attributes, each of which is a name/value pair of arbitrary size. Internally the file system must manage attributes that reside in the small_data area as well as those that live in the attribute directory.

Conceptually managing the two sets of attributes is straightforward. Each time a program requests an attribute operation, the file system checks if the attribute is in the small_data area. If not, it then looks in the attribute directory for the attribute. In practice, though, this adds considerable complexity to the code. For example, the write attribute operation uses the algorithm shown in Listing 5-1.

Subtleties such as deleting the attribute from the attribute directory after adding it to the small_data area are necessary in situations where rewriting an existing attribute causes the location of the attribute to change.

Manipulating attributes that live in the attribute directory of a file is eased because many of the operations can reuse the existing operations that work on files. Creating an attribute in the attribute directory uses the same underlying functions that create a file in a directory. Likewise, the operations that read, write, and remove attributes do so using the same routines as files. The glue code necessary for these operations has subtleties analogous to the operations on the small_data area (attributes need to be deleted from the small_data area if they exist when an attribute is written to the attribute directory, and so on).

File system reentrancy is another issue that adds some complexity to the situation. Because the file system uses the same operations for access to the attribute directory and attributes, we must be careful that the same resources are not ever locked a second time (which would cause a deadlock). Fortunately deadlock problems such as this are quite catastrophic if encountered, making it easy to detect when they happen (the file system locks up) and to correct (it is easy to examine the state of the offending code and to backtrack from there to a solution).

Attribute Summary

The basic concept of an attribute is a name and some chunk of data associated with that name. An attribute can be something simple:

```
Keywords = bass, guitar, drums
```

or it can be a much more complex piece of associated data. The data associated with an attribute is free-form and can store anything. In a file system, attributes are usually attached to files and store information about the contents of the file.

Implementing attributes is not difficult, although the straightforward implementation will suffer in performance. To speed up access to attributes, BFS supports a fast-attribute area directly in the i-node of a file. The fast-attribute area significantly reduces the cost of accessing an attribute.

5.2 Indexing

To understand indexing it is useful to imagine the following scenario: Suppose you went to a library and wanted to find a book. At the library, instead of a meticulously organized card catalog, you found a huge pile of cards, each card complete with the information (attributes) about a particular book. If there was no order to the pile of cards, it would be quite tedious to find the book you wanted. Since librarians prefer order to chaos, they keep three indices of information about books. Each catalog is organized alphabetically, one by book title, one by author name, and one by subject area. This makes it rather simple to locate a particular book by searching the author, title, or subject index cards.

Indexing in a file system is quite similar to the card catalog in a library. Each file in a file system can be thought of as equivalent to a book in a library. If the file system does not index the information about a file, then finding a particular file can result in having to iterate over all files to find the one that matches. When there are many files, such an exhaustive search is slow. Indexing items such as the name of a file, its size, and the time it was last modified can significantly reduce the amount of time it takes to find a file.

In a file system, an index is simply a list of files ordered on some criteria. With the presence of additional attributes that a file may have, it is natural to allow indexing of other attributes besides those inherent to the file. Thus a file system could index the `Phone Number` attribute of a person, the `From` field of email addresses, or the `Keywords` of a document. Indexing additional attributes opens up considerable flexibility in the ways in which users can locate information in a file system.

If a file system indexes attributes about a file, a user can ask for sophisticated queries such as "find all email from Bob Lewis received in the last week." The file system can search its indices and produce the list of files that match the criteria. Although it is true that an email program could do the same, doing the indexing in the file system with a general-purpose mechanism allows all applications to have built-in database functionality without requiring them to each implement their own database.

A file system that supports indexing suddenly takes on many characteristics of a traditional database, and the distinction between the two blurs. Although a file system that supports attributes and indexing is quite similar to a database, the two are not the same because their goals push the two in subtly different directions. For example, a database trades some flexibility (a database usually has fixed-size entries, it is difficult to extend a record after the database is created, etc.) for features (greater speed and ability to deal with larger numbers of entries, richer query interface). A file system offers more generality at the expense of overhead: storing millions of 128-byte records as files in a file system would have considerable overhead. So although on the surface a file system with indices and a database share much functionality, the different design goals of each keep them distinct.

By simplifying many details, the above examples give a flavor for what is possible with indices. The following sections discuss the meatier issues involved.

What Is an Index?

The first question we need to answer is, What is an index? An index is a mechanism that allows efficient lookups of input values. Using our card catalog example, if we look in the author index for "Donald Knuth," we will find references to books written by Donald Knuth, and the references will allow us to locate the physical copy of the book. It is efficient to look up the value "Knuth" because the catalog is in alphabetical order. We can jump directly to the section of cards for authors whose name begins with "K" and from there jump to those whose name begins with "Kn" and so on.

In computer terms, an index is a data structure that stores key/value pairs and allows efficient lookups of keys. The key is a string, integer, floating-point number, or other data item that can be compared. The value stored with a key is usually just a reference to the rest of the data associated with the key. For a file system the value associated with a key is the i-node number of the file associated with the key.

The keys of an index must always have a consistent order. That is, if the index compares key A against key B, they must always have the same relation—either A is less than B, greater than B, or equal to B. Unless the value of A or B changes, their relation cannot change. With integral computer types such as strings and integers, this is not a problem. Comparing more complex structures can make the situation less clear.

Many textbooks expound on different methods of managing sorted lists of data. Usually each approach to keeping a sorted list of data has some advantages and some disadvantages. For a file system there are several requirements that an indexing data structure must meet:

- It must be an on-disk structure.
- It must have a reasonable memory footprint.
- It must have efficient lookups.
- It must support duplicate entries.

First, any indexing method used by a file system must inherently be an on-disk data structure. Most common indexing methods only work in memory, making them inappropriate for a file system. File system indices must exist on permanent storage so that they will survive reboots and crashes. Further, because a file system is merely a supporting piece of an entire OS and not the focal point, using indices cannot impose undue requirements on the rest of the system. Consequently, the entire index cannot be kept in memory nor can a significant chunk of it be loaded each time the file system accesses an index. There may be many indices on a file system, and a file system needs to be able to have any number of them loaded at once and be able to switch between them as needed without an expensive performance hit each time it accesses a new index. These constraints eliminate from consideration a number of indexing techniques commonly used in the commercial database world.

The primary requirement of an index is that it can efficiently look up keys. The efficiency of the lookup operation can have a dramatic effect on the overall performance of the file system because every access to a file name must perform a lookup. Thus it is clear that lookups must be the most efficient operation on an index.

The final requirement, and perhaps the most difficult, is the need to support duplicate entries in an index. At first glance, support for duplicate entries may seem unnecessary, but it is not. For example, duplicate entries are indispensable if a file system indexes file names. There will be many duplicate names because it is possible for files to have the same name if they live in different directories. Depending on the usage of the file system, the number of duplicates may range from only a few per index to many tens of thousands per index. Performance can suffer greatly if this issue is not dealt with well.

Data Structure Choices

Although many indexing data structures exist, there are only a few that a file system can consider. By far the most popular data structure for storing an on-disk index is the B-tree or any of its variants (B*tree, B+tree, etc.). Hash tables are another technique that can be extended to on-disk data structures. Each of these data structures has advantages and disadvantages. We'll briefly discuss each of the data structures and their features.

B-trees

A B-tree is a treelike data structure that organizes data into a collection of nodes. As with real trees, B-trees begin at a root, the starting node. Links from the root node refer to other nodes, which, in turn, have links to other nodes, until the links reach a leaf node. A leaf node is a B-tree node that has no links to other nodes.

Each B-tree node stores some number of key/value pairs (the number of key/value pairs depends on the size of the node). Alongside each key/value pair is a link pointer to another node. The keys in a B-tree node are kept in order, and the link associated with a key/value pair points to a node whose keys are all less than the current key.

Figure 5-4 shows an example of a B-tree. Here we can see that the link associated with the word *cat* points to nodes that only contain values lexicographically less than the word *cat*. Likewise, the link associated with the word *indigo* refers to a node that contains a value less than *indigo* but greater than *deluxe*. The bottom row of nodes (*able*, *ball*, etc.) are all leaf nodes because they have no links.

One important property of B-trees is that they maintain a relative ordering between nodes. That is, all the nodes referred to by the link from *man* in the root node will have entries greater than *cat* and less than *man*. The B-tree search routine takes advantage of this property to reduce the amount of work needed to find a particular node.

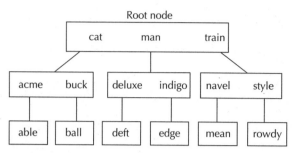

Figure 5-4   An example B-tree.

Knowing that B-tree nodes are sorted and the links for each entry point to nodes with keys less than the current key, we can perform a search of the B-tree. Normally searching each node uses a binary search, but we will illustrate using a sequential search to simplify the discussion. If we wanted to find the word *deft* we would start at the root node and search through its keys for the word *deft*. The first key, *cat*, is less than *deft*, so we continue. The word *deft* is less than *man*, so we know it is not in this node. The word *man* has a link though, so we follow the link to the next node. At the second-level node (*deluxe indigo*) we compare *deft* against *deluxe*. Again, *deft* is less than *deluxe*, so we follow the associated link. The final node we reach contains the word *deft*, and our search is successful. Had we searched for the word *depend*, we would have followed the link from *deluxe* and discovered that our key was greater than *deft*, and thus we would have stopped the search because we reached a leaf node and our key was greater than all the keys in the node.

The important part to observe about the search algorithm is how few nodes we needed to look at to do the search (3 out of 10 nodes). When there are many thousands of nodes, the savings is enormous. When a B-tree is well balanced, as in the above example, the time it takes to search a tree of N keys is proportional to $\log_k(N)$. The base of the logarithm, k, is the number of keys per node. This is a very good search time when there are many keys and is the primary reason that B-trees are popular as an indexing technique.

The key to the performance of B-trees is that they maintain a reasonable balance. An important property of B-trees is that no one branch of the tree is significantly taller than any other branch. Maintaining this property is a requirement of the insertion and deletion operations, which makes their implementation much more complex than the search operation.

Insertion into a B-tree first locates the desired insertion position (by doing a search operation), and then it attempts to insert the key. If inserting the key would cause the node to become overfull (each node has a fixed maximum size), then the node is split into two nodes, each getting half of the keys. Splitting a node requires modifications to the parent nodes of the node that is split. The parent nodes of a split node need to change their pointers to the child node because there are now two. This change may propagate all the way back up to the root node, perhaps even changing the root node (and thus creating a new root).

Deletion from a B-tree operates in much the same way as insertion. Instead of splitting a node, however, deletion may cause pairs of nodes to coalesce into a single node. Merging adjacent nodes requires modification of parent nodes and may cause a similar rebalancing act as happens with insertions.

These descriptions of the insertion and deletion algorithms are not meant to be implementation guides but rather to give an idea of the process involved. If you are interested in this topic, you should refer to a file structures textbook for the specifics of implementing B-trees, such as Folk, Zoellick, and Riccardi's book.

Another benefit of B-trees is that their structure is inherently easy to store on disk. Each node in a B-tree is usually a fixed size, say, 1024 or 2048 bytes, a size that corresponds nicely to the disk block size of a file system. It is very easy to store a B-tree in a single file. The links between nodes in a B-tree are simply the offsets in the file of the other nodes. Thus if a node is located at position 15,360 in a file, storing a pointer to it is simply a matter of storing the value 15,360. Retrieving the node stored there requires seeking to that position in the file and reading the node.

As keys are added to a B-tree, all that is necessary to grow the tree is to increase the size of the file that contains the B-tree. Although it may seem that splitting nodes and rebalancing a tree may be a potentially expensive operation, it is not because there is no need to move significant chunks of data. Splitting a node into two involves allocating extra space at the end of the file, but the other affected nodes only need their pointers updated; no data must be rearranged to make room for the new node.

B-tree Variants

There are several variants of a standard B-tree, some of which have even better properties than traditional B-trees. The simplest modification, B*trees, increases how full a node can be before it is split. By increasing the number of keys per node, we reduce the height of the tree and speed up searching.

The other more significant variant of a B-tree is a B+tree. A B+tree adds the restriction that all key/value pairs may only reside in leaf nodes. The interior nodes of a B+tree only contain index values to guide searches to the correct leaf nodes. The index values stored in the interior nodes are copies of the keys in the leaf nodes, but the index values are only used for searching, never for retrieval. With this extension, it is useful to link the leaf nodes together left to right (so, for example, in the B-tree defined above, the node *able* would contain a link to *ball*, etc.). By linking the leaf nodes together, it becomes easy to iterate sequentially over the contents of the B+tree. The other benefit is that interior nodes can have a different format than leaf nodes, making it easy to pack as much data as possible into an interior node (which makes for a more efficient tree).

If the data being indexed is a string of text, another technique can be applied to compact the tree. In a prefix B+tree the interior nodes store only as much of the keys as necessary to traverse the tree and still arrive at the correct leaf node. This modification can reduce the amount of data that needs to be stored in the interior nodes. By reducing the amount of information stored in the interior nodes, the prefix B+tree stays shorter than if the compaction were not done.

Hashing

Hashing is another technique for storing data on disk. Hashing is a technique where the input keys are fed through a function that generates a hash value for the key. The same key value should always generate the same hash value. A hash function accepts a key and returns an integer value. The hash value of a key is used to index the hash table by taking the hash value modulo the size of the table to generate a valid index into the table. The items stored in the table are the key/value pairs just as with B-trees. The advantage of hashing is that the cost to look for an item is constant: the hash function is independent of the number of items in the hash table, and thus lookups are extremely efficient.

Except under special circumstances where all the input values are known ahead of time, the hash value for an input key is not always unique. Different keys may generate the same hash value. One method to deal with multiple keys colliding on the same hash value is to chain together in a linked list all the values that hash to the same table index (that is, each table entry stores a linked list of key/value pairs that map to that table entry). Another method is to rehash using a second hash function and to continue rehashing until a free spot is found. Chaining is the most common technique since it is the easiest to implement and has the most well-understood properties.

Another deficiency of hash tables is that hashing does not preserve the order of the keys. This makes an in-order traversal of the items in a hash table impossible.

One problem with hashing as an indexing method is that as the number of keys inserted into a table increases, so do the number of collisions. If a hash table is too small for the number of keys stored in it, then the number of collisions will be high and the cost of finding an entry will go up significantly (as the chain is just a linked list). A large hash table reduces the number of collisions but also increases the amount of wasted space (table entries with nothing in them). Although it is possible to change the size of a hash table, this is an expensive task because all the key/value pairs need to be rehashed. The expense of resizing a hash table makes it a very difficult choice for a general-purpose file system indexing method.

A variation on regular hashing, *extendible hashing*, divides a hash table into two parts. In extendible hashing there is a file that contains a directory of bucket pointers and a file of buckets (that contain the data). Extendible hashing uses the hash value of a key to index the directory of bucket pointers. Not all of the bits of the hash value are used initially. When a bucket overflows, the solution is to increase the number of bits of the hash value that are used as an index in the directory of bucket pointers. Increasing the size of the directory file is an expensive operation. Further, the use of two files complicates the use of extendible hashing in a file system.

Indexing in a file system should not waste space unnecessarily and should accommodate both large and small indices. It is difficult to come up with a set of hashing routines that can meet all these criteria, still maintain adequate efficiency, and not require a lengthy rehashing or reindexing operation. With additional work, extendible hashing could be made a viable alternative to B-trees for a file system.

Data Structure Summary

For file systems, the choice between hash tables and B-trees is an easy one. The problems that exist with hash tables present significant difficulties for a general-purpose indexing method when used as part of a file system. Resizing a hash table would potentially lock the entire file system for a long period of time while the table is resized and the elements rehashed, which is unacceptable for general use. B-trees, on the other hand, lend themselves very well to compact sizes when there are few keys, grow easily as the number of keys increases, and maintain a good search time (although not as good as hash tables). BFS uses B+trees for all of its indexing.

Connections: Indexing and the Rest of the File System

The most obvious questions to ask at this point are, How is the list of indices maintained? And where do individual indices live? That is, where do indices fit into the standard set of directories and files that exist on a file system? As with attributes, it is tempting to define new data structures for maintaining this information, but there is no need. BFS uses the normal directory structure to maintain the list of indices. BFS stores the data of each index in regular files that live in the index directory.

Although it is possible to put the index files into a user-visible directory with special protections, BFS instead stores the list of indices in a hidden directory created at file system creation time. The superblock stores the i-node number of the index directory, which establishes the connection with the rest of the file system. The superblock is a convenient place to store hidden information such as this. Storing the indices in a hidden directory prevents accidental deletion of indices or other mishaps that could cause a catastrophic situation for the file system. The disadvantage of storing indices in a hidden directory is that it requires a special-purpose API to access. This is the sort of decision that could go either way with little or no repercussions.

The API to operate on and access indices is simple. The operations that operate on entire indices are

- create index
- delete index
- open index directory
- read index directory
- stat index

It would be easy to extend this list of operations to support other common file operations (rename, etc.). But since there is little need for such operations on indices, BFS elects not to provide that functionality.

The create index operation simply takes an index name and the data type of the index. The name of the index connects the index with the corresponding attributes that will make use of the index. For example, the BeOS mail daemon adds an attribute named MAIL:from to all email messages it receives, and it also creates an index whose name is MAIL:from. The data type of the index should match the data type of the attributes. BFS supports the following data types for indices:

- String (up to 255 bytes)
- Integer (32-bit)
- Integer (64-bit)
- Float
- Double

Other types are certainly possible, but this set of data types covers the most general functionality. In practice almost all indices are string indices.

One "gotcha" when creating an index is that the name of an index may match files that already have that attribute. For example, if a file has an attribute named Foo and a program creates an index named Foo, the file that already had the attribute is not added to the newly created index. The difficulty is that there is no easy way to determine which files have the attribute without iterating over all files. Because creating indices is a relatively uncommon occurrence, it could be acceptable to iterate over all the files to find those that already have the attribute. BFS does not do this and pushes the responsibility onto the application developer. This deficiency of BFS is unfortunate, but there was no time in the development schedule to address it.

Deleting an index is a straightforward operation. Removing the file that contains the index from the index directory is all that is necessary. Although it is easy, deleting an index should be a rare operation since re-creating the index will not reindex all the files that have the attribute. For this reason an index should only be deleted when the only application that uses it is removed from the system and the index is empty (i.e., no files have the attribute).

The remaining index operations are simple housekeeping functions. The index directory functions (open, read, and close) allow a program to iterate over the index directory much like a program would iterate over a regular directory. The stat index function allows a program to check for the existence of an index and to obtain information about the size of the index. These routines all have trivial implementations since all the data structures involved are identical to that of regular directories and files.

Automatic Indices

In addition to allowing users to create their own indices, BFS supports built-in indices for the integral file attributes: name, size, and last modification. The file system itself must create and maintain these indices because it is the one that maintains those file attributes. Keep in mind that the name, size, and last modification time of a file are not regular attributes; they are integral parts of the i-node and not managed by the attribute code.

The name index keeps a list of all file names on the entire system. Every time a file name changes (creation, deletion, or rename), the file system must also update the name index. Adding a new file name to the name index happens after everything else about the file has been successfully created (i-node allocated and directory updated). The file name is then added to the name index. The insertion into the name index must happen as part of the file creation transaction so that should the system fail, the entire operation is undone as one transaction. Although it rarely happens, if the file name cannot be added to the name index (e.g., no space left), then the entire file creation must be undone.

Deletion of a file name is somewhat less problematic because it is unlikely to fail (no extra space is needed on the drive). Again though, deleting the name from the file name index should be the last operation done, and it should be done as part of the transaction that deletes the file so that the entire operation is atomic.

A rename operation is the trickiest operation to implement (in general and for the maintenance of the indices). As expected, updating the name index is the last thing done as part of the rename transaction. The rename operation itself decomposes into a deletion of the original name (if it exists) and an insertion of the new name into the index. Undoing a failure to insert the new name is particularly problematic. The rename operation may have deleted a file if the new name already existed (this is required for rename to be an atomic operation). However, because the other file is deleted (and its resources freed), undoing such an operation is extremely complex. Due to the complexity involved and the unlikeliness of the event even happening, BFS does not attempt to handle this case. Were the rename operation to be unable to insert the new name of a file into the name index, the file system would still be consistent, just not up-to-date (and the disk would most likely be 100% full as well).

Updates to the size index happen when a file changes size. As an optimization the file system only updates the size index when a file is closed. This prevents the file system from having to lock and modify the global size index for every write to any file. The disadvantage is that the size index may be slightly out-of-date with respect to certain files that are actively being written. The trade-off between being slightly out-of-date versus updating the size index on every write is well worth it—the performance hit is quite significant.

The other situation in which the size index can be a severe bottleneck is when there are many files of the same size. This may seem like an unusual situation, but it happens surprisingly often when running file system benchmarks that create and delete large numbers of files to test the speed of the file system. Having many files of the same size will stress the index structure and how it handles duplicate keys. BFS fares moderately well in this area, but performance degrades nonlinearly as the number of duplicates increases. Currently more than 10,000 or so duplicates causes the performance of modifications to the size index to lag noticeably.

The last modification time index is the final inherent file attribute that BFS indexes. Indexing the last modification time makes it easy for users to find recently created files or old files that are no longer needed. As expected, the last modification time index receives updates when a file is closed. The update consists of deleting the old last modification time and inserting a new time.

Knowing that an inherent index such as the last modification time index could be critical to system performance, BFS uses a slightly underhanded technique to improve the efficiency of the index. Since the last modification time has only 1-second granularity and it is possible to create many hundreds of files in 1 second, BFS scales the standard 32-bit time variable to 64 bits and adds in a small random component to reduce the potential number of duplicates. The random component is masked off when doing comparisons or passing the information to/from the user. In retrospect it would have been possible to use a 64-bit microsecond resolution timer and do similar masking of time values, but since the POSIX APIs only support 32-bit time values with 1-second resolution, there wasn't much point in defining a new, parallel set of APIs just to access a larger time value.

In addition to these three inherent file attributes, there are others that could also have been indexed. Early versions of BFS did in fact index the creation time of files, but we deemed this index to not be worth the performance penalty it cost. By eliminating the creation time index, the file system received roughly a 20% speed boost in a file create and delete benchmark. The trade-off is that it is not possible to use an index to search for files on their creation time, but we did not feel that this presented much of a loss. Similarly it would have been possible to index file access permissions, ownership information, and so on, but we chose not to because the cost of maintaining the indices outweighed the benefit they would provide. Other file systems with different constraints might choose differently.

Other Attribute Indices

Aside from the inherent indices of name, size, and last modification time, there may be any number of other indices. Each of these indices corresponds to an attribute that programs store with files. As mentioned earlier, the BeOS mail system stores incoming email in individual files, tagging each file with attributes such as who the mail is from, who it is to, when it was sent, the subject, and so on. When first run, the mail system creates indices for each of the attributes that it writes. When the mail daemon writes one of these attributes to a file, the file system notices that the attribute name has a corresponding index and therefore updates the index as well as the file with the attribute value.

For every write to an attribute, the file system must also look in the index directory to see if the attribute name is the same as an index name. Although this may seem like it would slow the system down, the number of indices tends to be small (usually less than 100), and the cost of looking for an attribute is cheap since the data is almost always cached. When writing to an attribute, the file system also checks to see if the file already had the attribute. If so, it must delete the old value from the index first. Then the file system can add the new value to the file and insert the value into the corresponding attribute index. This all happens transparently to the user program.

When a user program deletes an attribute from a file, a similar set of operations happens. The file system must check if the attribute name being deleted has an index. If so, it must delete the attribute value from the index and then delete the attribute from the file.

The maintenance of indices complicates attribute processing but is necessary. The automatic management of indices frees programs from having to deal with the issue and offers a guarantee to programs that if an attribute index exists, the file system will keep it consistent with the state of all attributes written after the index is created.

BFS B+trees

BFS uses B+trees to store the contents of directories and all indexed information. The BFS B+tree implementation is a loose derivative of the B+trees described in the first edition Folk and Zoellick file structures textbook and owes a great deal to the public implementation of that data structure by Marcus J. Ranum. The B+tree code supports storing variable-sized keys along with a single disk offset (a 64-bit quantity in BFS). The keys stored in the tree can be strings, integers (32- and 64-bit), floats, or doubles. The biggest departure from the original data structure was the addition of support for storing duplicate keys in the B+tree.

The API

The interface to the B+trees is also quite simple. The API has six main functions:

- Open/create a B+tree
- Insert a key/value pair
- Delete a key/value pair
- Find a key and return its value
- Go to the beginning/end of the tree
- Traverse the leaves of the tree (forwards/backwards)

The function that creates the B+tree has several parameters that allow specification of the node size of the B+tree, the data type to be stored in the tree, and various other bits of housekeeping information. The choice of node size for the B+tree is important. BFS uses a node size of 1024 bytes regardless of the block size of the file system. Determining the node size was a simple matter of experimentation and practicality. BFS supports file names up to 255 characters in length, which made a B+tree node size of 512 bytes too small. Larger B+trees tended to waste space because each node is never 100% full. This is particularly a problem for small directories. A size of 1024 bytes was chosen as a reasonable compromise.

The insertion routine accepts a key (whose type should match the data type of the B+tree), the length of the key, and a value. The value is a 64-bit i-node number that identifies which file corresponds to the key stored in the tree. If the key is a duplicate of an existing key and the tree does not allow duplicates, an error is returned. If the tree does support duplicates, the new value is inserted. In the case of duplicates, the value is used as a secondary key and must be unique (it is considered an error to insert the same key/value pair twice).

The delete routine takes a key/value pair as input and will search the tree for the key. If the key is found and it is not a duplicate, the key and its value are deleted from the tree. If the key is found and it has duplicate entries, the value passed in is searched for in the duplicates and that value removed.

The most basic operation is searching for a key in the B+tree. The find operation accepts an input key and returns the associated value. If the key contains duplicate entries, the first is returned.

The remaining functions support traversal of the tree so that a program can iterate over all the entries in the tree. It is possible to traverse the tree either forwards or backwards. That is, a forward traversal returns all the entries in ascending alphabetical or numerical order. A backwards traversal of the tree returns all the entries in descending order.

The Data Structure

The simplicity of the B+tree API belies the complexity of the underlying data structure. On disk, the B+tree is a collection of nodes. The very first node in all B+trees is a header node that contains a simple data structure that describes the rest of the B+tree. In essence it is a superblock for the B+tree. The structure is

```
long     magic;
int      node_size;
int      max_number_of_levels;
int      data_type;
off_t    root_node_pointer;
off_t    free_node_pointer;
off_t    maximum_size;
```

The `magic` field is simply a magic number that identifies the block. Storing magic numbers like this aids in reconstructing file systems if corruption should occur. The next field, `node_size`, is the node size of the tree. Every node in the tree is always the same size (including the B+tree header node). The next field, `max_number_of_levels`, indicates how many levels deep the B+tree is. This depth of the tree is needed for various in-memory data structures. The `data_type` field encodes the type of data stored in the tree (either 32-bit integers, 64-bit integers, floats, doubles, or strings).

The `root_node_pointer` field is the most important field. It contains the offset into the B+tree file of the root node of the tree. Without the address of the root node, it is impossible to use the tree. The root node must always be read to do any operation on a tree. The root node pointer, as with all disk offsets, is a 64-bit quantity.

The `free_node_pointer` field contains the address of the first free node in the tree. When deletions cause an entire node to become empty, the node is linked into a list that begins at this offset in the file. The list of free nodes is kept by linking the free nodes together. The link stored in each free node is simply the address of the next free node (and the last free node has a link address of −1).

The final field, `maximum_size`, records the maximum size of the B+tree file and is used to error-check node address requests. The `maximum_size` field is also used when requesting a new node and there are no free nodes. In that case the B+tree file is simply extended by writing to the end of the file. The address of the new node is the value of `maximum_size`. The `maximum_size` field is then incremented by the amount contained in the `node_size` variable.

The structure of interior and leaf nodes in the B+tree is the same. There is a short header followed by the packed key data, the lengths of the keys, and finally the associated values stored with each key. The header is enough to distinguish between leaf and interior nodes, and, as in all B+trees, only leaf nodes contain user data. The structure of nodes is

```
off_t      left link
off_t      right link
off_t      overflow link
short      count of keys in the node
short      length of all the keys
           key data
short      key length index
off_t      array of the value for each key
```

The left and right links are used for leaf nodes to link them together so that it is easy to do an in-order traversal of the tree. The overflow link is used in interior nodes and refers to another node that effectively continues this node. The count of the keys in the node simply records how many keys exist in this node. The length of all the keys is added to the size of the header and then rounded up to a multiple of four to get to the beginning of the key length index. Each entry in the key length index stores the ending offset of the key (to compute the byte position in the node, the header size must also be added). That is, the first entry in the index contains the offset to the end of the first key. The length of a key can be computed by subtracting the previous entry's length (the first element's length is simply the value in the index). Following the length index is the array of key values (the value that was stored with the key). For interior nodes the value associated with a key is an offset to the corresponding node that contains elements less than this key. For leaf nodes the value associated with a key is the value passed by the user.

Duplicates

In addition to the interior and leaf nodes of the tree, there are also nodes that store the duplicates of a key. For reasons of efficiency, the handling of duplicates is rather complex. There are two types of duplicate nodes in the B+trees that BFS uses: duplicate fragment nodes and full duplicate nodes. A duplicate fragment node contains duplicates for several different keys. A full duplicate node stores duplicates for only one key.

The distinction between fragment node types exists because it is more common to have a small number of duplicates of a key than it is to have a large number of duplicates. That is, if there are several files with the same name in several different directories, it is likely that the number of duplicate names is less than eight. In fact, simple tests on a variety of systems reveal that as many as 35% of all file names are duplicates and have eight or fewer duplicates. Efficiently handling this case is important. Early versions of the BFS B+trees did not use duplicate fragments and we discovered that, when duplicating a directory hierarchy, a significant chunk of all the I/O being done was on behalf of handling duplicates in the name and size indices. By adding support for duplicate fragments, we were able to significantly reduce the amount of I/O that took place and sped up the time to duplicate a folder by nearly a factor of two.

When a duplicate entry must be inserted into a leaf node, instead of storing the user's value, the system stores a special value that is a pointer to either a fragment node or a full duplicate node. The value is special because it has its high bit(s) set. The BFS B+tree code reserves the top 2 bits of the value field to indicate if a value refers to duplicates. In general, this would not be acceptable, but because the file system only stores i-node numbers in the value field, we can be assured that this will not be a problem. Although this attitude has classically caused all sorts of headaches when a system grows, we are free from guilt in this instance. The safety of this approach stems from the fact that i-node numbers are disk block addresses, so they are at least 10 bits smaller than a raw disk byte address (because the minimum block size in BFS is 1024 bytes). Since the maximum disk size is 2^{64} bytes in BeOS and BFS uses a minimum of 1024-byte blocks, the maximum i-node number is 2^{54}. The value 2^{54} is small enough that it does not interfere with the top 2 bits used by the B+tree code.

When a duplicate key is inserted into a B+tree, the file system looks to see if any other keys in the current leaf node already have a duplicate fragment. If there is a duplicate fragment node that has space for another fragment, we insert our duplicate value into a new fragment within that node. If there are no other duplicate fragment nodes referenced in the current node, we create a new duplicate fragment node and insert the duplicate value there. If the key we're adding already has duplicates, we insert the duplicate into the fragment. If the fragment is full (it can only hold eight items), we allocate a full duplicate node and copy the existing duplicates into the new node. The full duplicate node contains space for more duplicates than a fragment, but there may still be more duplicates. To manage an arbitrary number of duplicates, full duplicate nodes contain links (forwards and backwards) to additional full duplicate pages. The list of duplicates is kept in sorted order based on the value associated with the key (i.e., the i-node number of the file that contains this key value as an attribute). This linear list of duplicates can become extremely slow to access when there are more than 10,000 or so duplicates. Unfortunately during the development of BFS there was not time to explore a better solution (such as storing another B+tree keyed on the i-node values).

Integration

In the abstract, the structure we have described has no connection to the rest of the file system; that is, it exists, but it is not clear how it integrates with the rest of the file system. The fundamental abstraction of BFS is an i-node that stores data. Everything is built up from this most basic abstraction. B+trees, which BFS uses to store directories and indices, are based on top of i-nodes. That is, the i-node manages the disk space allocated to the

B+tree, and the B+tree organizes the contents of that disk space into an index the rest of the system uses to look up information.

The B+trees use two routines, `read_data_stream()` and `write_data_stream()`, to access file data. These routines operate directly on i-nodes and provide the lowest level of access to file data in BFS. Despite their low-level nature, `read/write_data_stream()` have a very similar API to the higher-level `read()` and `write()` calls most programmers are familiar with. On top of this low-level I/O, the B+tree code implements the features discussed previously. The rest of the file system wraps around the B+tree functionality and uses it to provide directory and index abstractions. For example, creating a new directory involves creating a file and putting an empty B+tree into the file. When a program needs to enumerate the contents of a directory, the file system requests an in-order traversal of the B+tree. Opening a file contained in a directory is a lookup operation on the B+tree. The value returned by the lookup operation (if successful) is the i-node of the named file (which in turn is used to gain access to the file data). Creating a file inserts a new name/i-node pair into the B+tree. Likewise, deleting a file simply removes a name/i-node pair from a B+tree. Indices use the B+trees in much the same way as directories but allow duplicates where a directory does not.

5.3   Queries

If all the file system did with the indices was maintain them, they would be quite useless. The reason the file system bothers to manage indices is so that programs can issue queries that use the indices to efficiently obtain the results. The use of indices can speed up searches considerably over the brute-force alternative of examining every file in the file system.

In BFS, a query is simply a string that contains an expression about file attributes. The expression evaluates to true or false for any given file. If the expression is true for a file, then the file is in the result of the query. For example, the query

```
name == "main.c"
```

will only evaluate to true for files whose name is exactly `main.c`. The file system will evaluate this query by searching the name index to find files that match. Using the name index for this type of query is extremely efficient because it is a $\log(N)$ search on the name index B+tree instead of a linear search of all files. The difference in speed depends on the number of files on the file system, but for even a small system of 5000 files, the search time using the index is orders of magnitude faster than iterating over the files individually.

The result of a query is a list of files that match. The query API follows the POSIX directory iteration function API. There are three routines: open query, read query, and close query.

The open query routine accepts a string that represents the query and a flags argument that allows for any special options (such as live queries, which we will discuss later in this section). We will discuss the format of the query string next. The read query routine is called repeatedly; each time it returns the next file that matches the query until there are no more. When there are no more matching files, the read query routine returns an end-of-query indicator. The close query routine disposes of any resources and state associated with the query.

This simple API hides much of the complexity associated with processing queries. Query processing is the largest single chunk of code in BFS. Parsing queries, iterating over the parse trees, and deciding which files match a query requires a considerable amount of code. We now turn our attention to the details of that code.

Query Language

The query language that BFS supports is straightforward and very "C looking." While it would have been possible to use a more traditional database query language like SQL, it did not seem worth the effort. Because BFS is not a real database, we would have had considerable difficulty matching the semantics of SQL with the facilities of a file system. The BFS query language is built up out of simple expressions joined with logical AND or logical OR connectives. The grammar for a simple expression is

```
<attr-name>  [logical-op]  <value>
```

The `attr-name` is a simple text string that corresponds to the name of an attribute. The strings `MAIL:from`, `PERSON:email`, `name`, or `size` are all examples of valid `attr-name`s. At least one of the attribute names in an expression must correspond to an index with the same name.

The `logical-op` component of the expression is one of the following operators:

- = (equality)
- ! = (inequality)
- < (less than)
- > (greater than)
- >= (greater than or equal to)
- <= (less than or equal to)

The `value` of an expression is a string. The string may be interpreted as a number if the data type of the attribute is numeric. If the `value` field is a string type, the `value` may be a regular expression (to allow wildcard matching).

These simple expressions may be grouped using logical AND (&&) or logical OR (||) connectives. Parentheses may also be used to group simple expressions and override the normal precedence of AND over OR. Finally, a logical

NOT may be applied to an entire expression by prefixing it with a "!" operator. The precedence of operators is the same as in the C programming language.

It is helpful to look at a few example queries to better understand the format. The first query we'll consider is

```
name == "*.c" && size > 20000
```

This query asks to find all files whose name is *.c (that is, ends with the characters .c) and whose size is greater than 20,000 bytes.

The query

```
(name == "*.c" || name == "*.h") && size > 20000
```

will find all files whose name ends in either .c or .h and whose size is greater than 20,000 bytes. The parentheses group the OR expression so that the AND conjunction (size > 20000) applies to both halves of the OR expression.

A final example demonstrates a fairly complex query:

```
(last_modified < 81793939  && size > 5000000) ||
(name == "*.backup" && last_modified < 81793939)
```

This query asks to find all files last modified before a specific date and whose size is greater than 5 million bytes, OR all files whose name ends in .backup and who were last modified before a certain date. The date is expressed as the number of seconds since January 1, 1970 (i.e., it's in POSIX ctime format). This query would find very large files that have not been modified recently and backup files that have not been modified recently. Such a query would be useful for finding candidate files to erase or move to tape storage when trying to free up disk space on a full volume.

The query language BFS supports is rich enough to express almost any query about a set of files but yet still simple enough to be easily read and parsed.

Parsing Queries

The job of the BFS open query routine is to parse the query string (which also determines if it is valid) and to build a parse tree that represents the query. The parsing is done with a simple recursive descent parser (handwritten) that generates a tree as it parses through the query. If at any time the parser detects an error in the query string, it bubbles the error back to the top level and returns an error to the user. If the parse is successful, the resulting query tree is kept as part of the state associated with the object returned by the open query routine.

The parse tree that represents a query begins with a top-level node that maintains state about the entire query. From that node, pointers extend out to nodes representing AND and OR connectives. The leaves of the tree are simple expressions that evaluate one value on a specific attribute. The leaves of the tree drive the evaluation of the query.

After parsing the query, the file system must decide how to evaluate the query. Deciding the evaluation strategy for the parse tree uses heuristics to walk the tree and find an optimal leaf node for beginning the evaluation. The heuristics BFS uses could, as always, stand some improvement. Starting at the root node, BFS attempts to walk down to a leaf node by picking a path that will result in the fewest number of matches. For example, in the query

```
name == "*.c" && size > 20000
```

there are two nodes, one that represents the left half (name == "*.c") and one for the right half (size > 20000). In choosing between these two expressions, the right half is a "tighter" expression because it is easier to evaluate than the left half. The left half of the query is more difficult to evaluate because it involves a regular expression. The use of a regular expression makes it impossible to take advantage of any fast searches of the name index since a B+tree is organized for exact matches. The right half of the query (size > 20000), on the other hand, can take advantage of the B+tree to find the first node whose size is 20,000 bytes and then to iterate in order over the remaining items in the tree (that are greater than the value 20,000).

The evaluation strategy also looks at the sizes of the indices to help it decide. If one index were significantly smaller in size than another, it makes more sense to iterate over the smaller index since it inherently will have fewer entries than the larger index. The logic controlling this evaluation is fairly convoluted. The complexity pays off though because picking the best path through a tree can result in significant savings in the time it takes to evaluate the query.

Read Query—The Real Work

The open query routine creates the parse tree and chooses an initial leaf node (i.e., query piece) to begin evaluation at. The real work of finding which files match the query is done by the read query routine. The read query routine begins iterating at the first leaf node chosen by the open query routine. Examining the leaf node, the read routine calls functions that know how to iterate through an index of a given data type and find files that match the leaf node expression.

Iterating through an index is complicated by the different types of logical operations that the query language supports. A less-than-or-equal comparison on a B+tree is slightly different than a less-than and is the inverse of a greater-than query. The number of logical comparisons (six) and the number of data types the file system supports (five) create a significant amount of similar but slightly different code.

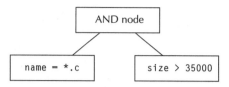

Figure 5-5   The parse tree for an AND query.

The process of iterating through all the values that match a particular query piece (e.g., a simple expression like `size < 500`) begins by finding the first matching item in the index associated with the query piece. In the case of an expression like `size < 500`, the iteration routine first finds the value 500, then traverses backward through the leaf items of the index B+tree to find the first value less than 500. If the traversal reaches the beginning of the tree, there are no items less than 500, and the iterator returns an error indicating that there are no more entries in this query piece. The iteration over all the matching items of one query piece is complicated because only one item is returned each iteration. This requires saving state between calls to be able to restart the search.

Once a matching file is found for a given query piece, the query engine must then travel back up the parse tree to see if the file matches the rest of the query. If the query in question was

```
name == *.c && size > 35000
```

then the resulting parse tree would be as shown in Figure 5-5.

The query engine would first descend down the right half of the parse tree because the `size > 35000` query piece is much less expensive to evaluate than the `name = *.c` half. For each file that matches the expression `size > 35000`, the query engine must also determine if it matches the expression `name = *.c`. Determining if a file matches the rest of the parse tree does not use other indices. The evaluation merely performs the comparison specified in each query piece directly against a particular file by reading the necessary attributes from the file.

The not-equal (`!=`) comparison operator presents an interesting difficulty for the query iterator. The interpretation of what "not equal" means is normally not open to discussion: either a particular value is not equal to another or it is. In the context of a query, however, it become less clear what the meaning is.

Consider the following query:

```
MAIL:status == New && MAIL:reply_to != mailinglist@noisy.com
```

This is a typical filter query used to only display all email not from a mailing list. The problem is that not all regular email messages will have a `Reply-To:` field in the message and thus will not have a `MAIL:reply_to` attribute. Even if an email message does not have a `Reply-To:` field, it should still match the query. The original version of BFS required the attribute to be present for the file to match, which resulted in undesired behavior with email filters such as this.

To better support this style of querying, BFS changed its interpretation of the not-equal comparison. Now, if BFS encounters a not-equal comparison and the file in question does not have the attribute, then the file is still considered a match. This change in behavior complicates processing not-equal queries when the not-equal comparison is the only query piece. A query with a single query piece that has a not-equal comparison operator must now iterate through all files and cannot use any indexing to speed the search. All files that do not have the attribute will match the query, and those files that do have the attribute will only match if the value of the attribute is not equal to the value in the query piece. Although iterating over all files is dreadfully slow, it is necessary for the query engine to be consistent.

String Queries and Regular Expression Matching

By default, string matching in BFS is case-sensitive. This makes it easy to take advantage of the B+tree search routines, which are also case-sensitive. Queries that search for an exact string are extremely fast because this is exactly what B+trees were designed to do. Sadly, from a human interface standpoint, having to remember an exact file name, including the case of all the letters, is not acceptable. To allow more flexible searches, BFS supports string queries using regular expressions.

The regular expression matching supported by BFS is simple. The regular expression comparison function supports

- *—match any number of characters (including none)
- ?—match any single character
- [...]—match the range/class of characters in the []
- [^ ...]—match the negated range/class of characters in the []

The character class expressions allow matching specific ranges of characters. For example, all lowercase characters would be specified as [a-z]. The negated range expression, [^], allows matching everything but that range/class of characters. For example, [^0-9] matches everything that is not a digit.

The typical query issued by the Tracker (the GUI file browser of the BeOS) is a case-insensitive substring query. That is, using the Tracker's find panel to search for the name "slow" translates into the following query:

```
name = "*[sS][lL][oO][wW]*"
```

Such a query must iterate through all the leaves of the name index and do a regular expression comparison on each name in the name index.

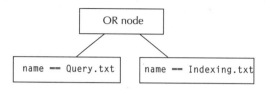

Figure 5-6   The parse tree for an OR query.

Unfortunately this obviates any benefit of B+trees and is much slower than doing a normal B+tree search. It is what end users expect, however, and that is more important than the use of an elegant B+tree search algorithm.

Additional Duties for Read Query

The read query routine also maintains additional state because it is repeatedly called to return results. The read query routine must be able to restart iterating over a query each time it is called. This requires saving the position in the query tree where the evaluation was as well as the position in the B+tree the query was iterating over.

Once a particular leaf node exhausts all the files in that index, the read query routine backs up the parse tree to see if it must descend down to another leaf node. In the following query:

```
name == Query.txt  || name == Indexing.txt
```

the parse tree will have two leaves and will look like Figure 5-6.

The read query routine will iterate over the left half of the query, and when that exhausts all matches (most likely only one file), read query will back up to the OR node and descend down the right half of the tree. When the right half of the tree exhausts all matches, the query is done and read query returns its end-of-query indicator.

Once the query engine determines that a file matches a query, it must be returned to the program that called the read query routine. The result of a file match by the query engine is an i-node (recall that an index only stores the i-node number of a file in the index). The process of converting the result of a query into something appropriate for a user program requires the file system to convert an i-node into a file name. Normally this would not be possible, but BFS stores the name of a file (not the complete path, just the name) as an attribute of the file. Additionally, BFS stores a link in the file i-node to the directory that contains the file. This enables us to convert from an i-node address into a complete path to a file. It is quite unusual to store the name of a file in the file i-node, but BFS does this explicitly to support queries.

Live Queries

Live queries are another feature built around the query engine of BFS. A live query is a persistent query that monitors all file operations and reports additions to and deletions from the set of matching files. That is, if we issue the following as a live query:

```
name = *.c
```

the file system will first return to us all existing files whose name ends in .c. The live aspect of the query means that the file system will continue to inform us when any new files are created that match the query or when any existing files that matched are deleted or renamed. A more useful example of a live query is one that watches for new email. A live query with the predicate MAIL:status = New will monitor for newly arrived email and not require polling. A system administrator might wish to issue the live query size > 50000000 to monitor for files that are growing too large. Live queries reduce unnecessary polling in a system and do not lag behind the actual event as is common with polling.

To support this functionality the file system tags all indices it encounters when parsing the query. The tag associated with each index is a link back to the original parse tree of the query. Each time the file system modifies the index, it also traverses the list of live queries interested in modifications to the index and, for each, checks if the new file matches the query. Although this sounds deceptively simple, there were many subtle locking issues that needed to be dealt with properly to be able to traverse from indices to parse trees and then back again.

5.4   Summary

This lengthy chapter touched on numerous topics that relate to indexing in the Be File System. We saw that indices provide a mechanism for efficient access to all the files with a certain attribute. The name of an index corresponds to an attribute name. Whenever an attribute is written and its name matches an index, the file system also updates the index. The attribute index is keyed on the value written to the attribute, and the i-node address of the file is stored with the value. Storing the i-node address of the file that contains the attribute allows the file system to map from the entry in the index to the original file.

The file system maintains three indices that are inherent to a file (name, size, and last modification time). These indices require slightly special treatment because they are not real attributes in the same sense as attributes added by user programs. An index may or may not exist for other attributes added to a file.

We discussed several alternative approaches for the data structure of the index: B-trees, their variants, and hash tables. B-trees win out over hash tables because B-trees are more scalable and because there are no unexpected costly operations on B-trees like resizing a hash table.

The chapter then discussed the details of the BFS implementation of B+trees, their layout on disk, and how they handle duplicates. We observed that the management of duplicates in BFS is adequate, though perhaps not as high-performance as we would like. Then we briefly touched on how B+trees in BFS hook into the rest of the file system.

The final section discussed queries, covering what queries are, some of the parsing issues, how queries iterate over indices to generate results, and the way results are processed. The discussion also covered live queries and how they manage to send updates to a query when new files are created or when old files are deleted.

The substance of this chapter—attributes, indexing, and queries—is the essence of why BFS is interesting. The extensive use of these features in the BeOS is not seen in other systems.

6

Allocation Policies

6.1 Where Do You Put Things on Disk?

The Be File System views a disk as an array of blocks. The blocks are numbered beginning at zero and continuing up to the maximum disk block of the device. This view of a storage device is simple and easy to work with from a file system perspective. But the geometry of a physical disk is more than a simple array of disk blocks. The policies that the file system uses to arrange where data is on disk can have a significant impact on the overall performance of the file system. This chapter explains what allocation policies are, different ways to arrange data on disk, and other mechanisms for improving file system throughput by taking advantage of physical properties of disks.

6.2 What Are Allocation Policies?

An *allocation policy* is the set of rules and heuristics a file system uses to decide where to place items on a disk. The allocation policy dictates the location of file system metadata (i-nodes, directory data, and indices) as well as file data. The rules used for this task range from trivial to complex. Fortunately the effectiveness of a set of rules does not always match the complexity.

The goal of an allocation policy is to arrange data on disk so that the layout provides the best throughput possible when retrieving the data later. Several factors influence the success of an allocation policy. One key factor in defining good allocation policies is knowledge of how disks operate. Knowing what disks are good at and what operations are more costly can help when constructing an allocation policy.

6.3 Physical Disks

A physical disk is a complex mechanism comprising many parts (see Figure 3-1 in Chapter 3). For the purposes of our discussion, we need to understand only three parts of a disk: the platters, tracks, and heads. Every disk is made up of a collection of *platters*. Platters are thin, circular, and metallic. Modern disks use platters that are 2–5 inches in diameter. Platters have two sides, each of which is divided into tracks. A *track* is a narrow circular ring around the platter. Any particular track is always the same distance from the center of the platter. There are typically between 2000 and 5000 tracks per inch on each side of a platter. Each track is divided into sectors (or disk blocks). A *sector* is the smallest indivisible unit that a disk drive can read or write. A sector is usually 512 bytes in size.

There are two disk heads per platter, one for the top side and one for the bottom. All disk heads are attached to a single arm, and all heads are in line. Often all the tracks under each of the heads are referred to collectively as a *cylinder* or *cylinder group*. All heads visit the same track on each platter at the same time. Although it would be interesting, it is not possible for some heads to read one track and other heads to read a different track.

Performing I/O within the same cylinder is very fast because it requires very little head movement. Switching from one head to another within the same cylinder is much faster than repositioning to a different track because only minor adjustments must be made to the head position to read from the same track on a different head.

Moving from one track to another involves what is known as a *seek*. Seeking from track to track requires physical motion of the disk arm from one location to another on the disk. Repositioning the disk arm over a new track requires finding the new position to within 0.05–0.1 mm accuracy. After finding the position, the disk arm and heads must settle before I/O can take place. The distance traveled in the seek also affects the amount of time to complete the seek. Seeking to an adjacent track takes less time than seeking from the innermost track to the outermost track. The time it takes to seek from one track to another before I/O can take place is known as the *seek time*. Seek time is typically 5–20 milliseconds. This is perhaps the slowest operation possible on a modern computer system.

Although the preceding paragraphs discussed the very low-level geometry of disk drives, most modern disk drives go to great lengths to hide this information from the user. Even if an operating system extracts the physical geometry information, it is likely that the drive fabricated the information to suit its own needs. Disk drives do this so that they can map logical disk block addresses to physical locations in a way that is most optimal for a particular drive. Performing the mapping in the disk drive allows the manufacturer to use intimate knowledge of the drive; if the host system tried to use physical knowledge of a drive to optimize access patterns, it could only do so in a general fashion.

Even though disk drives do much to hide their physical geometry, understanding the latency issues involved with different types of operations affects the design of the file system allocation policies. Another important consideration when constructing an allocation policy is to know what disks are good at. The fastest operation any disk can perform is reading contiguous blocks of data. Sequential I/O is fast because it is the easiest to make fast. I/O on large contiguous chunks of memory allows the OS to take advantage of DMA (direct memory access) and burst bus transfers. Further, at the level of the disk drive, large transfers take advantage of any on-board cache and allow the drive to fully exploit its block remapping to reduce the amount of time required to transfer the data to/from the platters.

A simple test program helps illustrate some of the issues involved. The test program opens a raw disk device, generates a random list of block addresses (1024 of them), and then times how long it takes to read that list of blocks in their natural random order versus when they are in sorted order. On the BeOS with several different disk drives (Quantum, Seagate, etc.), we found that the difference in time to read 1024 blocks in sorted versus random order was nearly a factor of two. That is, simply sorting the list of blocks reduced the time to read all the blocks from 16 seconds to approximately 8.5 seconds. To illustrate the difference between random I/O and sequential I/O, we also had the program read the same total amount of data (512K) in a single read operation. That operation took less than 0.2 seconds to complete. Although the absolute numbers will vary depending on the hardware configuration used in the test, the importance of these numbers is in how they relate to each other. The difference is staggering: sequential I/O for a large contiguous chunk of data is nearly 50 times faster than even a sorted list of I/Os, and nearly 100 times faster than reading the same amount of data in pure random order.

Two important points stand out from this data: contiguous I/O is the fastest operation a disk can do by at least an order of magnitude. Knowing the extreme difference in the speed of sequential I/O versus random I/O, we can see that there is no point in wasting time trying to compact data structures at the expense of locality of data. It is faster to read a large contiguous data structure, even if it is as much as 10 times the size of a more compact but spread-out structure. This is quite counterintuitive.

The other salient point is that when I/O must take place to many different locations, batching multiple transactions is wise. By batching operations together and sorting the resulting list of block addresses before performing the I/O, the file system can take advantage of any locality between different operations and amortize the cost of disk seeks over many operations. This technique can halve the time it takes to perform the I/O.

6.4 What Can You Lay Out?

The first step in defining allocation policies is to decide what file system structures the policies will affect. In BFS there are three main structures that require layout decisions:

- File data
- Directory data
- I-node data

First, the allocation policy for file data will have the largest effect on how effectively the file system can utilize the disk's bandwidth. A good allocation policy for file data will try to keep the file data contiguous. If the file data is not contiguous or is spread around the disk, the file system will never be able to issue large-enough requests to take advantage of the real disk speed.

Measuring the effectiveness of the file data allocation policy is simple: compare the maximum bandwidth possible doing I/O to a file versus accessing the device in a raw fashion. The difference in bandwidth is an indication of the overhead introduced by the file data allocation policy. Minimizing the overhead of the file system when doing I/O to a file is important. Ideally the file system should introduce as little overhead as possible.

The next item of control is directory data. Even though directories store their contents in regular files, we separate directory data from normal file data because directories contain file system metadata. The storage of file system metadata has different constraints than regular user data. Of course, maintaining contiguous allocations for directory data is important, but there is another factor to consider: Where do the corresponding i-nodes of the directory live? Forcing a disk arm to make large sweeps to go from a directory entry to the necessary i-node could have disastrous effects on performance.

The placement of i-node data is important because all accesses to files must first load the i-node of the file being referenced. The organization and placement of i-nodes has the same issues as directory data. Placing directory data and file i-nodes near each other can produce a very large speed boost because when one is needed, so is the other. Often all i-nodes exist in one fixed area on disk, and thus the allocation policy is somewhat moot. When i-nodes can exist anywhere on disk (as with BFS), the allocation policy is much more relevant.

There are several different ways to measure the effectiveness of the directory data and i-node allocation policies. The simplest approach is to measure the time it takes to create varying numbers of files in a directory. This is a crude measurement technique but gives a good indication of how much overhead there is in the creation and deletion of files. Another technique is to measure how long it takes to iterate over the contents of a directory (optionally also retrieving information about each file, i.e., a stat()).

To a lesser degree, the placement of the block bitmap and the log area can also have an effect on performance. The block bitmap is frequently written when allocating space for files. Choosing a good location for the block bitmap can avoid excessively long disk seeks. The log area of a journaled file system also receives a heavy amount of I/O. Again, choosing a good location for the log area can avoid long disk seeks.

There are only a small number of items that a file system allocation policy has control over. The primary item that an allocation policy has control over is file data. The allocation policy regarding file system metadata, such as directory data blocks and i-nodes, also plays an important role in the speed of various operations.

6.5   Types of Access

Different types of access to a file system behave differently based on the allocation policy. One type of access may fare poorly under a certain allocation policy, while another access pattern may fare extremely well. Further, some allocation policies may make space versus time trade-offs that are not appropriate in all situations.

The types of operations a file system performs that are interesting to optimize are

- open a file
- create a file
- write data to a file
- delete a file
- rename a file
- list the contents of a directory

Of this list of operations, we must choose which to optimize and which to ignore. Improving the speed of one operation may slow down another, or the ideal policy for one operation may conflict with the goals of other operations.

Opening a file consists of a number of operations. First, the file system must check the directory to see if it contains the file we would like to open. Searching for the name in the directory is a directory lookup operation, which may entail either a brute-force search or some other more intelligent algorithm. If the file exists, we must load the associated i-node.

In the ideal situation, the allocation policy would place the directory and i-node data such that both could be read in a single disk read. If the only thing a file system needed to do was to arrange data perfectly, this would be an easy task. In the real world, files are created and deleted all the time, and maintaining a perfect relationship between directory and i-node data is quite difficult. Some file systems embed the i-nodes directly in the directory, which does maintain this relationship but at the expense of added complexity elsewhere in the file system. As a general rule, placing directory data and i-nodes near each other is a good thing to do.

Creating a file modifies several data structures—at a minimum, the block bitmap and directory, as well as any indices that may need maintainence. The allocation policy must choose an i-node and a place in the directory for the new file. Picking a good location for an i-node on a clean disk is easy, but the more common case is to have to pick an i-node after a disk has had many files created and deleted.

The allocation policy for writing data to a file faces many conflicting goals. Small files should not waste disk space, and packing many of them together helps avoid fragmentation. Large files should be contiguous and avoid large skips in the block addresses that make up the file. These goals often conflict, and in general it is not possible to know how much data will eventually be written to a file.

When a user deletes a file, the file system frees the space associated with the file. The hole left by the deleted file could be compacted, but this presents significant difficulties because the file system must move data. Moving data could present unacceptable lapses in performance. Ideally the file system will reuse the hole left by the previous file when the next file is created.

Renaming a file is generally not a time-critical operation, and so it receives less attention. The primary data structures modified during a rename are the directory data and a name index if one exists on the file system. Since in most systems the rename operation is not that frequent, there is not enough I/O involved in a rename operation to warrant spending much time optimizing it.

The speed of listing the contents of a directory is directly influenced by the allocation policy and its effectiveness in arranging data on disk. If the contents of the directory are followed by the i-node data, prefetching will bring in significant chunks of relevant data in one contiguous I/O. This layout is fairly easy to ensure on an empty file system, but it is harder to maintain under normal use when files are deleted and re-created often.

The allocation policy applied to these operations will affect the overall performance of the file system. Based on the desired goals of the file system, various choices can be made as to how and where to place file system structures. If the ultimate in compactness is desired, it may make sense to delete the holes left by removing a file. Alternatively, it may be more efficient to ignore the hole and to fill it with a new file when one is created. Weighing these conflicting goals and deciding on the proper solution is the domain of file system allocation policy.

6.6 Allocation Policies in BFS

Now let's look at the allocation policies chosen for BFS.

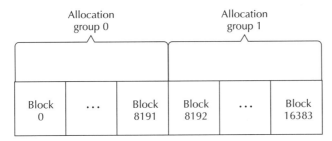

Figure 6-1   The relationship of allocation groups to physical blocks.

Allocation Groups: The Underlying Organization

To help manage disk space, BFS introduces a concept called *allocation groups*. An allocation group is a soft structure in that there is no corresponding data structure that exists on disk. An allocation group is a way to divide up the blocks that make up a file system into chunks for the purposes of the allocation policy.

In BFS an allocation group is a collection of at least 8192 file system blocks. Allocation group boundaries fall on block-sized chunks of the disk block bitmap. That is, an allocation group is always at least one block of the file system block bitmap. If a file system has a block size of 1024 bytes (the preferred and smallest allowed for BFS), then one bitmap block would contain the state of up to 8192 different blocks (1024 bytes in one block multiplied by eight, the number of bits in 1 byte). Very large disks may have more than one bitmap block per allocation group.

If a file system has 16,384 1024-byte blocks, the bitmap would be two blocks long (2 × 8192). That would be sufficient for two allocation groups, as shown in Figure 6-1.

An allocation group is a conceptual aid to help in deciding where to put various file system data structures. By breaking up the disk into fixed-size chunks, we can arrange data so that related items are near each other. The rules for placement are just that—rules—which means they are meant to be broken. The heuristics used to guide placement of data structures are not rigid. If disk space is tight or the disk is very fragmented, it is acceptable to use any disk block for any purpose.

Even though allocation groups are a soft structure, proper sizing can affect several factors of the performance of the overall file system. Normally an allocation group is only 8192 blocks long (i.e., one block of the bitmap). Thus, a block_run has a maximum size of 8192 blocks since a block_run cannot span more than one allocation group. If a single block_run can only map 8192 blocks, this places a maximum size on a file. Assuming perfect allocations (i.e., every block_run is fully allocated), the maximum amount of data that a file can store is approximately 5 GB:

12 direct block_runs = 96 MB	(8192K per block_run)
512 indirect block_runs = 4 GB	(512 block_runs of 8192K each)
256,000 double-indirect block_runs = 1 GB	(256K block_runs of 4K each)

Total data mapped = 5.09 GB

On a drive smaller than 5 GB, such a file size limit is not a problem, but on larger drives it becomes more of an issue. The solution is quite simple. Increasing the size of each allocation group increases the amount of data that each block_run can map, up to the maximum of 64K blocks per block_run. If each allocation group were 65,536 blocks long, the maximum file size would be over 33 GB:

12 direct block_runs = 768 MB	(64 MB per block_run)
512 indirect block_runs = 32 GB	(512 block_runs of 64 MB each)
256,000 double-indirect block_runs = 1 GB	(256K block_runs of 4K each)

Total data mapped = 33.76 GB

The amount of space mapped by the double-indirect blocks can also be increased by making each block_run map 8K or more, instead of 4K. And, of course, increasing the file system block size increases the maximum file size. If even larger file sizes are necessary, BFS has an unused triple-indirect block, which would increase file sizes to around 512 GB.

When creating a file system, BFS chooses the size of the allocation group such that the maximum file size will be larger than the size of the device. Why doesn't the file system always make allocation groups 65,536 blocks long? Because on smaller volumes such large allocation groups would cause all data to fall into one allocation group, thus defeating the purpose of clustering directory data and i-nodes separately from file data.

Directory and Index Allocation Policy

BFS reserves the first eight allocation groups as the preferred area for indices and their data. BFS reserves these eight allocation groups simply by convention; nothing prevents an i-node or file data block from being allocated in this area of the disk. If the disk becomes full, BFS will use the disk blocks in the first eight allocation groups for whatever is necessary. Segregating the indices to the first eight allocation groups provides them with at least 64 MB of disk space to grow and prevents file data or normal directory data from becoming intermixed with the index data. The advantage of this approach is that indices tend to grow slowly, and this allows them space to grow without becoming fragmented by normal file data.

The root directory for all BFS file systems begins in the eighth allocation group (i.e., starting at block 65,536). The root directory i-node is usually

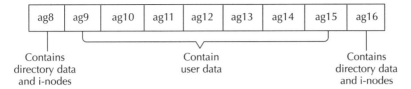

| ag8 | ag9 | ag10 | ag11 | ag12 | ag13 | ag14 | ag15 | ag16 |

Contains
directory data
and i-nodes

Contain
user data

Contains
directory data
and i-nodes

Figure 6-2   Use of allocation groups by BFS to distribute metadata and user data.

i-node number 65,536 unless a disk is very large. When a disk is very large
(i.e., greater than 5 GB), more blocks are part of each allocation group, and the
root directory i-node block would be pushed out further.

All data blocks for a directory are allocated from the same allocation group
as the directory i-node (if possible). File i-nodes are also put in the same allocation group as the directory that contains them. The result is that directory
data and i-node blocks for the files in the directory will be near each other.
The i-node block for a subdirectory is placed eight allocation groups further
away. This helps to spread data around the drive so that not too much is con-
centrated in one allocation group. File data is placed in the allocation groups
that exist between allocation groups that contain directory and i-node data.
That is, every eighth allocation group contains primarily directory data and
i-node data; the intervening seven allocation groups contain user data (see
Figure 6-2).

File Data Allocation Policy

In BFS, the allocation policy for file data tries hard to ensure that files are as
contiguous as possible. The first step is to preallocate space for a file when it
is first written or when it is grown. If the amount of data written to a file is
less than 64K and the file needs to grow to accommodate the new data, BFS
preallocates 64K of space for the file. BFS chooses a preallocation size of 64K
for several reasons. Because the size of most files is less than 64K, by preal-
locating 64K we virtually guarantee that most files will be contiguous. The
other reason is that for files larger than 64K, allocating contiguous chunks
of 64K each allows the file system to perform large I/Os to contiguous disk
blocks. A size of 64K is (empirically) large enough to allow the disk to transfer data at or near its maximum bandwidth. Preallocation also has another
benefit: it amortizes the cost of growing the file over a larger amount of I/O.
Because BFS is journaled, growing a file requires starting a new transaction. If
we had to start a new transaction each time a few bytes of data were written,
the performance of writing to a file would be negatively impacted by the cost
of the transactions. Preallocation ensures that most file data is contiguous
and at the same time reduces the cost of growing a file by only growing it
once per 64K of data instead of on every I/O.

Preallocation does have some drawbacks. The actual size of a file is hardly ever exactly 64K, so the file system must trim back the unused preallocated space at some point. For regular files the file system trims any unused preallocated space when the file is closed. Trimming the preallocated space is another transaction, but it is less costly than we might imagine because another transaction is already necessary at file close time to maintain the size and last modification time indices. Trimming the space not used by the file also modifies the same bitmap blocks as were modified during the allocation, so it is easy for BFS to collapse the multiple modifications to the file into a single log transaction, which further reduces the cost.

Dangers of Preallocation and File Contiguity

BFS tries hard to ensure that file data is contiguous on disk and succeeds quite well in the common case when the disk is not terribly fragmented. But not all disks remain unfragmented, and in certain degenerate situations, preallocation and the attempt of the file system to allocate contiguous blocks of disk space can result in very poor performance. During the development of BFS we discovered that running a disk fragmenter would cause havoc the next time the system was rebooted. On boot-up the virtual memory system would ask to create a rather large swap file, which BFS would attempt to do as contiguously as possible. The algorithms would spend vast amounts of time searching for contiguous block_runs for each chunk of the file that it tried to allocate. The searches would iterate over the entire bitmap until they found that the largest consecutive free block_run was 4K or so, and then they would stop. This process could take several minutes on a modest-sized disk.

The lesson learned from this is that the file system needs to be smart about its allocation policies. If the file system fails too many times while trying to allocate large contiguous runs, the file system should switch policies and simply attempt to allocate whatever blocks are available. BFS uses this technique as well as several hints in the block bitmap to allow it to "know" when a disk is very full and therefore the file system should switch policies. Knowing when a disk is no longer full is also important lest the file system switch policies in only one direction. Fortunately these sorts of policy decisions are easy to modify and tinker with and do not affect the on-disk structure. This allows later tuning of a file system without affecting existing structures.

Preallocation and Directories

Directories present an interesting dilemma for preallocation policies. The size of a directory will grow, but generally it grows much more slowly than a file. A directory grows in size as more files are added to it, but, unlike a file, a directory has no real "open" and "close" operations (i.e., a directory need not be opened to first create a file in it). This makes it less clear when preallocated blocks in the directory should be trimmed back. BFS trims directory data when the directory i-node is flushed from memory. This approach to trimming the preallocated data has several advantages. The preallocation of data for the directory allows the directory to grow and still remain contiguous. By delaying the trimming of data until the directory is no longer needed, the file system can be sure that all the contents of the directory are contiguous and that it is not likely to grow again soon.

6.7   Summary

This chapter discussed the issues involved in choosing where to place data structures on disk. The physical characteristics of hard disks play a large role in allocation policies. The ultimate goal of file system allocation policies is to lay out data structures contiguously and to minimize the need for disk seeks. Where a file system chooses to place i-nodes, directory data, and file data can significantly impact the overall performance of the file system.

7

Journaling

J*ournaling*, also referred to as *logging*, is a mechanism for ensuring the correctness of on-disk data structures. The goal of this chapter is to explain what journaling is, how a file system implements it, and techniques to improve journaling performance.

To understand journaling, we first need to understand the problem that it tries to solve. If a system crashes while updating a data structure on disk, the data structure may become corrupted. Operations that need to update multiple disk blocks are at risk if a crash happens between updates. A crash that happens between two modifications to a data structure will leave the operation only partially complete. A partially updated structure is essentially a corrupt structure, and thus a file system must take special care to avoid that situation.

A disk can only guarantee that a write to a single disk block succeeds. That is, an update to a single disk block either succeeds or it does not. A write to a single block on a disk is an indivisible (i.e., atomic) event; it is not possible to only partially write to a disk block. If a file system never needs to update more than a single disk block for any operation, then the damage caused by a crash is limited: either the disk block is written or it isn't. Unfortunately on-disk data structures often require modifications to several different disk blocks, all of which must be written properly to consider the update complete. If only some of the blocks of a data structure are modified, it may cause the software that manipulates the data structure to corrupt user data or to crash.

If a catastrophic situation occurs while modifying the data structure, the next time the system initiates accesses to the data structure, it must carefully verify the data structure. This involves traversing the entire data structure to repair any damage caused by the previous system halt—a tedious and lengthy process.

Journaling, a technique invented by the database community, guarantees the correctness of on-disk data structures by ensuring that each update to the structure happens completely or not at all, even if the update spans multiple disk blocks. If a file system uses journaling, it can assume that, barring bugs or disk failure, its on-disk data structures will remain consistent regardless of crashes, power failures, or other disastrous conditions. Further, recovery of a journaled file system is independent of its size. Crash recovery of a journaled volume takes on the order of seconds, not tens of minutes as it does with large nonjournaled file systems. Guaranteed consistency and speedy recovery are the two main features journaling offers.

Without knowing the details, journaling may seem like magic. As we will see, it is not. Furthermore, journaling does not protect against all kinds of failures. For example, if a disk block goes bad and can no longer be read from or written to, journaling does not (and cannot) offer any guarantees or protection. Higher-level software must always be prepared to deal with physical disk failures. Journaling has several practical limits on the protection it provides.

7.1 The Basics

In a journaling file system, a *transaction* is the complete set of modifications made to the on-disk structures of the file system during one operation. For example, creating a file is a single transaction that consists of all disk blocks modified during the creation of the file. A transaction is considered atomic with respect to failures. Either a transaction happens completely (e.g., a file is created), or it does not happen at all. A transaction finishes when the last modification is made. Even though a transaction finishes, it is not complete until all modified disk blocks have been updated on disk. This distinction between a finished transaction and a completed transaction is important and will be discussed later. A transaction is the most basic unit of journaling.

An alternative way to think about the contents of a transaction is to view them at a high level. At a high level, we can think of a transaction as a single operation such as "create file X" or "delete file Y." This is a much more compact representation than viewing a transaction as a sequence of modified blocks. The low-level view places no importance on the contents of the blocks; it simply records which blocks were modified. The more compact, higher-level view requires intimate knowledge of the underlying data structures to interpret the contents of the log, which complicates the journaling implementation. The low-level view of transactions is considerably simpler to implement and has the advantage of being independent of the file system data structures.

When the last modification of a transaction is complete (i.e., it is finished), the contents of the transaction are written to the *log*. The log is a fixed-size, contiguous area on the disk that the journaling code uses as a circular buffer.

Another term used to refer to the log is the *journal*. The journaling system records all transactions in the log area. It is possible to put the log on a different device than the rest of the file system for performance reasons. The log is only written during normal operation, and when old transactions complete, their space in the log is reclaimed. The log is central to the operation of journaling.

When a transaction has been written to the log, it is sometimes referred to as a *journal entry*. A journal entry consists of the addresses of the modified disk blocks and the data that belongs in each block. A journal entry is usually stored as a single chunk of memory and is written to the log area of a volume.

When a journaled system reboots, if there are any journal entries that were not marked as completed, the system must *replay* the entries to bring the system up-to-date. Replaying the journal prevents partial updates because each journal entry is a complete, self-contained transaction.

Write-ahead logging is when a journaling system writes changes to the log before modifying the disk. All journaling systems that we know of use write-ahead logging. We assume that journaling implies write-ahead logging and mention it only for completeness.

Supporting the basic concept of a transaction and the log are several in-memory data structures. These structures hold a transaction in memory while modifications are being made and keep track of which transactions have successfully completed and which are pending. These structures of course vary depending on the journaling implementation.

7.2   How Does Journaling Work?

The basic premise of journaling is that all modified blocks used in a transaction are locked in memory until the transaction is finished. Once the transaction is finished, the contents of the transaction are written to the log and the modified blocks are unlocked. When all the cached blocks are eventually flushed to their respective locations on disk, the transaction is considered complete. Buffering the transaction in memory and first writing the data to the log prevents partial updates from happening.

The key to journaling is that it writes the contents of a transaction to the log area on disk *before* allowing the writes to happen to their normal place on disk. That is, once a transaction is successfully written to the log, the blocks making up the transaction are unlocked from the cache. The cached blocks are then allowed to be written to their regular locations on disk at some point in the future (i.e., whenever it is convenient for the cache to flush them to disk). When the cache flushes the last block of a transaction to disk, the journal is updated to reflect that the transaction completed.

The "magic" behind journaling is that the disk blocks modified during a transaction are not written until after the entire transaction is successfully written to the log. By buffering the transaction in memory until it

Figure 7-1 A simplified transaction to create a file and the places where it can crash.

is complete, journaling avoids partially written transactions. If the system crashes before successfully writing the journal entry, the entry is not considered valid and the transaction never happens. If the system crashes after writing the journal entry, when it reboots it examines the log and replays the outstanding transactions. This notion of replaying a transaction is the crux of the journaling consistency guarantee.

When a journaling system replays a transaction, it effectively redoes the transaction. If the journal stores the modified disk blocks that are part of a transaction, replaying a transaction is simply a matter of writing those disk blocks to their correct locations on disk. If the journal stores a high-level representation of a transaction, replaying the log involves performing the actions over again (e.g., create a file). When the system is done replaying the log, the journaling system updates the log so that it is marked clean. If the system crashes while replaying the log, no harm is done and the log will be replayed again the next time the system boots. Replaying transactions brings the system back to a known consistent state, and it must be done before any other access to the file system is performed.

If we follow the time line of the events involved in creating a file, we can see how journaling guarantees consistency. For this example (shown in Figure 7-1), we will assume that only two blocks need to be modified to create a file, one block for the allocation of the i-node and one block to add the new file name to a directory.

If the system crashes at time A, the system is still consistent because the file system has not been modified yet (the log has nothing written to it and no blocks are modified). If the system crashes at any point up to time C, the transaction is not complete and therefore the journal considers the transaction not to have happened. The file system is still consistent despite a crash at any point up to time C because the original blocks have not been modified.

If the system crashes between time C and D (while writing the journal entry), the journal entry is only partially complete. This does not affect the consistency of the system because the journal always ignores partially completed transactions when examining the log. Further, no other blocks were modified, so it is as though the transaction never happened.

If the system crashes at time D, the journal entry is complete. In the case of a crash at time D or later, when the system restarts, it will replay the log, updating the appropriate blocks on disk, and the file will be successfully created. A crash at times E or F is similar to a crash at time D. Just as before, the file system will replay the log and write the blocks in the log to their correct locations on disk. Even though some of the actual disk blocks may have been updated between time D and E, no harm is done because the journal contains the same values as the blocks do.

A crash after time F is irrelevant with respect to our transaction because all disk blocks were updated and the journal entry marked as completed. A crash after time F would not even be aware that the file was created since the log was already updated to reflect that the transaction was complete.

7.3   Types of Journaling

In file systems there are two main forms of journaling. The first style, called old-value/new-value logging, records both the old value and the new value of a part of a transaction. For example, if a file is renamed, the old name and the new name are both recorded to the log. Recording both values allows the file system to abort a change and restore the old state of the data structures. The disadvantage to old-value/new-value logging is that twice as much data must be written to the log. Being able to back out of a transaction is quite useful, but old-value/new-value logging is considerably more difficult to implement and is slower because more data is written to the log.

To implement old-value/new-value logging, the file system must record the state of any disk block before modifying the disk block. This can complicate algorithms in a B+tree, which may examine many nodes before making a modification to one of them. Old-value/new-value logging requires changes to the lowest levels of code to ensure that they properly store the unmodified state of any blocks they modify.

New-value-only logging is the other style of journaling. New-value-only logging records only the modifications made to disk blocks, not the original value. Supporting new-value-only logging in a file system is relatively trivial because everywhere that code would perform a normal block write simply becomes a write to the log. One drawback of new-value-only logging is that it does not allow aborting a transaction. The inability to abort a transaction complicates error recovery, but the trade-off is worth it. New-value-only logging writes half as much data as old-value/new-value logging does and thus is faster and requires less memory to buffer the changes.

7.4   What Is Journaled?

One of the main sources of confusion about journaling is what exactly a journal contains. A journal only contains modifications made to file system metadata. That is, a journal contains changes to a directory, the bitmap, i-nodes, and, in BFS, changes to indices. A journal does not contain modifications to user data stored in a file (or attribute in the case of BFS). That means that if a text editor saves a new file, the contents of the new file are not in the log, but the new directory entry, the i-node, and the modified bitmap blocks are stored in the journal entry. This is an important point about journaling.

Not only does journaling not store user data in the log, it cannot. If a journal were to also record user data, the amount of data that could be written to the log would be unbounded. Since the log is a fixed size, transactions cannot ever be larger than the size of the log. If a user were to write more data than the size of the log, the file system would be stuck and have no place to put all the user data. A user program can write more data than it is possible to store in the fixed-size log, and for this reason user data is not written to the log.

Journaling only guarantees the integrity of file system data structures. Journaling does not guarantee that user data is always completely up-to-date, nor does journaling guarantee that the file system data structures are up-to-date with respect to the time of a crash. If a journaled file system crashes while writing data to a new file, when the system reboots, the file data may not be correct, and furthermore the file may not even exist. How up-to-date the file system is depends on how much data the file system and the journal buffer.

An important aspect of journaling is that, although the file system may be consistent, it is not a requirement that the system also be up-to-date. In a journaled system, a transaction either happens completely or not at all. That may mean that even files created successfully (from the point of view of a program before the crash) may not exist after a reboot.

It is natural to ask, Why can't journaling also guarantee that the file system is up-to-date? Journaling can provide that guarantee if it only buffers at most one transaction. By buffering only one transaction at a time, if a crash occurs, only the last transaction in progress at the time of the crash would be undone. Only buffering one transaction increases the number of disk writes to the log, which slows the file system down considerably. The slowdown introduced by buffering only one transaction is significant enough that most file systems prefer to offer improved throughput instead of better consistency guarantees. The consistency needs of the rest of the system that the file system is a part of dictate how much or how little buffering should be done by the journaling code.

7.5 Beyond Journaling

The Berkeley Log Structured File System (LFS) extends the notion of journaling by treating the entire disk as the log area and writing everything (including user data) to the log. In LFS, files are never deleted, they are simply rewritten. LFS reclaims space in the log by finding transactions that have been superseded by later transactions.

LFS writes its log transactions in large contiguous chunks, which is the fastest way to write to a disk. Unfortunately when a disk becomes nearly full (the steady state of disks), LFS may have to search through a lot of log entries to find a free area. The cost of that search may offset the benefit of doing the large write. The task of reclaiming log space can be quite time-consuming and requires locking the file system. LFS assumes that reclaiming log space is the sort of task that can run late at night. This assumption works fine for a Unix-style system that is running continually, but works less well for a desktop environment, which may not always be running.

Interestingly, because LFS never overwrites a file, it has the potential to implicitly version all files. Because LFS does not rewrite a file in place, it would be possible to provide hooks to locate the previous version of a file and to retrieve it. Such a feature would also apply to undeleting files and even undoing a file save. The current version of LFS does not do this, however.

Log structured file systems are still an area of research. Even though LFS shipped with BSD 4.4, it is not generally used in commercial systems because of the drawbacks associated with reclaiming space when the disk is full. The details of LFS are beyond the scope of this book (for more information about log structured file systems, refer to the papers written by Mendel Rosenblum).

7.6 What's the Cost?

Journaling offers two significant advantages to file systems: guaranteed consistency of metadata (barring hardware failures) and quick recovery in the case of failure. The most obvious cost of journaling is that metadata must be written twice (once to the log and once to its regular place). Surprisingly, writing the data twice does not impact performance—and in some cases can even improve performance!

How is it possible that writing twice as much file system metadata can improve performance? The answer is quite simple: the first write of the data is to the log area and is batched with other metadata, making for a large contiguous write (i.e., it is fast). When the data is later flushed from the cache, the cache manager can sort the list of blocks by their disk address, which minimizes the seek time when writing the blocks. The difference that sorting the blocks can make is appreciable. The final proof is in the performance numbers. For various file system metadata-intensive benchmarks (e.g., creating and deleting files), a journaled file system can be several times faster than a traditional synchronous write file system, such as the Berkeley Fast File System (as used in Solaris). We'll cover more details about performance in Chapter 9.

The biggest bottleneck that journaled file systems face is that all transactions write to a single log. With a single log, all transactions must lock access to the log before making modifications. A single log effectively forces the file system into a single-threaded model for updates. This is a serious disadvantage if it is necessary to support a great deal of concurrent modifications to a file system.

The obvious solution to this is to support multiple log files. A system with multiple log files would allow writing to each log independently, which would allow transactions to happen in parallel. Multiple logs would necessitate timestamping transactions so that log playback could properly order the transactions in the different logs. Multiple logs would also require revisiting the locking scheme used in the file system.

Another technique to allow more concurrent access to the log is to have each transaction reserve a fixed number of blocks and then to manage that space independently of the other transactions. This raises numerous locking and ordering issues as well. For example, a later transaction may take less time to complete than an earlier transaction, and thus flushing that transaction may require waiting for a previous transaction to complete. SGI's XFS uses a variation of this technique, although they do not describe it in detail in their paper.

The current version of BFS does not implement either of these techniques to increase concurrent access to the log. The primary use of BFS is not likely to be in a transaction-oriented environment, and so far the existing performance has proved adequate.

7.7   The BFS Journaling Implementation

The BFS journaling implementation is rather simple. The journaling API used by the rest of the file system consists of three functions. The code to implement journaling and journal playback (i.e., crash recovery) is less than 1000 lines. The value of journaling far outweighs the cost of its implementation.

The log area used to write journal entries is a fixed area allocated at file system initialization. The superblock maintains a reference to the log area as well as two roving indices that point to the start and end of the active area of the log. The log area is used in a circular fashion, and the start and end indices simply mark the bounds of the log that contain active transactions.

In Figure 7-2 we see that there are three transactions that have finished but not yet completed. When the last block of journal entry 1 is flushed to disk by the cache, the log start index will be bumped to point to the beginning of journal entry 2. If a new transaction completes, it would be added in the area beyond journal entry 3 (wrapping around to the beginning of the log area if needed), and when the transaction finishes, the log end index would be incremented to point just beyond the end of the transaction. If the system

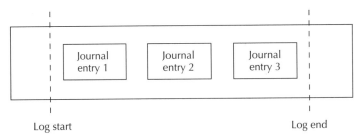

Figure 7-2   A high-level overview of the entire log area on disk.

were to crash with the log in the state shown in Figure 7-2, each of the three journal entries would be replayed, which would bring the file system into a consistent state.

The BFS journaling API comprises three functions. The first function creates a structure used to represent a transaction:

```
struct log_handle *start_transaction(bfs_info *bfs);
```

The input to the function is simply a pointer to an internal structure that represents a file system. This pointer is always passed to all file system routines so it is always available. The handle returned is ostensibly an opaque data type and need not be examined by the calling code. The handle represents the current transaction and holds state information.

The first task of start_transaction() is to acquire exclusive access to the log. Once start_transaction() acquires the log semaphore, it is held until the transaction completes. The most important task start_transaction() performs is to ensure that there is enough space available in the log to hold this transaction. Transactions are variably sized but must be less than a maximum size. Fixing the maximum size of a transaction is necessary to guarantee that any new transaction will have enough space to complete. It would also be possible to pass in the amount of space required by the code calling start_transaction().

Checking the log to see if there is enough space is easy. Some simple arithmetic on the start and end indices maintained in the superblock (reachable from the bfs_info struct) reveal how much space is available. If there is enough space in the log, then the necessary transaction structures and a buffer to hold the transaction are allocated, and a handle returned to the calling code.

If there is not enough space in the log, the caller cannot continue until there is adequate space to hold the new transaction. The first technique to free up log space is to force flushing blocks out of the cache, preferably those that were part of previous transactions. By forcing blocks to flush to disk, previous log transactions can complete, which thereby frees up log space (we will see how this works in more detail later). This may still not be sufficient to free up space in the log. As we will also discuss later, BFS groups multiple transactions and batches them into one transaction. For this reason it may be necessary to release the log semaphore, force a log flush, and then reacquire the log semaphore. This is a very rare circumstance and can only happen if the currently buffered log transaction is nearly as large as the entire log area.

Writing to the Log

Once start_transaction() completes, the calling code can begin making modifications to the file system. Each time the code modifies an on-disk data structure, it must call the function

```
ssize_t log_write_blocks(bfs_info      *bfs,
                         struct log_handle *lh,
                         off_t          block_number,
                         const void     *data,
                         int            number_of_blocks);
```

The log_write_blocks() routine commits the modified data to the log and locks the data in the cache as well. One optimization made by log_write_blocks() is that if the same block is modified several times in the same transaction, only one copy of the data is buffered. This works well since transactions are all or nothing—either the entire transaction succeeds or it doesn't.

During a transaction, any code that modifies a block of the file system metadata must call log_write_blocks() on the modified data. If this is not strictly adhered to, the file system will not remain consistent if a crash occurs.

There are several data structures that log_write_blocks() maintains. These data structures maintain all the state associated with the current transaction. The three structures managed by log_write_blocks() are

- the log_handle, which points to
- an entry_list, which has a pointer to
- a log_entry, which stores the data of the transaction.

Their relationship is shown in Figure 7-3.

The log_handle structure manages the overall information about the transaction. The structure contains

- the total number of blocks in the transaction
- the number of entry_list structures
- a block_run describing which part of the log area this transaction uses
- a count of how many blocks have been flushed

The block_run describing the log area and the count of the number of flushed blocks are only maintained after the transaction is finished.

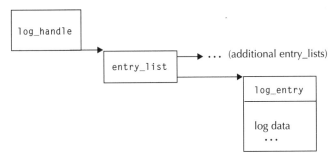

Figure 7-3   The in-memory data structures associated with BFS journaling.

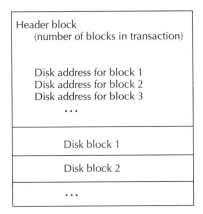

Figure 7-4   The layout of a BFS journal entry.

In memory a transaction is simply a list of buffers that contain the modified blocks. BFS manages this with the `entry_list` and `log_entry` structures. The `entry_list` keeps a count of how many blocks are used in the `log_entry`, a pointer to the `log_entry`, and a pointer to the next `entry_list`. Each `log_entry` is really nothing more than a chunk of memory that can hold some number of disk blocks (128 in BFS). The `log_entry` reserves the first block to keep track of the block numbers of the data blocks that are part of the transaction. The first block, which contains the block numbers of the remaining blocks in the `log_handle`, is written out as part of the transaction. The block list is essential to be able to play back the log in the event of a failure. Without the block list the file system would not know where each block belongs on the disk.

On disk, a transaction has the structure shown in Figure 7-4. The on-disk layout of a transaction mirrors its in-memory representation.

It is rare that a transaction uses more than one `entry_list` structure, but it can happen, especially with batched transactions (discussed later in this section). The maximum size of a transaction is a difficult quantity to compute because it not only depends on the specific operation but also on the item being operated on. The maximum size of a transaction in BFS is equal to the size of the log area (by default 2048 blocks). It is possible for a single operation to require more blocks than are in the log area, but fortunately such situations are pathological enough that we can expect that they will only occur in testing, not the real world. One case that came up during testing was deleting a file with slightly more than three million attributes. In that case, deleting all the associated attributes caused the file system to modify more blocks than the maximum number of blocks in the log area (2048). Such extreme situations are rare enough that BFS does not concern itself with them. It is conceivable that BFS could improve its handling of this situation.

The End of a Transaction

When a file system operation finishes making modifications and an update is complete, it calls

```
int end_transaction(bfs_info *bfs, struct log_handle *lh);
```

This function completes a transaction. After calling end_transaction() a file system operation can no longer make modifications to the disk unless it starts a new transaction.

The first step in flushing a log transaction involves writing the in-memory transaction buffer out to the log area of the disk. Care must be taken because the log area is a circular buffer. Writing the log_entry to disk must handle the wraparound case if the current start index is near the end of the log area and the end index is near the beginning.

To keep track of which parts of the log area are in use, the file system keeps track of start and end indices into the log. On a fresh file system the start and end indices both refer to the start of the log area and the entire log is empty. When a transaction is flushed to disk, the end index is incremented by the size of the transaction.

After flushing the log buffer, end_transaction() iterates over each block in the log buffer and sets a callback function for each block in the cache. The cache will call the callback immediately after the block is flushed to its regular location on disk. The callback function is the connection that the log uses to know when all of the blocks of a transaction have been written to disk. The callback routine uses the log_handle structure to keep track of how many blocks have been flushed. When the last one is flushed, the transaction is considered complete.

When a transaction is considered complete, the log space may be reclaimed. If there are no other outstanding transactions in the log before this transaction, all that must be done is to bump up the log start index by the size of the transaction. A difficulty that arises is that log transactions may complete out of order. If a later transaction completes before an earlier transaction, the log code cannot simply bump up the log start index. In this case the log completion code must keep track of which log transactions completed and which are still outstanding. When all the transactions spanning the range back to the current value of the start index are complete, then the start index can increment over the range.

As alluded to earlier, BFS does not write a journal entry every time a transaction completes. To improve performance, BFS batches multiple transactions into a group and flushes the whole group at once. For this reason end_transaction() does not necessarily flush the transaction to disk. In most cases end_transaction() records how much of the transaction buffer is used, releases the log semaphore, and returns. If the log buffer is mostly full, then end_transaction() flushes the log to disk.

Batching Transactions

Let's back up for a minute to consider the implications of buffering multiple transactions in the same buffer. This turns out to be a significant performance win. To better understand this, it is useful to look at an example, such as extracting files from an archive. Extracting the files will create many files in a directory. If we made each file creation a separate transaction, the data blocks that make up the directory would be written to disk numerous times. Writing the same location more than once hurts performance, but not as much as the inevitable disk seeks that would also occur. Batching multiple file creations into one transaction minimizes the number of writes of directory data. Further, it is likely that the i-nodes will be allocated sequentially if at all possible, which in turn means that when they are flushed from the cache, they will be forced out in a single write (because they are contiguous).

The technique of batching multiple transactions into a single transaction is often known as *group commit*. Group commit can offer significant speed advantages to a journaling file system because it amortizes the cost of writing to disk over many transactions. This effectively allows some transactions to complete entirely in memory (similar to the Linux ext2 file system) while still maintaining file system consistency guarantees because the system is journaled.

Adjusting the size of the log buffer and the size of the log area on disk directly influences how many transactions can be held in memory and how many transactions will be lost in the event of a crash. In the degenerate case, the log buffer can only hold one transaction, and the log area is only large enough for one transaction. At the other end of the spectrum, the log buffer can hold all transactions in memory, and nothing is ever written to disk. Reality lies somewhere in between: the log buffer size depends on the memory constraints of the system, and the size of the log depends on how much disk space can be dedicated to the log.

7.8   What Are Transactions?—A Deeper Look

The operations considered by BFS to be a single atomic transaction are

- create a file/directory
- delete a file/directory
- rename a file (including deletion of the existing name)
- change the size of a file (growing or shrinking)
- write data to an attribute
- delete an attribute
- create an index
- delete an index
- update a file's attributes

Each of these operations typically correspond to a user-level system call. For example, the `write()` system call writes data to a file. Implicit in that is that the file will grow in size to accommodate the new data. Growing the file to a specific size is one atomic operation—that is, a transaction. The other operations all must define the starting and ending boundaries of the transaction—what is included in the transaction and what is not.

Create File/Directory

In BFS, creating a file or directory involves modifying the bitmap (to allocate the i-node), adding the file name to a directory, and inserting the name into the name index. When creating a directory, the file system must also write the initial contents of the directory. All blocks modified by these suboperations would be considered part of the create file or create directory transaction.

Delete

Deleting a file is considerably more complex than creating a file. The file name is first removed from the directory and the main file system indices (name, size, last modified time). This is considered one transaction. When all access to the file is finished, the file data and attributes are removed in a separate transaction. Removing the data belonging to a file involves stepping through all the blocks allocated to the file and freeing them in the bitmap. Removing attributes attached to the file is similar to deleting all the files in a directory—each attribute must be deleted the same as a regular file. Potentially a delete transaction may touch many blocks.

Rename

The rename operation is by far the most complex operation the file system supports. The semantics of a rename operation are such that if a file exists with the new name, it is first deleted and the old file is then renamed. Consequently, a rename may touch as many blocks as a delete does, in addition to all the blocks necessary to delete the old file name from the directory (and indices) and then to reinsert the new name in the directory (and indices).

Change a File Size

In comparison to rename, changing the size of a file is a trivial operation. Adjusting the size of a file involves modifying the i-node of the file, any indirect blocks written with the addresses of new data blocks, and the bitmap blocks the allocation happened in. A large allocation that involves double-indirect blocks may touch many blocks as part of the transaction. The number of blocks that may be touched in a file creation is easy to calculate by knowing the allocation policy of BFS. First, the default allocation size for indirect and double-indirect block_runs is 4K. That is, the indirect block is 4K, and the double-indirect block is 4K and points to 512 indirect block_runs (each of 4K). Knowing these numbers, the maximum number of blocks touched by growing a file is

$$
\begin{array}{r}
1 \text{ for the i-node} \\
4 \text{ for the indirect block} \\
4 \text{ for the first-level double-indirect block} \\
512 \times 4 \text{ for the second-level double-indirect blocks} \\
\hline
2057 \text{ total blocks}
\end{array}
$$

This situation would occur if a program created a file, seeked to a file position 9 GB out, and then wrote a byte. Alternatively, on a perfectly fragmented file system (i.e., every other disk block allocated), this would occur with a 1 GB file. Both of these situations are extremely unlikely.

The Rest

The remaining operations decompose into one of the above operations. For example, creating an index is equivalent to creating a directory in the index directory. Adding attributes to a file is equivalent to creating a file in the attribute directory attached to the file. Because the other operations are equivalent in nature to the preceding basic operations, we will not consider them further.

7.9 Summary

Journaling is a technique borrowed from the database community and applied to file systems. A journaling file system prevents corruption of its data structures by collecting modifications made during an operation and batching those modifications into a single transaction that the file system records in its journal. Journaling can prevent corruption of file system data structures but does not protect data written to regular files. The technique of journaling can also improve the performance of a file system, allowing it to write large contiguous chunks of data to disk instead of synchronously writing many individual blocks.

8

The Disk Block Cache

Whenever two devices with significantly mismatched speeds need to work together, the faster device will often end up waiting for the slower device. Depending on how often the system accesses the slower device, the overall throughput of the system can effectively be reduced to that of the slower device. To alleviate this situation, system designers often incorporate a *cache* into a design to reduce the cost of accessing a slow device.

A cache reduces the cost of accessing a device by providing faster access to data that resides on the slow device. To accomplish this, a cache keeps copies of data that exists on a slow device in an area where it is faster to retrieve. A cache works because it can provide data much more quickly than the same data could be retrieved from its real location on the slow device. Put another way, a cache interposes itself between a fast device and a slow device and transparently provides the faster device with the illusion that the slower device is faster than it is.

This chapter is about the issues involved with designing a disk cache, how to decide what to keep in the cache, how to decide when to get rid of something from the cache, and the data structures involved.

8.1 Background

A cache uses some amount of buffer space to hold copies of frequently used data. The buffer space is faster to access than the underlying slow device. The buffer space used by a cache can never hold all the data of the underlying device. If a cache could hold all of the data of a slower device, the cache would simply replace the slower device. Of course, the larger the buffer space, the more effective the cache is. The main task of a cache system is the management of the chunks of data in the buffer.

A disk cache uses system memory to hold copies of data that resides on disk. To use the cache, a program requests a disk block, and if the cache has the block already in the cache, the block is simply read from or written to and the disk not accessed. On a read, if a requested block is not in the cache, the cache reads the block from the disk and keeps a copy of the data in the cache as well as fulfilling the request. On a write to a block not in the cache, the cache makes room for the new data, marks it as dirty, and then returns. Dirty data is flushed at a later, more convenient, time (perhaps batching up many writes into a single write).

Managing a cache is primarily a matter of deciding what to keep in the cache and what to kick out of the cache when the cache is full. This management is crucial to the performance of the cache. If useful data is dropped from the cache too quickly, the cache won't perform as well as it should. If the cache doesn't drop old data from the cache when appropriate, the useful size and effectiveness of the cache are greatly reduced.

The effectiveness of a disk cache is a measure of how often data requested is found in the cache. If a disk cache can hold 1024 different disk blocks and a program never requests more than 1024 blocks of data, the cache will be 100% effective because once the cache has read in all the blocks, the disk is no longer accessed. At the other end of the spectrum, if a program randomly requests many tens of thousands of different disk blocks, then it is likely that the effectiveness of the cache will approach zero, and every request will have to access the disk. Fortunately, access patterns tend to be of a more regular nature, and the effectiveness of a disk cache is higher.

Beyond the number of blocks that a program may request, the locality of those references also plays a role in the effectiveness of the cache. A program may request many more blocks than are in the cache, but if the addresses of the disk blocks are sequential, then the cache may still prove useful. In other situations the number of disk blocks accessed may be more than the size of the cache, but some amount of those disk blocks may be accessed many more times than the others, and thus the cache will hold the important blocks, reducing the cost of accessing them. Most programs have a high degree of locality of reference, which helps the effectiveness of a disk cache.

8.2 Organization of a Buffer Cache

A disk cache has two main requirements. First, given a disk block number, the cache should be able to quickly return the data associated with that disk block. Second, when the cache is full and new data is requested, the cache must decide what blocks to drop from the cache. These two requirements necessitate two different methods of access to the underlying data. The first task, to efficiently find a block of data given a disk block address, uses the

Hash table (indexed by block number)

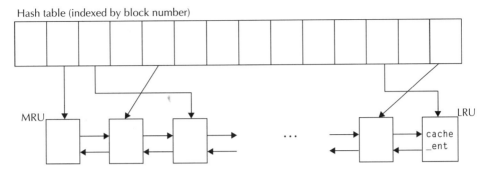

Figure 8-1   A disk block cache data structure showing the hash table and the LRU list.

obvious hash table solution. The second method of access requires an organization that enables quick decisions to be made about which blocks to flush from the cache. There are a few possible implementations to solve this problem, but the most common is a doubly linked list ordered from the most recently used (MRU) block to the least recently used (LRU). A doubly linked list ordered this way is often referred to as an *LRU list* (the head of which is the MRU end, and the tail is the LRU end). The hash table and LRU list are intimately interwoven, and access to them requires careful coordination.

The cache management we discuss focuses on this dual structure of hash table and LRU list. Instead of an LRU list to decide which block to drop from the cache, we could have used other algorithms, such as random replacement, the working set model, a clock-based algorithm, or variations of the LRU list (such as least frequently used). In designing BFS, it would have been nice to experiment with these other algorithms to determine which performed the best on typical workloads. Unfortunately, time constraints dictated that the cache get implemented, not experimented with, and so little exploration was done of other possible algorithms.

Underlying the hash table and LRU list are the blocks of data that the cache manages. The BeOS device cache manages the blocks of data with a data structure known as a cache_ent. The cache_ent structure maintains a pointer to the block of data, the block number, and the next/previous links for the LRU list. The hash table uses its own structures to index by block number to retrieve a pointer to the associated cache_ent structure.

In Figure 8-1 we illustrate the interrelationship of the hash table and the doubly linked list. We omit the pointers from the cache_ent structures to the data blocks for clarity.

Cache Reads

First, we will consider the case where the cache is empty and higher-level code requests a block from the cache. A hash table lookup determines that the block is not present. The cache code must then read the block from disk

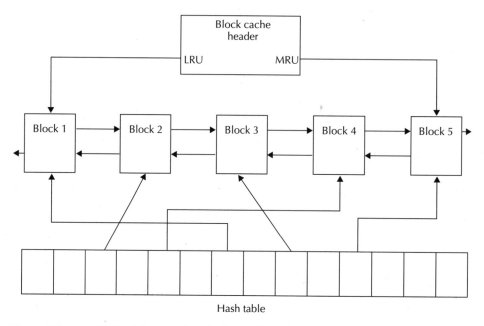

Figure 8-2   An old block is moved to the head of the list.

and insert it into the hash table. After inserting the block into the hash table, the cache inserts the block at the MRU end of the LRU list. As more blocks are read from disk, the first block that was read will migrate toward the LRU end of the list as other blocks get inserted in front of it.

If our original block is requested again, a probe of the hash table will find it, and the block will be moved to the MRU end of the LRU list because it is now the most recently used block (see Figure 8-2). This is where a cache provides the most benefit: data that is frequently used will be found and retrieved at the speed of a hash table lookup and a memcpy() instead of the cost of a disk seek and disk read, which are orders of magnitude slower.

The cache cannot grow without bound, so at some point the number of blocks managed by the cache will reach a maximum. When the cache is full and new blocks are requested that are not in the cache, a decision must be made about which block to kick out of the cache. The LRU list makes this decision easy. Simply taking the block at the LRU end of the list, we can discard its contents and reuse the block to read in the newly requested block (see Figure 8-3). Throwing away the least recently used block makes sense inherently: if the block hasn't been used in a long time, it's not likely to be needed again. Removing the LRU block involves not only deleting it from the LRU list but also deleting the block number from the hash table. After reclaiming the LRU block, the new block is read into memory and put at the MRU end of the LRU list.

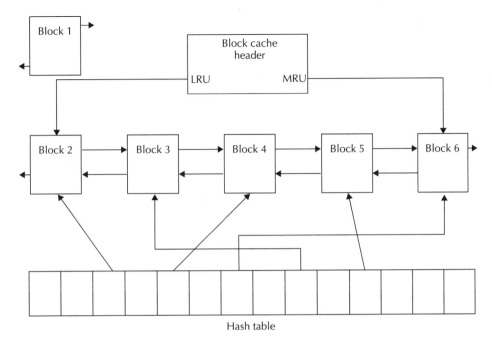

Figure 8-3 **Block 1 drops from the cache and block 6 enters.**

Cache Writes

There are two scenarios for a write to a cache. The first case is when the block being written to is already in the cache. In this situation the cache can memcpy() the newly written data over the data that it already has for a particular disk block. The cache must also move the block to the MRU end of the LRU list (i.e., it becomes the most recently used block of data). If a disk block is written to and the disk block is not in the cache, then the cache must make room for the new disk block. Making room in the cache for a newly written disk block that is not in the cache is the same as described previously for a miss on a cache read. Once there is space for the new disk block, the data is copied into the cache buffer for that block, and the cache_ent is added to the head of the LRU list. If the cache must perform write-through for data integrity reasons, the cache must also write the block to its corresponding disk location.

The second and more common case is that the block is simply marked dirty and the write finishes. At a later time, when the block is flushed from the cache, it will be written to disk because it has been marked dirty. If the system crashes or fails while there is dirty data in the cache, the disk will not be consistent with what was in memory.

Dirty blocks in the cache require a bit more work when flushing the cache. In the situations described previously, only clean blocks were in the cache, and flushing them simply meant reusing their blocks of data to hold new data. When there are dirty blocks, the cache must first write the dirty data to disk before allowing reuse of the associated data block. Proper handling of dirty blocks is important. If for any reason a dirty block is not flushed to disk before being discarded, the cache will lose changes made to the disk, effectively corrupting the disk.

8.3 Cache Optimizations

Flushing the cache when there are dirty blocks presents an interesting opportunity. If the cache always only flushed a single block at a time, it would perform no better at writing to the disk than if it wrote directly through on each write. However, by waiting until the cache is full, the cache can do two things that greatly aid performance. First, the cache can batch multiple changes together. That is, instead of only flushing one block at a time, it is wiser to flush multiple blocks at the same time. Flushing multiple blocks at once amortizes the cost of doing the flush over several blocks, and more importantly it enables a second optimization. When flushing multiple blocks, it becomes possible to reorder the disk writes and to write contiguous disk blocks in a single disk write. For example, if higher-level code writes the following block sequence:

$$971 \quad 245 \quad 972 \quad 246 \quad 973 \quad 247$$

when flushing the cache, the sequence can be reorganized into

$$245 \quad 246 \quad 247 \quad 971 \quad 972 \quad 973$$

which allows the cache to perform two disk writes (each for three consecutive blocks) and one seek, instead of six disk writes and five seeks. The importance of this cannot be overstated. Reorganizing the I/O pattern into an efficient ordering substantially reduces the number of seeks a disk has to make, thereby increasing the overall bandwidth to the disk. Large consecutive writes outperform sequential single-block writes by factors of 5–10 times, making this optimization extremely important. At a minimum, the cache should sort the list of blocks to be flushed, and if possible, it should coalesce writes to contiguous disk locations.

In a similar manner, when a cache miss occurs and a read of a disk block must be done, if the cache only reads a single block at a time, it would not perform very well. There is a fixed cost associated with doing a disk read, regardless of the size of the read. This fixed cost is very high relative to the amount of time that it takes to transfer one or two disk blocks. Therefore it is better to amortize the cost of doing the disk read over many blocks. The BeOS cache will read 32K on a cache miss. The cost of reading the extra data is insignificant in comparison to the cost of reading a single disk block. Another benefit of this scheme is that it performs read-ahead for the file system. If the file system is good at allocating files contiguously, then the extra data that is read is likely to be data that will soon be needed. Performing read-ahead of 32K also increases the effective disk bandwidth seen by the file system because it is much faster than performing 32 separate 1K reads.

One drawback to performing read-ahead at the cache level is that it is inherently imperfect. The cache does not know if the extra data read will be useful or not. It is possible to introduce special parameters to the cache API to control read-ahead, but that complicates the API and it is not clear that it would offer significant benefits. If the file system does its job allocating files contiguously, it will interact well with this simple cache policy. In practice, BFS works very well with implicit read-ahead.

In either case, when reading or writing, if the data refers to contiguous disk block addresses, there is another optimization possible. If the cache system has access to a scatter/gather I/O primitive, it can build a scatter/gather table to direct the I/O right to each block in memory. A scatter/gather table is a table of pointer and length pairs. A scatter/gather I/O primitive takes this table and performs the I/O directly to each chunk of memory described in the table. This is important because the blocks of data that the cache wants to perform I/O to are not likely to be contiguous in memory even though they refer to contiguous disk blocks. Using a scatter/gather primitive, the cache can avoid having to copy the data through a contiguous temporary buffer.

Another feature provided by the BeOS cache is to allow modification of data directly in the cache. The cache API allows a file system to request a disk block and to get back a pointer to the data in that block. The cache reads the disk block into its internal buffer and returns a pointer to that buffer. Once a block is requested in this manner, the block is locked in the cache until it is released. BFS uses this feature primarily for i-nodes, which it manipulates directly instead of copying them to another location (which would require twice as much space). When such a block is modified, there is a cache call to mark the block as dirty so that it will be properly written back to disk when it is released. This small tweak to the API of the cache allows BFS to use memory more efficiently.

8.4 I/O and the Cache

One important consideration in the design of a cache is that it should not remain locked while performing I/O. Not locking the cache while performing I/O allows other threads to enter the cache and read or write data that is already in the cache. This approach is known as *hit-under-miss* and is important in a multithreaded system such as the BeOS.

There are several issues that arise in implementing hit-under-miss. Unlocking the cache before performing I/O allows other threads to enter the cache and read/write to blocks of data. It also means that other threads will manipulate the cache data structures while the I/O takes place. This has the potential to cause great mayhem. To prevent a chaotic situation, before releasing the cache lock, any relevant data structures must be marked as busy so that any other threads that enter the cache will not delete them or otherwise invalidate them. Data structures marked busy must not be modified until the busy bit clears. In the BeOS cache system, a cache_ent may be marked busy. If another thread wishes to access the block that the cache_ent represents, then it must relinquish the cache lock, sleep for a small amount of time and then reacquire the cache lock, look up the block again, and check the status of the busy bit. Although the algorithm sounds simple, it has a serious implication. The unlock-sleep-and-retry approach does not guarantee forward progress. Although it is unlikely, the thread waiting for the block could experience starvation if enough other threads also wish to access the same block. The BeOS implementation of this loop contains code to detect if a significant amount of time has elapsed waiting for a block to become available. In our testing scenarios we have seen a thread spend a significant amount of time waiting for a block when there is heavy paging but never so long that the thread starved. Although it appears in practice that nothing bad happens, this is one of those pieces of code that makes you uneasy every time it scrolls by on screen.

Returning to the original situation, when an I/O completes, the cache lock must be reobtained and any stored pointers (except to the cache_ent in question) need to be assigned again because they may have changed in the interim. Once the correct state has been reestablished, the cache code can finish its manipulation of the cache_ent. The ability to process cache hits during outstanding cache misses is very important.

Sizing the Cache

Sizing a cache is a difficult problem. Generally, the larger a cache is, the more effective it is (within reason, of course). Since a cache uses host memory to hold copies of data that reside on disk, letting the cache be too large reduces the amount of memory available to run user programs. Not having enough memory to run user programs may force those programs to swap unnecessarily, thereby incurring even more disk overhead. It is a difficult balance to maintain.

The ideal situation, and that offered by most modern versions of Unix, is to allow the cache to dynamically grow and shrink as the memory needs of user programs vary. A dynamic cache such as this is often tightly integrated with the VM system and uses free memory to hold blocks of data from disk. When the VM system needs more memory, it uses the least recently used blocks of cached data to fill program requests for memory. When memory is freed up, the VM system allows the cache to use the memory to hold additional blocks of data from disk. This arrangement provides the best use of memory. If there is a program running that does not use much memory but does reference a lot of disk-based data, it will be able to cache more data in memory. Likewise, if there is a program running that needs more memory than it needs disk cache, the cache will reduce in size and the memory will instead be allocated for program data.

Sadly, the BeOS does not have an integrated VM and disk buffer cache. The BeOS disk cache is a fixed size, determined at boot time based on the amount of memory in the system. This arrangement works passably well, but we plan to revise this area of the system in the future. The BeOS allocates 2 MB of cache for every 16 MB of system memory. Of course the obvious disadvantage to this is that the kernel uses one-eighth of the memory for disk cache regardless of the amount of disk I/O performed by user programs.

Journaling and the Cache

The journaling system of BFS imposes two additional requirements on the cache. The first is that the journaling system must be able to lock disk blocks in the cache to prevent them from being flushed. The second requirement is that the journaling system must know when a disk block is flushed to disk. Without these features, the journaling system faces serious difficulties managing the blocks modified as part of a transaction.

When a block is modified as part of a transaction, the journaling code must ensure that it is not flushed to disk until the transaction is complete and the log is written to disk. The block must be marked dirty and locked. When searching for blocks to flush, the cache must skip locked blocks. This is crucial to the correct operation of the journal. Locking a block in the cache is different than marking a block busy, as is done when performing I/O on a block. Other threads may still access a locked block; a busy block cannot be accessed until the busy bit is clear.

When the journal writes a transaction to the on-disk log, the blocks in the cache can be unlocked. However, for a transaction to complete, the journal needs to know when each block is flushed from the cache. In the BeOS this is achieved with a callback function. When a transaction finishes in memory, the journal writes the journal entry and sets a callback for each block in the transaction. As each of those blocks is flushed to disk by the cache, the journaling callback is called and it records that the block was flushed. When the callback function sees that the last block of a transaction has been flushed to disk, the transaction is truly complete and its space in the log can be reclaimed. This callback mechanism is unusual for caches but is necessary for the proper operation of a journal.

The BeOS cache supports obtaining pointers to cached blocks of data, and BFS takes advantage of this to reference i-node data directly. This fact, coupled with the requirements of journaling, presents an interesting problem. If a modification is made to an i-node, the i-node data is written to the log (which locks the corresponding disk block in the cache). When the transaction is complete, the journaling code unlocks the block and requests a callback when the block is flushed to disk. However, the rest of BFS already has a pointer to the block (since it is an i-node), and so the block is not actually free to be flushed to disk until the rest of the file system relinquishes access to the block. This is not the problem though.

The problem is that the journal expects the current version of the block to be written to disk, but because other parts of the system still have pointers to this block of data, it could potentially be modified before it is flushed to disk. To ensure the integrity of journaling, when the cache sets a callback for a block, the cache *clones* the block in its current state. The cloned half of the block is what the cache will flush when the opportunity presents itself. If the block already has a clone, the clone is written to disk before the current block is cloned. Cloning of cached blocks is necessary because the rest of the system has pointers directly to the cached data. If i-node data was modified after the journal was through with it but before it was written to disk, the file system could be left in an inconsistent state.

When Not to Use the Cache

Despite all the benefits of the cache, there are times when it makes sense not to use it. For example, if a user copies a very large file, the cache becomes filled with two copies of the same data; if the file is large enough, the cache won't be able to hold all of the data either. Another example is when a program is streaming a large amount of data (such as video or audio data) to disk. In this case the data is not likely to be read again after it is written, and since the amount of data being written is larger than the size of the cache, it will have to be flushed anyway. In these situations the cache simply winds up causing an extra memcpy() from a user buffer into the cache, and the cache has zero effectiveness. This is not optimal. In cases such as this it is better to bypass the cache altogether and do the I/O directly.

The BeOS disk cache supports bypassing the cache in an implicit manner. Any I/O that is 64K in size or larger bypasses the cache. This allows programs to easily skip the cache and perform their I/O directly to the underlying device. In practice this works out quite well. Programs manipulating large amounts of data can easily bypass the cache by specifying a large I/O buffer size. Those programs that do not care will likely use the default stdio buffer size of 4K and therefore operate in a fully buffered manner.

There are two caveats to this. The cache cannot simply pass large I/O transactions straight through without first checking that the disk blocks being written to are not already in the cache. If a block is written with a large I/O and that block is already in the cache, then the cached version of the block must also be updated with the newly written data. Likewise on a read, if a block is already in the cache, the user buffer must be patched up with the in-memory version of the block since it may be more current than what is on disk. These two caveats are small but important for the consistent operation of the cache.

There are times when this feature results in more disk traffic than necessary. If a program were to repeatedly read the same block of data but the block was larger than 64K, the disk request would be passed through each time; instead of operating at `memcpy()` speeds, the program would operate at the speed of the disk. Although rare, this can happen. If performance is an issue, it is easy to recode such a program to request the data in smaller chunks that will be cached.

One outcome of this cache bypass policy is that it is possible for a device to transfer data directly from a user buffer, straight to disk, without having to perform a `memcpy()` through the cache (i.e., it uses DMA to transfer the data). When bypassing the cache in this manner, the BeOS is able to provide 90–95% (and sometimes higher) of the raw disk bandwidth to an application. This is significant because it requires little effort on the part of the programmer, and it does not require extra tuning, special options, or specially allocated buffers. As an example, a straightforward implementation of a video capture program (capture a field of 320×240, 16-bit video and write it to disk) achieved 30 fields per second of bandwidth without dropping frames simply by doing large writes. Cache bypass is an important feature of the BeOS.

8.5   Summary

A disk cache can greatly improve the performance of a file system. By caching frequently used data, the cache significantly reduces the number of accesses made to the underlying disk. A cache has two modes of access. The first method of access is for finding disk blocks by their number; the other method orders the disk blocks by a criteria that assists in determining which ones to dispose of when the cache is full and new data must be put in the cache. In the BeOS cache this is managed with a hash table and a doubly linked list ordered from most recently used (MRU) to least recently used (LRU). These two data structures are intimately interwoven and must always remain self-consistent.

There are many optimizations possible with a cache. In the simplest, when flushing data to disk, the cache can reorder the writes to minimize the number of disk seeks required. It is also possible to coalesce writes to contiguous disk blocks so that many small writes are replaced by a single large write. On a cache read where the data is not in the cache, the cache can perform read-ahead to fetch more data that is likely to be needed soon. If the file system does its job and lays data out contiguously, the read-ahead will eliminate future reads. These optimizations can significantly increase the effective throughput of the disk because they take advantage of the fact that disks are good at bulk data transfer.

When the cache does perform I/O, it is important that the cache not be locked while the I/O takes place. Keeping the cache unlocked allows other threads to read data that is in the cache. This is known as hit-under-miss and is important in a multithreaded system such as the BeOS.

Journaling imposes several constraints on the cache. To accommodate the implementation of journaling in BFS, the BeOS disk cache must provide two main features. The first feature is that the journaling code must be able to lock blocks in the cache when they are modified as part of a transaction. The second feature is that the journaling system needs to be informed when a disk block is flushed. The BeOS cache supports a callback mechanism that the journaling code makes use of to allow it to know when a transaction is complete. Because BFS uses pointers directly to cached data, the cache must clone blocks when they are released by the journaling code. Cloning the block ensures that the data written to disk will be an identical copy of the block as it was modified during the transaction.

The last subsection of this chapter discussed when it is inappropriate to use the cache. Often when copying large files or when streaming data to disk, the cache is not effective. If it is used, it imposes a rather large penalty in terms of effective throughput. The BeOS cache performs I/O directly to/from a user's buffer when the size of the I/O is 64K or larger. This implicit cache bypass is easy for programmers to take advantage of and tends not to interfere with most normal programs that use smaller I/O buffers.

9

File System Performance

Measuring and analyzing file system performance is an integral part of writing a file system. Without some metric by which to measure a file system implementation, there is no way to gauge its quality. We could judge a file system by some other measure—for example, reliability—but we assume that, before even considering performance, reliability must be a given. Measuring performance is useful for understanding how applications will perform and what kind of workload the file system is capable of handling.

9.1 What Is Performance?

The performance of a file system has many different aspects. There are many different ways to measure a file system's performance, and it is an area of active research. In fact, there is not even one commonly used disk benchmark corresponding to the SPEC benchmarks for CPUs. Unfortunately it seems that with every new file system that is written, new benchmarks are also written. This makes it very difficult to compare file systems.

There are three main categories of file system measurement that are interesting:

- Throughput benchmarks (megabytes per second of data transfers)
- Metadata-intensive benchmarks (number of operations per second)
- Real-world workloads (either throughput or transactions per second)

Throughput benchmarks measure how many megabytes per second of data transfer a file system can provide under a variety of conditions. The simplest situation is sequential reading and writing of files. More complex throughput measurements are also possible using multiple threads, varying file sizes and number of files used. Throughput measurements are very dependent on the disks used, and consequently, absolute measurements, although useful, are difficult to compare between different systems unless the same hard disk is used. A more useful measure is the percentage of the raw disk bandwidth that the file system achieves. That is, performing large sequential I/Os directly to the disk device yields a certain data transfer rate. Measuring file system throughput for sequential I/O as a percentage of the raw disk bandwidth yields a more easily compared number since the percentage is in effect a normalized number. File systems with transfer rates very close to the raw drive transfer rate are ideal.

Metadata-intensive benchmarks measure the number of operations per second that a file system can perform. The major metadata-intensive operations performed by a file system are open, create, delete, and rename. Of these operations, rename is not generally considered a performance bottleneck and is thus rarely looked at. The other operations can significantly affect the performance of applications using the file system. The higher the number of these operations per second, the better the file system is.

Real-world benchmarks utilize a file system to perform some task such as handling email or Internet news, extracting files from an archive, compiling a large software system, or copying files. Many different factors besides the file system affect the results of real-world benchmarks. For example, if the virtual memory system and disk buffer cache are integrated, the system can more effectively use memory as a disk cache, which improves performance. Although a unified VM and buffer cache improve performance of most disk-related tests, it is independent of the quality (or deficiency) of the file system. Nevertheless, real-world benchmarks provide a good indication of how well a system performs a certain task. Focusing on the performance of real-world tasks is important so that the system does not become optimized to run just a particular synthetic benchmark.

9.2   What Are the Benchmarks?

There are a large number of file system benchmarks available but our preference is toward simple benchmarks that measure one specific area of file system performance. Simple benchmarks are easy to understand and analyze. In the development of BFS, we used only a handful of benchmarks. The two primary tests used were IOZone and lat_fs.

IOZone, written by Bill Norcott, is a straightforward throughput measurement test. IOZone sequentially writes and then reads back a file using an I/O block size specified on the command line. The size of the file is also specified on the command line. By adjusting the I/O block size and the total file size, it is easy to adjust the behavior of IOZone to reflect many different types of sequential file I/O. Fortunately sequential I/O is the predominant type of

I/O that programs perform. Further, we expect that the BeOS will be used to stream large quantities of data to and from disk (in the form of large audio and video files), and so IOZone is a good test.

The second test, lat_fs, is a part of Larry McVoy's lmbench test suite. lat_fs first creates 1000 files and then deletes them. The lat_fs test does this for file sizes of 0 bytes, 1K, 4K, and 10K. The result of the benchmark is the number of files per second that the file system can create and delete for each of the file sizes. Although it is extremely simple, the lat_fs test is a straightforward way to measure the two most important metadata-intensive operations of a file system. The single drawback of the lat_fs test is that it creates only a fixed number of files. To observe the behavior of a larger number of files, we wrote a similar program to create and delete an arbitrary number of files in a single directory.

In addition to using these two measurements, we also ran several real-world tests in an attempt to get an objective result of how fast the file system was for common tasks. The first real-world test simply times archiving and unarchiving large (10–20 MB) archives. This provides a good measure of how the file system behaves with realistic file sizes (instead of all files of a fixed size) and is a large enough data set not to fit entirely in cache.

The second real-world test was simply a matter of compiling a library of source files. It is not necessarily the most disk-intensive operation, but because many of the source files are small, they spend a great deal of time opening many header files and thus involve a reasonable amount of file system operations. Of course, we do have some bias in choosing this benchmark because improving its speed directly affects our day-to-day work (which consists of compiling lots of code)!

Other real-world tests are simply a matter of running practical applications that involve significant disk I/O and observing their performance. For example, an object-oriented database package that runs on the BeOS has a benchmark mode that times a variety of operations. Other applications such as video capture work well as real examples of how applications behave. Not all real-world tests result in a specific performance number, but their ability to run successfully is a direct measure of how good the file system is.

Other Benchmarks

As mentioned, there are quite a few other file system benchmark programs. The most notable are

- Andrew File System Benchmark
- Bonnie
- IOStone
- SPEC SFS
- Chen's self-scaling benchmark
- PostMark

The first three benchmarks (Andrew, Bonnie, and IOStone) are no longer particularly interesting benchmarks because they often fit entirely in the file system buffer cache. The Andrew benchmark has a small working set and is dominated by compiling a large amount of source code. Although we do consider compiling code a useful measurement, if that is all that the Andrew benchmark will tell us, then it is hardly worth the effort to port it.

Both Bonnie and IOStone have such small working sets that they easily fit in most file system buffer caches. That means that Bonnie and IOStone wind up measuring the memcpy() speed from the buffer cache into user space—a useful measurement, but it has very little to do with file systems.

The SPEC SFS benchmark (formerly known as LADDIS) is targeted toward measuring Network File System (NFS) server performance. It is an interesting benchmark, but you must be a member of the SPEC organization to obtain it. Also, because it is targeted at testing NFS, it requires NFS and several clients. The SPEC SFS benchmark is not really targeted at stand-alone file systems nor is it an easy benchmark to run.

Chen's self-scaling benchmark addresses a number of the problems that exist with the Andrew, Bonnie, and IOStone benchmarks. By scaling benchmark parameters to adjust to the system under test, the benchmark adapts much better to different systems and avoids statically sized parameters that eventually become too small. The self-scaling of the benchmark takes away the ability to compare results across different systems. To solve this problem, Chen uses "predicted performance" to calculate a performance curve for a system that can be compared to other systems. Unfortunately the predicted performance curve is expressed solely in terms of megabytes per second and does little to indicate what areas of the system need improvement. Chen's self-scaling benchmark is a good general test but not specific enough for our needs.

The most recent addition to the benchmark fray is PostMark. Written at Network Appliance (an NFS server manufacturer), the PostMark test tries to simulate the workload of a large email system. The test creates an initial working set of files and then performs a series of transactions. The transactions read files, create new files, append to existing files, and delete files. All parameters of the test are configurable (number of files, number of transactions, amount of data read/written, percentage of reads/writes, etc.). This benchmark results in three performance numbers: number of transactions per second, effective read bandwidth, and effective write bandwidth. The default parameters make PostMark a very good small-file benchmark. Adjusting the parameters, PostMark can simulate a wide variety of workloads.

Two other key features of PostMark are that the source is freely downloadable and that it is portable to Windows 95 and Windows NT. The portability to Windows 95 and Windows NT is important because often those two operating systems receive little attention from the Unix-focused research community. Few other (if any) benchmarks run unmodified under both the POSIX and the Win32 APIs. The ability to directly compare PostMark performance numbers across a wide variety of systems (not just Unix derivatives) is useful. Sadly, PostMark was only released in August 1997, and thus did not have an impact on the design of BFS.

Dangers of Benchmarks

The biggest pitfall of running any set of benchmarks is that it can quickly degenerate into a contest of beating all other file systems on a particular benchmark. Unless the benchmark in question is a real-world test of an important customer's application, it is unlikely that optimizing a file system for a particular benchmark will help improve general performance. In fact, just the opposite is likely to occur.

During the development of BFS, for a short period of time, the lat_fs benchmark became the sole focus of performance improvements. Through various tricks the performance of lat_fs increased considerably. Unfortunately the same changes slowed other much more common operations (such as extracting an archive of files). This is clearly not the ideal situation.

The danger of benchmarks is that it is too easy to focus on a single performance metric. Unless this metric is the sole metric of interest, it is rarely a good idea to focus on one benchmark. Running a variety of tests, especially real-world tests, is the best protection against making optimizations that only apply to a single benchmark.

Running Benchmarks

Benchmarks for file systems are almost always run on freshly created file systems. This ensures the best performance, which means that benchmark numbers can be somewhat misleading. However, it is difficult to accurately "age" a file system because there is no standardized way to age a file system so that it appears as it would after some amount of use. Although it doesn't present the full picture, running benchmarks on clean file systems is the safest way to compare file system performance numbers.

A more complete picture of file system performance can be obtained by running the system through a well-defined set of file system activity prior to running a benchmark. This is a difficult task because any particular set of file system activity is only likely to be representative of a single workload. Because of the difficulties in accurately aging a file system and doing so for a variety of workloads, it is not usually done. This is not to say that aging a file system is impossible, but unless it is done accurately, repeatably, and consistently, reporting file system benchmarks for aged file systems would be inaccurate and misleading.

9.3 Performance Numbers

Despite all the caveats that benchmarking suffers from, there is no substitute for hard numbers. The goal of these tests was not to demonstrate the superiority of any one file system but rather to provide a general picture of how each file system performs on different tests.

Test Setup

For tests of BeOS, Windows NT, and Linux, our test configuration was a dual-processor Pentium Pro machine. The motherboard was a Tyan Titan Pro (v3.03 10/31/96) with an Award Bios. The motherboard uses the Intel 440-FX chip set. We configured the machine with 32 MB of RAM. The disk used in the tests is an IBM DeskStar 3.2 GB hard disk (model DAQA-33240). The machine also had a Matrox Millennium graphics card and a DEC 21014 Ethernet card. All operating systems used the same partition on the same physical hard disk for their tests (to eliminate any differences between reading from inner cylinders or outer cylinders).

For the BeOS tests we installed BeOS Release 3 for Intel from a production CD-ROM, configured graphics (1024 × 768 in 16-bit color), and networking (TCP/IP). We installed no other software. On a system with 32 MB of system memory, the BeOS uses a fixed 4 MB of memory for disk cache.

For the Windows NT tests we installed Windows NT Workstation version 4.00 with ServicePak 3. We did a standard installation and selected no special options. As with the BeOS installation, we configured graphics and networking and did no other software installations. Using the Task Manager we observed that Windows NT uses as much as 20–22 MB of memory for disk cache on our test configuration.

The Linux ext2 tests used a copy of the RedHat 4.2 Linux distribution, which is based on the Linux v2.0.30 kernel. We performed a standard installation and ran all tests in text mode from the console. The system used approximately 28 MB of memory for buffer cache (measured by running `top` and watching the buffer cache stats during a run of a benchmark).

For the XFS tests we used a late beta of Irix 6.5 on an Onyx2 system. The Onyx2 is physically the same as an Origin-2000 but has a graphics board set. The machine had two 250 MHz R10000 processors and 128 MB of RAM. The disk was an IBM 93G3048 4 GB Fast & Wide SCSI disk connected to the built-in SCSI controller of an Onyx2. Irix uses a significant portion of total system memory for disk cache, although we were not able to determine exactly how much.

To obtain the numbers in the following tables, we ran all tests three times and averaged the results. All file systems were initialized before each set of tests to minimize the impact of the other tests on the results. We kept all systems as quiescent as possible during the tests so as not to measure other factors aside from file system performance.

Raw disk bandwidth (MB/sec)	
Write	5.92
Read	5.94

Table 9-1   Raw disk bandwidths (IBM DAQA-33240) for the test configuration.

Streaming I/O Benchmark

The IOZone benchmark tests how fast a system can write sequential chunks of data to a file. This is an interesting test for the BeOS because one of its intended uses is for streaming large amounts of media data to and from disk. This test does not measure intense file system metadata operations.

The IOZone benchmark has two parameters: the total amount of data to read/write and the size of each I/O to perform. The result of running IOZone is a bandwidth (in megabytes per second) for writing and reading data. The absolute numbers that IOZone reports are only moderately interesting since they depend on the details of the disk controller and disk used.

Instead of focusing on the absolute numbers reported by IOZone, it is more interesting to measure how much overhead the file system imposes when compared with accessing the underlying disk as a raw device. First measuring the raw device bandwidth and then comparing that to the bandwidth achieved writing through the file system yields an indication of how much overhead the file system and operating system introduce.

To measure the raw device bandwidth, under the BeOS we used IOZone on the raw disk device (no file system, just raw access to the disk). Under Windows NT we ran a special-purpose program that measures the bandwidth of the raw disk and observed nearly identical results. For the test configuration described previously, Table 9-1 shows the results.

All percentages for the IOZone tests are given relative to these absolute bandwidth numbers. It is important to note that these are sustained transfer rates over 128 MB of data. This rate is different than the often-quoted "peak transfer rate" of a drive, which is normally measured by repeatedly reading the same block of data from the disk.

We ran IOZone with three different sets of parameters. We chose the file sizes to be sufficiently large so as to reduce the effects of disk caching (if present). We chose large I/O chunk sizes to simulate streaming large amounts of data to disk. Tables 9-2 through 9-4 present the results.

In these tests BFS performs exceptionally well because it bypasses the system cache and performs DMA directly to and from the user buffer. Under the BeOS, the processor utilization during the test was below 10%. The same tests under NT used 20–40% of the CPU; if any other action happened during the test (e.g., a mouse click on the desktop), the test results would plummet because of heavy paging. Linux ext2 performs surprisingly well given that it passes data through the buffer cache. One reason for this is that the speed of

File system	Write (MB/sec and % of peak)	Read (MB/sec and % of peak)
BFS	5.88 (99%)	5.91 (99%)
ext2	4.59 (78%)	4.97 (84%)
NTFS	3.77 (64%)	3.12 (52%)

Table 9-2   IOZone bandwidths for a 128 MB file written in 64K chunks.

File system	Write (MB/sec and % of peak)	Read (MB/sec and % of peak)
BFS	5.88 (99%)	5.91 (99%)
ext2	4.36 (74%)	5.75 (97%)
NTFS	3.81 (64%)	3.05 (51%)

Table 9-3   IOZone bandwidths for a 128 MB file written in 256K chunks.

File system	Write (MB/sec and % of peak)	Read (MB/sec and % of peak)
BFS	5.81 (98%)	5.84 (98%)
ext2	4.31 (73%)	5.51 (93%)
NTFS	3.88 (65%)	3.10 (52%)

Table 9-4   IOZone bandwidths for a 512 MB file written in 128K chunks.

the disk (about 6 MB/sec) is significantly less than the memcpy() bandwidth of the machine (approximately 50 MB/sec). If the disk subsystem were faster, Linux would not perform as well relative to the maximum speed of the disk. The BeOS approach to direct I/O works exceptionally well in this situation and scales to higher-performance disk subsystems.

File Creation/Deletion Benchmark

The lmbench test suite by Larry McVoy and Carl Staelin is an extensive benchmark suite that encompasses many areas of performance. One of the tests from that suite, lat_fs, tests the speed of create and delete operations on a file system. Although highly synthetic, this benchmark provides an easy yardstick for the cost of file creation and deletion.

We used the systems described previously for these tests. We also ran the benchmark on a BFS volume created with indexing turned off. Observing the speed difference between indexed and nonindexed BFS gives an idea of the cost of maintaining the default indices (name, size, and last modified time). The nonindexed BFS case is also a fairer comparison with NTFS and XFS since they do not index anything.

We used lat_fs v1.6 from the original lmbench test suite (not lmbench 2.0) because it was easier to port to NT. The lat_fs test creates 1000 files (writing

File system	0K	1K	4K	10K
ext2	1377	1299	1193	1027
NTFS	1087	178	164	151
BFS-noindex	844	475	318	163
BFS	487	292	197	115
XFS	296	222	260	248

Table 9-5   lat_fs **results for creating files of various sizes (number of files per second).**

File system	0K	1K	4K	10K
ext2	24453	19217	17062	13250
BFS-noindex	2096	1879	1271	800
NTFS	1392	591	482	685
BFS	925	821	669	498
XFS	359	358	359	361

Table 9-6   lat_fs **results for deleting files of various sizes (number of files per second).**

a fixed amount of data to each file) and then goes back and deletes all the files. The test iterates four times, increasing the amount of data written in each phase. The amount of data written for each iteration is 0K, 1K, 4K, and then 10K. The result of the test is the number of files per second that a file system can create or delete for each given file size (see Tables 9-5 and 9-6).

The results of this test require careful review. First, the Linux ext2 numbers are virtually meaningless because the ext2 file system did not touch the disk once during these benchmarks. The ext2 file system (as discussed in Section 3.2) offers no consistency guarantees and therefore performs all operations in memory. The lat_fs benchmark on a Linux system merely tests how fast a user program can get into the kernel, perform a memcpy(), and exit the kernel. We do not consider the ext2 numbers meaningful except to serve as an upper limit on the speed at which a file system can operate in memory.

Next, it is clear that NTFS has a special optimization to handle creating 0-byte files because the result for that case is totally out of line with the rest of the NTFS results. BFS performs quite well until the amount of data written starts to fall out of the paltry 4 MB BeOS disk cache. BFS suffers from the lack of unified virtual memory and disk buffer cache.

Overall, BFS-noindex exhibits good performance, turning in the highest scores in all but two cases. XFS and NTFS file creation performance is relatively stable, most likely because all the file data written fits in their disk cache and they are limited by the speed that they can write to their journal. One conclusion from this test is that BFS would benefit significantly from a better disk cache.

File system	Transactions/sec	Read (KB/sec)	Write (KB/sec)
ext2	224	624.92	759.52
XFS	48	129.13	156.94
NTFS	48	141.38	171.83
BFS-noindex	35	104.91	127.51
BFS	17	50.44	61.30

Table 9-7   PostMark results for 1000 initial files and 10,000 transactions.

From Tables 9-5 and 9-6 we can also make an inference about the cost of indexing on a BFS volume. By default, BFS indexes the name, size, and last modified time of all files. In all cases the speed of BFS-noindex is nearly twice that of regular BFS. For some environments the cost of indexing may not be worth the added functionality.

The PostMark Benchmark

The PostMark benchmark, written by Jeffrey Katcher of Network Appliance (*www.netapp.com*), is a simulation of an email or NetNews system. This benchmark is extremely file system metadata intensive. Although there are many parameters, the only two we modified were the base number of files to start with and the number of transactions to perform against the file set. The test starts by creating the specified number of base files, and then it iterates over that file set, randomly selecting operations (create, append, and delete) to perform. PostMark uses its own random number generator and by default uses the same seed, which means that the test always performs the same work and results from different systems are comparable.

For each test, the total amount of data read and written is given as an absolute number in megabytes. The number is slightly misleading, though, because the same data may be read many times, and some files may be written and deleted before their data is ever written to disk. So although the amount of data read and written may seem significantly larger than the buffer cache, it may not be.

The first test starts with 1000 initial files and performs 10,000 transactions over those files. This test wrote 37.18 MB of data and read 30.59 MB.

The results (shown in Table 9-7) are not surprising. Linux ext2 turns in an absurdly high result, indicating that the bulk of the test fit in its cache. As we will see, the ext2 performance numbers degrade drastically as soon as the amount of data starts to exceed its cache size.

Plain BFS (i.e., with indexing) turns in a paltry 17 transactions per second for a couple of reasons: The cost of indexing is high, and the amount of data touched falls out of the cache very quickly. BFS-noindex performs about twice as fast (as expected from the lat_fs results), although it is still

File system	Transactions/sec	Read (KB/sec)	Write (KB/sec)
ext2	45	109.47	221.46
XFS	27	52.73	106.67
NTFS	24	57.91	117.14
BFS-noindex	20	53.76	108.76
BFS	10	25.05	50.01

Table 9-8   PostMark results for 5000 initial files and 10,000 transactions.

File system	Transactions/sec	Read (KB/sec)	Write (KB/sec)
ext2	18	33.61	106.13
XFS	18	28.56	90.19
NTFS	13	28.88	99.19
BFS-noindex	13	32.14	101.50
BFS	6	12.90	40.75

Table 9-9   PostMark results for 20,000 initial files and 20,000 transactions.

somewhat behind NTFS and XFS. Again, the lack of a real disk cache hurts BFS.

For the next test, we upped the initial set of files to 5000. In this test the total amount of data read was 28.49 MB, while 57.64 MB were written. The results are shown in Table 9-8. This amount of data started to spill out of the caches of ext2, NTFS, and XFS, which brought their numbers down a bit. BFS-noindex holds its own, coming close to NTFS. The regular version of BFS comes in again at half the performance of a nonindexed version of BFS.

The last PostMark test is the most brutal: it creates an initial file set of 20,000 files and performs 20,000 transactions on that file set. This test reads 52.76 MB of data and writes 166.61 MB. This is a sufficiently large amount of data to blow all the caches. Table 9-9 shows the results. Here all of the file systems start to fall down and the transactions per second column falls to an abysmal 18, even for mighty (and unsafe) ext2. Plain BFS turns in the worst showing yet at 6 transactions per second. This result for indexed BFS clearly indicates that indexing is not appropriate for a high-volume file server.

Analysis

Overall there are a few conclusions that we can draw from these performance numbers:

- BFS performs extremely well for streaming data to and from disk. Achieving as much as 99% of the available bandwidth of a disk, BFS introduces very little overhead in the file I/O process.

- BFS performs well for metadata updates when the size of the data mostly fits in the cache. As seen in the 0K, 1K, and 4K lat_fs tests, BFS outperforms all other systems except the ext2 file system (which is fair since ext2 never touches the disk during the test).
- The lack of a unified virtual memory and buffer cache system hurts BFS performance considerably in benchmarks that modify large amounts of data in many small files (i.e., the PostMark benchmark). As proof, consider the last PostMark test (the 20,000/20,000 run). This test writes enough data to nullify the effects of caching in the other systems, and in that case (nonindexed) BFS performs about as well as the other file systems.
- The default indexing done by BFS results in about a 50% performance hit on metadata update tests, which is clearly seen in the PostMark benchmark results.

In summary, BFS performs well for its intended purpose of streaming media to and from disk. For metadata-intensive benchmarks, BFS fares reasonably well until the cost of indexing and the lack of a dynamic buffer cache slow it down. For systems in which transaction-style processing is most important, disabling indexing is a considerable performance improvement. However, until the BeOS offers a unified virtual memory and buffer cache system, BFS will not perform as well as other systems in a heavily transaction-oriented system.

9.4 Performance in BFS

During the initial development of BFS, performance was not a primary concern, and the implementation progressed in a straightforward fashion. As other engineers started to use the file system, performance became more of an issue. This required careful examination of what the file system actually did under normal operations. Looking at the I/O access patterns of the file system turned out to be the best way to improve performance.

File Creation

The first "benchmark" that was an issue for BFS was the performance of extracting archives of our daily BeOS builds. After a few days of use, BFS would degenerate until it could only extract about one file per second. This abysmal performance resulted from a number of factors that were very obvious when examining the I/O log of the file system. By inserting a print statement for each disk I/O performed and analyzing the block numbers written and the size of each I/O, it was easy to see what was happening.

First, at the time BFS only kept one transaction per log buffer. This forced an excessive number of writes to the on-disk log. Second, when the cache flushed data, it did not coalesce contiguous writes. This meant that the cache effectively wrote one file system block (usually 1024 bytes) at a time and thus severely undercut the available disk bandwidth. To alleviate these problems I extended the journaling code to support multiple transactions per log buffer. The cache code was then modified to batch flushing of blocks and to coalesce writes to contiguous locations.

These two changes improved performance considerably, but BFS still felt sluggish. Again, examining the I/O log revealed another problem. Often one block would be modified several times as part of a transaction, and it would be written once per modification. If a block is part of a single log buffer (which may contain multiple transactions), there is no need to consume space in the log buffer for multiple copies of the block. This modification drastically cut down the number of blocks used in the log buffer because often the same directory block is modified many times when extracting files.

The Cache

When examining the I/O performed by the cache, it became obvious that a simple sort of the disk block addresses being flushed would help reduce disk arm movement, making the disk arm operate in one big sweep instead of random movements. Disk seeks are by far the slowest operation a disk can perform, and minimizing seek times by sorting the list of blocks the cache needs to flush helps performance considerably.

Unfortunately at the time the caching code was written, BeOS did not support scatter/gather I/O. This made it necessary to copy contiguous blocks to a temporary buffer and then to DMA them to disk from the temporary buffer. This extra copying is inefficient and eventually will be unnecessary when the I/O subsystem supports scatter/gather I/O.

Allocation Policies

Another factor that helped performance was tuning the allocation policies so that file system data structures were allocated in an optimal manner when possible. When a program sequentially creates a large number of files, the file system has the opportunity to lay out its data structures in an optimal manner. The optimal layout for sequentially created files is to allocate i-nodes contiguously, placing them close to the directory that contains them and placing file data contiguously. The advantage is that read-ahead will get information for many files in one read. BFS initially did not allocate file data in a contiguous fashion. The problem was that preallocation of data blocks for a file caused gaps between successive files. The preallocated space for a file was not freed until much later after the file was closed. Fixing this problem was easy (trimming preallocated data blocks now happens at `close()` time) once the problem was discovered through closely examining the I/O patterns generated by the file system.

The Duplicate Test

In the final stages of BFS development, a few real-world tests were run to see how the nearly complete version of BFS stood up against its competitor on the same hardware platform (the Mac OS). Much to my amazement the Mac OS was significantly faster than the BeOS at duplicating a folder of several hundred files. Even though the BeOS must maintain three indices (name, size, and last modified time), I still expected it to be faster than the Mac OS file system HFS. Understanding the problem once again required examining the disk access patterns. The disk access patterns showed that BFS spent about 30% of its time updating the name and size indices. Closer examination revealed that the B+tree data structure was generating a lot of traffic to manage the duplicate entries that existed for file names and sizes.

The way in which the B+trees handled duplicate entries was not acceptable. The B+trees were allocating 1024 bytes of file space for each value that was a duplicate and then only writing two different i-node numbers (16 bytes) in the space. The problem is that when a hierarchy of files is duplicated, every single file becomes a duplicate in the name and size indices (and the last modification time index if the copy preserves all the attributes). Additional investigation into the number of duplicate file names that exist on various systems showed that roughly 70% of the duplicate file names had fewer than eight files with the same name. This information suggested an obvious solution. Instead of having the B+tree code allocate one 1024-byte chunk of space for each duplicate, it could instead divide that 1024-byte chunk into a group of fragments, each able to hold a smaller number of duplicates. Sharing the space allocated for one duplicate among a number of duplicates greatly reduced the amount of I/O required because each duplicate does not require writing to its own area of the B+tree. The other beneficial effect was to reduce the size of the B+tree files on disk. The cost was added complexity in managing the B+trees. After making these modifications to BFS, we reran the original tests and found that BFS was as fast or faster than HFS at duplicating a set of folders, even though BFS maintains three extra indices for all files.

The Log Area

Yet another area for performance tuning is the log area on disk. The size of the log area directly influences how many outstanding log transactions are possible and thus influences how effectively the disk buffer cache may be used. If the log area is small, then only a few transactions will happen before it fills up. Once the log area is full, the file system must force blocks to flush to disk so that transactions will complete and space will free up in the log. If the log area is small, hardly any transactions will be buffered in memory, and thus the cache will be underutilized. Increasing the size of the log allows better use of the disk buffer cache and thus allows for more transactions to complete in memory instead of requiring constant flushing to disk. BFS increased the log size from 512K to 2048K and saw a considerable increase in performance. Further tuning of the log area based on the amount of memory in the machine would perhaps be in order, but, once created, the log area on disk is fixed in size even if the amount of memory in the computer changes. Regardless, it is worthwhile to at least be aware of this behavior.

9.5 Summary

Many factors affect performance. Often it requires careful attention to I/O access patterns and on-disk data structure layout to help tune a file system to achieve optimal performance. BFS gained many improvements by examining the access patterns of the file system and tuning data structures and allocation policies to reduce the amount of I/O traffic.

10

The Vnode Layer

An operating system almost always has its own native file system format, but it is still often necessary to access other types of file systems. For example, CD-ROM media frequently use the ISO-9660 file system to store data, and it is desirable to access this information. In addition there are many other reasons why accessing different file systems is necessary: data transfer, interoperability, and simple convenience. All of these reasons are especially true for the BeOS, which must coexist with many other operating systems.

The approach taken by the BeOS (and most versions of Unix) to facilitate access to different file systems is to have a file system independent layer that mediates access to different file systems. This layer is often called a virtual file system layer or vnode (virtual node) layer. The term *vnode layer* originated with Unix. A vnode is a generic representation of a file or directory and corresponds to an i-node in a real file system. The vnode layer provides a uniform interface from the rest of the kernel to files and directories, regardless of the underlying file system.

The vnode layer separates the implementation of a particular file system from the rest of the system by defining a set of functions that each file system implements. The set of functions defined by the vnode layer abstracts the generic notion of files and directories. Each file system implements these functions and maps from each of the generic operations to the details of performing the operation in a particular file system format.

This chapter describes the BeOS vnode layer, the operations it supports, the protocols that file systems are expected to follow, and some details about the implementation of file descriptors and how they map to vnodes.

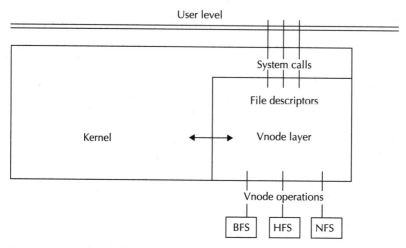

Figure 10-1   Where the BeOS vnode layer resides in the BeOS kernel.

10.1   Background

To understand the BeOS vnode layer, it is useful to first describe the framework in which the BeOS vnode layer operates. The BeOS kernel manages threads and teams ("processes" in Unix parlance), but file descriptors and all I/O are the sole purview of the vnode layer. Figure 10-1 illustrates how the vnode layer meshes with the rest of the kernel and several file systems. The vnode layer interfaces with user programs through file descriptors and communicates to different file systems through vnode operations. In Figure 10-1 there are three file systems (BFS, the Macintosh HFS, and NFS).

The vnode layer in the BeOS completely hides the details of managing file descriptors, and the rest of the kernel remains blissfully unaware of their implementation. File descriptors are managed on a per-thread basis. The BeOS thread structure maintains a pointer, ioctx, to an I/O context for each thread. The ioctx structure is opaque to the rest of the kernel; only the vnode layer knows about it. Within the ioctx structure is all the information needed by the vnode layer.

Figure 10-2 illustrates all of the structures that work together to support the concept of file descriptors at the user level. Although the overall structure appears complex, each piece is quite simple. To describe the structure, we will start at the thread_rec structure and work our way through the figure all the way to the structures used by the underlying file system.

Each thread has its own ioctx structure. The ioctx contains a pointer to the current working directory (cwd) of each thread, a pointer to the array of open file descriptors (fdarray), and a list of monitored vnodes (mon; we will discuss this later). The fdarray maintains state about the file descriptors,

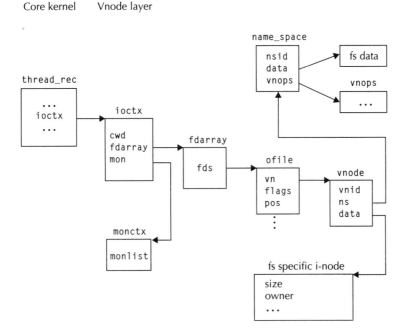

Figure 10-2   The BeOS vnode layer data structures.

but the primary member is a pointer, `fds`, that points to an array of `ofile` structures. The `fdarray` is shared between all threads in the same team. Each `ofile` maintains information about how the file was opened (read-only, etc.) and the position in the file. However, the most interesting field of the `ofile` structure is the `vn` pointer. The `vn` field points to a `vnode` structure, which is the lowest level of the vnode layer.

Each `vnode` structure is the abstract representation of a file or directory. The `data` member of the `vnode` structure keeps a pointer that refers to file-system-specific information about the vnode. The `data` field is the connection between the abstract notion of a file or directory and the concrete details of a file or directory on a particular file system. The `ns` field of a vnode points to a `name_space` structure that keeps generic information about the file system that this file or directory resides on. The `name_space` structure also keeps a pointer to a per-file system structure in a similar manner to the `data` field of the vnode.

There are several key points about this overall structure. Each thread in a team has a pointer to the same `fdarray`, which means that all threads in the same team share file descriptors. Each entry in the `fdarray` points to an `ofile` structure, which in turn points to a vnode. Different entries in the `fdarray` can point to the same ofile structure. The POSIX call dup() depends on this functionality to be able to duplicate a file descriptor. Similarly, different ofile structures can point to the same vnode, which corresponds to the ability to open a file multiple times in the same program or in different programs. The separation of the information maintained in the ofile structure and the vnode that it refers to is important.

Another important thing to notice about the above diagram is that every vnode structure has a vnode-id. In the BeOS, every vnode has a vnode-id that uniquely identifies a file on a single file system. For convenience, we abbreviate the term "vnode-id" to just "vnid." Given a vnid, a file system should be able to access the i-node of a file. Conversely, given a name in a directory, a file system should be able to return the vnid of the file.

To better understand how this structure is used, let's consider the concrete example of how a write() on a file descriptor actually takes place. It all starts when a user thread executes the following line of code:

```
write(4, "hello world\n", 12);
```

In user space, the function write() is a system call that traps into the kernel. Once in kernel mode, the kernel system call handler passes control to the kernel routine that implements the write() system call. The kernel write() call, sys_write(), is part of the vnode layer. Starting from the calling thread's ioctx structure, sys_write() uses the integer file descriptor (in this case, the value 4) to index the file descriptor array, fdarray (which is pointed to by the ioctx). Indexing into fdarray yields a pointer to an ofile structure. The ofile structure contains state information (such as the position we are currently at in the file) and a pointer to the underlying vnode associated with this file descriptor. The vnode structure refers to a particular vnode and also has a pointer to a structure containing information about the file system that this vnode resides on. The structure containing the file system information has a pointer to the table of functions supported by this file system as well as a file system state structure provided by the file system. The vnode layer uses the table of function pointers to call the file system write() with the proper arguments to write the data to the file associated with the file descriptor.

Although it may seem like a circuitous and slow route, this path from user level through the vnode layer and down to a particular file system happens very frequently and must be rather efficient. This example is simplified in many respects (for example, we did not discuss locking at all) but serves to demonstrate the flow from user space, into the kernel, and through to a particular file system.

The BeOS vnode layer also manages the file system name space and handles all aspects of mounting and unmounting file systems. The BeOS vnode layer maintains the list of mounted file systems and where they are mounted in the name space. This information is necessary to manage programs traversing the hierarchy as they transparently move from one file system to another.

Although the vnode layer of the BeOS is quite extensive, it is also quite encapsulated from the rest of the kernel. This separation helps to isolate bugs when they do occur (a bug in the vnode layer usually does not damage the rest of a thread's state) and decouples changes in the I/O subsystem from affecting the rest of the kernel. This clean separation of I/O management from the other aspects of the system (thread management, VM, etc.) is quite pleasant to work with.

10.2   Vnode Layer Concepts

The most important concept at the vnode layer is the vnode. Within the vnode layer itself, a vnode is an abstract entity that is uniquely identified by a 64-bit vnid. The vnode layer assumes that every named entity in a file system has a unique vnid. Given a vnid the vnode layer can ask a file system to load the corresponding node.

Private Data

When the vnode layer asks a file system to load a particular vnid, it allows the file system to associate a pointer to private data with that vnid. A file system creates this private data structure in its read_vnode() routine. Once the vnid is loaded in memory, the vnode layer always passes the file system's private data pointer when calling the file system in reference to that node. There is a reference count associated with each vnode structure. When the reference count reaches zero, the vnode layer can flush the node from memory, at which time the file system is called to free up any resources associated with the private data.

It is important to observe that each vnode (and associated private data) is global in the sense that many threads operating on the same file will use the same vnode structure. This requires that the node be locked if it is going to be modified and, further, that the data structure is not the appropriate place to store state information specific to one file descriptor.

The vnode layer operates on names, vnids, and vnodes. When the vnode layer needs to communicate with a file system, it will either ask for the vnid of a name, pass the vnid of a file, or pass a pointer to the file system private data of a vnode corresponding to some vnid. A file system never sees vnode structures. Rather, a file system receives either a vnid or the per-node data structure that it allocated when the vnode layer asked it to load a vnid. The interface between the vnode layer and a file system only passes file-system-specific information to the file system, and a file system only makes requests of the vnode layer that involve vnids.

In addition to the file-system-specific information that is kept per vnode, the vnode layer also allows a file system to supply a structure global to the entire file system. This structure contains state information about a particular instance of the file system. The vnode layer always passes this structure to all interface operations defined by the vnode layer API. Thus with this global information and the per-vnode information, each file system operation deals only with its own data structures. Likewise, the vnode layer deals only with its own structures and merely calls into the file-system-specific layer passing pointers to the file-system-specific information that is opaque to the vnode layer.

Cookies

Some vnode layer operations require that the file system maintain state information that is specific to a single file descriptor. State that must be maintained on a per-file-descriptor basis cannot be kept in the private data area of a vnode because the vnode structure is global. To support private data per file descriptor, the vnode layer has a notion of *cookies*. A cookie is a pointer to private state information needed by a file system between successive calls to functions in the file system. The cookie lets the file system maintain state for each file descriptor although the file system itself never sees a file descriptor. Only the file system manipulates the contents of the cookie. The cookie is opaque to the vnode layer. The vnode layer only keeps track of the cookie and passes it to the file system for each operation that needs it.

The vnode layer makes the ownership of cookies explicitly the responsibility of the file system. A file system allocates a cookie and fills in the data structure. The vnode layer keeps track of a pointer to that cookie. The vnode layer ensures that the file system receives a pointer to the cookie in each operation that requires it, but the vnode layer does not ever examine the contents of the cookie. When there are no more outstanding references to a cookie, the vnode layer asks the file system to free the resources associated with that cookie. The responsibility for allocating a cookie, managing the data in it, and freeing it is solely the domain of the file system.

Vnode Concepts Summary

The concepts of a per-vnid data structure, the per-file-system state structure, and cookies help to isolate the vnode layer from the specifics of any particular file system. Each of these structures stores clearly defined pieces of information related to files and the file system. The per-vnid data structure stores information about a file that is to be used by everyone (such as the size of a file). The per-file-system structure stores information global to the entire file system (such as the number of blocks on the volume). The cookie stores per-file-descriptor information that is private to a particular file descriptor (such as the current position in the file).

10.3   Vnode Layer Support Routines

In addition to the API that a file system implements, the vnode layer has several support routines that file systems make use of to properly implement the vnode layer API. The support routines of the vnode layer are

```
int  new_vnode(nspace_id nsid, vnode_id vnid, void *data);
int  get_vnode(nspace_id nsid, vnode_id vnid, void **data);
int  put_vnode(nspace_id nsid, vnode_id vnid);

int  remove_vnode(nspace_id nsid, vnode_id vnid);
int  unremove_vnode(nspace_id nsid, vnode_id vnid);
int  is_vnode_removed(nspace_id nsid, vnode_id vnid);
```

These calls manage creating, loading, unloading, and removing vnids from the vnode layer pool of active vnodes. The routines operate on vnids and an associated pointer to file-system-specific data. The new_vnode() call establishes the association between a vnid and a data pointer. The get_vnode() call returns the pointer associated with a vnid. The put_vnode() call releases the resource associated with the vnid. Every call to get_vnode() should have a matching put_vnode() call. The vnode layer manages the pool of active and cached vnodes and keeps track of reference counts for each vnid so that the vnode is only loaded from disk once until it is flushed from memory. The serialization of loading and unloading vnids is important because it simplifies the construction of a file system.

The remove_vnode(), unremove_vnode(), and is_vnode_removed() functions provide a mechanism for a file system to ask the vnode layer to set, unset, or inquire about the removal status of a vnode. A file system marks a vnode for deletion so that the vnode layer can delete the file when there are no more active references to a file.

In addition to the preceding vnode layer routines that operate on vnids, the vnode layer also has a support routine that's used when manipulating symbolic links:

```
int  new_path(const char *path, char **copy);
```

This routine operates on strings and enables a clean division of ownership between the vnode layer and a file system. We defer detailed discussion of the routine till later in the chapter.

All of the vnode layer support routines are necessary for a file system to operate correctly. As we will see, the interface that these routines provide between the file system and the vnode layer is simple but sufficient.

10.4   How It Really Works

The BeOS vnode layer manages file systems in an abstract way. A file system implementation exports a structure containing 57 functions that the vnode layer can call when needed. A file system is passive in that it is only called upon by the vnode layer; it never initiates action on its own. The set of functions that a file system exports encapsulates all the functionality provided by the BeOS, including attribute, indexing, and query functions. Fortunately, not all file systems must implement every call since most of the functionality is not strictly needed. A file system implementing only about 20 functions could function at a basic level.

The most basic file system possible would only be able to iterate over a directory and to provide full information about files (i.e., a stat structure). Beyond that, all the other functions in the API are optional. A file system such as the root file system (which is an in-memory-only file system) can only create directories and symbolic links, and it only implements the calls necessary for those abstractions.

The vnode operations are given by the vnode_ops structure in Listing 10-1. Of the 57 vnode operations, BFS implements all but the following four:

- rename_index
- rename_attr
- secure_vnode
- link

The lack of the two rename functions has not presented any problems (their presence in the API was primarily for completeness, and in retrospect they could have been dropped). The secure_vnode function, related to securing access to a vnid, will be necessary to implement when security becomes more of an issue for the BeOS. The link function is used to create hard links, but because the BeOS C++ API does not support hard links, we elected not to implement this function.

Instead of simply describing the role of each function (which would get to be dreadfully boring for both you and me), we will describe how these functions are used by the BeOS vnode layer and what a file system must do to correctly implement the API.

In the Beginning ...

The first set of vnode layer calls we will discuss are those that deal with mounting, unmounting, and obtaining information about a file system. These operations operate at the level of an entire file system and do not operate on individual files (unlike most of the other operations).

The mount call of the vnode interface is the call that initiates access to a file system. The mount call begins as a system call made from user space.

```
typedef struct vnode_ops {
    op_read_vnode       (*read_vnode);
    op_write_vnode      (*write_vnode);
    op_remove_vnode     (*remove_vnode);
    op_secure_vnode     (*secure_vnode);
    op_walk             (*walk);
    op_access           (*access);

    op_create           (*create);
    op_mkdir            (*mkdir);
    op_symlink          (*symlink);
    op_link             (*link);
    op_rename           (*rename);
    op_unlink           (*unlink);
    op_rmdir            (*rmdir);
    op_readlink         (*readlink);

    op_opendir          (*opendir);
    op_closedir         (*closedir);
    op_free_cookie      (*free_dircookie);
    op_rewinddir        (*rewinddir);
    op_readdir          (*readdir);

    op_open             (*open);
    op_close            (*close);
    op_free_cookie      (*free_cookie);
    op_read             (*read);
    op_write            (*write);
    op_ioctl            (*ioctl);
    op_setflags         (*setflags);
    op_rstat            (*rstat);
    op_wstat            (*wstat);
    op_fsync            (*fsync);

    op_initialize       (*initialize);
    op_mount            (*mount);
    op_unmount          (*unmount);
    op_sync             (*sync);

    op_rfsstat          (*rfsstat);
    op_wfsstat          (*wfsstat);

    op_open_indexdir    (*open_indexdir);
    op_close_indexdir   (*close_indexdir);
    op_free_cookie      (*free_indexdircookie);
    op_rewind_indexdir  (*rewind_indexdir);
    op_read_indexdir    (*read_indexdir);

    op_create_index     (*create_index);
    op_remove_index     (*remove_index);
    op_rename_index     (*rename_index);
    op_stat_index       (*stat_index);

    op_open_attrdir     (*open_attrdir);
    op_close_attrdir    (*close_attrdir);
    op_free_cookie      (*free_attrdircookie);
    op_rewind_attrdir   (*rewind_attrdir);
    op_read_attrdir     (*read_attrdir);

    op_write_attr       (*write_attr);
    op_read_attr        (*read_attr);
    op_remove_attr      (*remove_attr);
    op_rename_attr      (*rename_attr);
    op_stat_attr        (*stat_attr);

    op_open_query       (*open_query);
    op_close_query      (*close_query);
    op_free_cookie      (*free_querycookie);
    op_read_query       (*read_query);
} vnode_ops;
```

Listing 10-1   The BeOS vnode operations structure that file systems implement.

The mount() system call allows a user to mount a file system of a particular type on a device at a particular place in the file name space. The mount call passes in arguments that name the device (if any) that the file system should use as well as a pointer to arbitrary data (from user space) that the file system may use to specify additional file-system-specific arguments.

When the vnode layer calls the mount operation of a particular file system, it is up to that file system to open() the device, verify the requested volume, and prepare any data structures it may need. For BFS, mounting a volume entails verifying the superblock, playing back the log if needed, and reading in the bitmap of the volume. A virtual file system such as the root file system may not need to do much but allocate and initialize a few data structures. If a file system finds that the volume is not in its format or that the volume is potentially corrupted, it can return an error code to the vnode layer, which will abort the request.

Assuming all the initialization checks pass, the file system can complete the mounting procedure. The first step in completing the mounting process is for the file system to tell the vnode layer how to access the root directory of the file system. This step is necessary because it provides the connection to the file hierarchy stored on the volume. BFS stores the root directory i-node number in the superblock, making it easy to load. After loading the root directory node, the file system publishes the root directory i-node number (its vnid) to the vnode layer with the new_vnode() call. The new_vnode() routine is the mechanism that a file system uses to publish a new vnode-id that the rest of the system can use. We will discuss the new_vnode() call more when we talk about creating files. The vnid of the root directory is also stored into a memory location passed into the mount call.

Every file system also has some global state that it must maintain. Global state for a file system includes items such as the file descriptor of the underlying volume, global access semaphores, and superblock data. The mount routine of a file system initializes whatever structure is needed by the file system. The vnode layer passes a pointer that the file system can fill in with a pointer to the file system's global state structure. The vnode layer passes this pointer each time it calls into a file system.

The unmount operation for a file system is very simple. It is guaranteed to only be called if there are no open files on the file system, and it will only be called once. The unmount operation should tear down any structures associated with the file system and release any resources previously allocated. The BFS unmount operation syncs and shuts down the log, frees allocated memory, flushes the cache, and then closes the file descriptor of the underlying device. Unmounting is more complicated in the vnode layer because it must ensure that the file system is not being accessed before the operation begins. Once the unmount has begun, no one else should be allowed to touch the file system.

The next two operations in this group of top-level vnode operations are those that retrieve and set file system global information. The rfsstat function reads a file system info structure. This structure contains items such as the name of the volume, the block size of the file system, the number of total blocks, the number of free blocks, and so on. This information is used by programs such as df or displayed by the Get Info menu item for a disk icon on the desktop.

The function wfsstat allows programs to set information about the file system. The only supported field that can be written is the name of the volume. It would be very difficult to support changing the block size of a file system, and no attempt is made.

The rfsstat and wfsstat routines are trivial to implement but are required to provide global information about a file system to the rest of the system and to allow editing of a volume name.

Vnode Support Operations

Beyond the mounting/unmounting file system issues, there are certain low-level vnode-related operations that all file systems must implement. These functions provide the most basic of services to the vnode layer, and all other vnode operations depend on these routines to operate correctly. These operations are

```
op_walk              (*walk);
op_read_vnode        (*read_vnode);
op_write_vnode       (*write_vnode);
```

Most vnode operations, such as read or write, have a user-level function of the same name or a very similar name. Such functions implement the functionality that underlies the user-level call of the same name. The functions walk, read_vnode, and write_vnode are not like the other vnode operations. They have no corresponding user-level call, and they are called with certain restrictions.

The first routine, walk(), is the the crux of the entire vnode layer API. The vnode layer uses the walk() function to parse through a file name as passed in by a user. That is, the vnode layer "walks" through a file name, processing each component of the path (separated by the "/" character) and asking the file system for the vnid that corresponds to that component of the full path.

A short aside on path name parsing is in order. The choice of "/" as a separator in path names is a given if you are used to traditional Unix path names. It is unusual for people used to MS-DOS (which uses "\") or the Macintosh (which uses ":" internally). The choice of "/" pleases us, but the separator could certainly have been made configurable. We deemed that the complexity that would have to be added to all APIs (both in the kernel and at user level) did not warrant the feature. Other systems might have more of a requirement for flexibility in this regard.

Back to the issue at hand, the two most important arguments to the `walk()` routine are a directory node and a name. The name is a single file name component (i.e., it has no "/" characters in it). Using whatever mechanism that is appropriate, the file system should look up the name in the directory and find the vnid of that name. If the name exists in the directory, `walk()` should load the vnid that belongs to that name and inform the vnode layer of the vnid. The vnode layer does not concern itself with how the lookup of the name happens. Each file system will do it differently. The vnode layer only cares that the file system return a vnid for the name and that it load the vnode associated with the name.

To load a particular vnid from disk, the file system `walk()` routine calls the vnode layer support routine, `get_vnode()`. The `get_vnode()` call manages the pool of active and cached vnodes in the system. If a vnid is already loaded, the `get_vnode()` call increments the reference count and returns the pointer to the associated file-system-specific data. If the vnid is not loaded, then `get_vnode()` calls the `read_vnode()` operation of the file system to load the vnid. Note that when a file system calls `get_vnode()`, the `get_vnode()` call may in turn reenter the file system by calling the `read_vnode()` routine. This reentrance to the file system requires careful attention if the file system has any global locks on resources.

A quick example helps illustrate the process of `walk()`. The simplest path name possible is a single component such as `foo`. Such a path name has no subdirectories and refers to a single entity in a file system. For our example, let's consider a program whose current directory is the root directory and that makes the call

```
open("foo", O_RDONLY)
```

To perform the `open()`, the vnode layer must transform the name `foo` into a file descriptor. The file name `foo` is a simple path name that must reside in the current directory. In this example the current directory of the program is the root directory of a file system. The root directory of a file system is known from the `mount()` operation. Using this root directory handle, the vnode layer asks the `walk()` routine to translate the name `foo` into a vnode. The vnode layer calls the file system `walk()` routine with a pointer to the file-system-specific data for the root directory and the name `foo`. If the name `foo` exists, the file system fills in the vnid of the file and calls `get_vnode()` to load that vnid from disk. If the name `foo` does not exist, the `walk()` routine returns ENOENT and the `open()` fails.

If the `walk()` succeeds, the vnode layer has the vnode that corresponds to the name `foo`. Once the vnode layer `open()` has the vnode of `foo`, it will call the file system `open()` function. If the file system `open()` succeeds with its permission checking and so on, the vnode layer then creates the rest of the necessary structures to connect a file descriptor in the calling thread with the vnode of the file `foo`. This process of parsing a path name and walking through the individual components is done for each file name passed to the vnode layer. Although our example had only a single path name component, more complicated paths perform the same processing but iterate over all of the components. The `walk()` operation performs the crucial step of converting a named entry in a directory to a vnode that the vnode layer can use.

Symbolic links are named entries in a directory that are not regular files but instead contain the name of another file. At the user level, the normal behavior of a symbolic link is for it to transparently use the file that the symbolic link points to. That is, when a program opens a name that is a symbolic link, it opens the file that the symbolic link points to, not the symbolic link itself. There are also functions at the user level that allow a program to operate directly on a symbolic link and not the file it refers to. This dual mode of operation requires that the vnode layer and the file system `walk()` function have a mechanism to support traversing or not traversing a link.

To handle either behavior, the `walk()` routine accepts an extra argument in addition to the directory handle and the name. The path argument of the `walk()` routine is a pointer to a pointer to a character string. If this pointer is nonnull, the file system is required to fill in the pointer with a pointer to the path contained in the symbolic link. Filling in the path argument allows the vnode layer to begin processing the file name argument contained in the symbolic link. If the path argument passed to the file system `walk()` routine is null, then `walk()` behaves as normal and simply loads the vnid of the symbolic link and fills in the vnid for the vnode layer.

If the name exists in the directory, the `walk()` routine always loads the associated vnode. Once the vnode is loaded, the file system can determine if the node is a symbolic link. If it is and the path argument is nonnull, the file system must fill in the path argument. To fill in the path argument, the `walk()` routine uses the vnode layer `new_path()` function. The `new_path()` routine has the following prototype:

```
int  new_path(const char *npath, char **copy);
```

The first argument is the string contained in the symbolic link (i.e., the name of the file that the symbolic link points to). The second argument is a pointer to a pointer that the vnode layer fills in with a copy of the string pointed to by the `npath` argument. If the `new_path()` function succeeds, the result can be stored in the path argument of `walk()`. The requirement to call `new_path()` to effectively copy a string may seem strange, but it ensures proper ownership of strings. Otherwise, the file system would allocate strings that the vnode layer would later free, which is "unclean" from a design standpoint. The call to `new_path()` ensures that the vnode layer is the owner of the string.

Once this new_path() function is called, the walk() routine can release the vnode of the symbolic link that it loaded. To release the vnode, the walk() function calls put_vnode(), which is the opposite of get_vnode(). From there the vnode layer continues parsing with the new path as filled in by walk().

Although the walk() routine may seem complex, it is not. The semantics are difficult to explain, but the actual implementation can be quite short (the BFS walk() routine is only 50 lines of code). The key point of walk() is that it maps from a name in a directory to the vnode that underlies the name. The walk() function must also handle symbolic links, either traversing the link and returning the path contained in the symbolic link, or simply returning the vnode of the symbolic link itself.

The read_vnode() operation of a file system has a straightforward job. It is given a vnid, and it must load that vnid into memory and build any necessary structures that the file system will need to access the file or directory associated with the vnid. The read_vnode() function is guaranted to be single threaded for any vnid. That is, no locking must be done, and although read_vnode() calls for multiple vnids may happen in parallel, the read_vnode() for any given vnid will never happen multiple times unless the vnid is flushed from memory.

If the read_vnode() function succeeds, it fills in a pointer to the data structure it allocated. If read_vnode() fails, it returns an error code. No other requirements are placed on read_vnode().

The write_vnode() operation is somewhat misnamed. No data is written to disk at the time write_vnode() is called. Rather write_vnode() is called after the reference count for a vnode drops to zero and the vnode layer decides to flush the vnode from memory. The write_vnode() call is also guaranteed to be called only once. The write_vnode() call need not lock the node in question because the vnode layer will ensure that no other access is made to the vnode. The write_vnode() call should free any resources associated with the node, including any extra allocated memory, the lock for the node, and so on. Despite its name, write_vnode() does not write data to disk.

The read_vnode() and write_vnode() calls always happen in pairs for any given vnid. The read_vnode() call is made once to load the vnid and allocate any necessary structures. The write_vnode() call is made once and should free all in-memory resources associated with the node. Neither call should ever modify any on-disk data structures.

Securing Vnodes

There are two other routines in this group of functions:

```
op_secure_vnode          (*secure_vnode);
op_access                (*access);
```

The access() routine is the vnode layer equivalent of the POSIX access() call. BFS honors this call and performs the required permission checking. The aim of the secure_vnode() function is to guarantee that a vnid that a program requests is indeed a valid vnode and that access to it is allowed. This call is currently unimplemented in BFS. The difference between secure_vnode() and access() is that secure_vnode() is called directly by the vnode layer when needed to ensure that a program requesting a particular vnid indeed has access to it. The access() call is only made in response to user programs making the access() system call.

Directory Functions

After mounting a file system, the most likely operation to follow is a call to iterate over the contents of the root directory. The directory vnode operations abstract the process of iterating over the contents of a directory and provide a uniform interface to the rest of the system regardless of the implementation in the file system. For example, BFS uses on-disk B+trees to store directories, while the root file system stores directories as an in-memory linked list. The vnode directory operations make the differences in implementations transparent.

The vnode layer operations to manipulate directories are

```
op_opendir              (*opendir);
op_closedir             (*closedir);
op_free_cookie          (*free_dircookie);
op_rewinddir            (*rewinddir);
op_readdir              (*readdir);
```

Aside from the free_dircookie function, these functions correspond closely to the POSIX directory functions of the same names.

The opendir function accepts a pointer to a node, and based on that node, it creates a state structure that will be used to help iterate through the directory. Of course, the state structure is opaque to the vnode layer. This state structure is also known as a *cookie*. The vnode layer stores the cookie in the ofile structure and passes it to the directory routines each time they are called. The file system is responsible for the contents of the cookie.

Recall that a cookie contains file-system-specific data about a file descriptor. This use of cookies is very common in the vnode layer interface and will reappear several times.

The vnode layer only calls the free_dircookie function when the open count of a file descriptor is zero and there are no threads using the file descriptor. There is an important distinction between a close operation and a free_cookie operation. The distinction arises because multiple threads can access a file descriptor. Although one thread calls close(), another thread may be in the midst of a read(). Only after the last thread is done accessing a file descriptor can the vnode layer call the file system free_cookie routine. BFS does almost no work in its closedir() routine. The free_dircookie routine, however, must free up any resources associated with the cookie passed to it. The vnode layer manages the counts associated with a cookie and ensures that the free_cookie routine is only called after the last close.

Another caveat when using cookies involves multithreading issues. The vnode layer performs no serialization or locking of any data structures when it calls into a file system. Unless otherwise stated, all file system routines need to perform whatever locking is appropriate to ensure proper serialization. Some file systems may serialize the entire file system with a single lock. BFS serializes access at the node level, which is the finest granularity possible. BFS must first lock a node before accessing the cookie passed in (or it should only access the cookie in a read-only fashion). Locking the node before accessing the cookie is necessary because there may be multiple threads using the same file descriptor concurrently, and thus they will use the same cookie. Locking the node first ensures that only one thread at a time will access the cookie.

Returning to our discussion of the directory vnode operations, the primary function for scanning through a directory is the readdir function. This routine uses the information passed in the cookie to iterate through the directory, each time returning information about the next file in the directory. The information returned includes the name and the i-node number of the file. The state information stored in the cookie should be sufficient to enable the file system to continue iterating through the directory on the next call to readdir. When there are no more entries in a directory, the readdir function should return that it read zero items.

The rewinddir function simply resets the state information stored in the cookie so that the next call to readdir will return the first item in the directory.

This style of iterating over a list of items in the file system is replicated several times. Attributes and indices both use a nearly identical interface. The query interface is slightly different but uses the same basic principles. The key concept of the directory operations is the readdir operation, which returns the next entry in a directory and stores state in the cookie to enable it to continue iterating through the directory on the next call to readdir. The use of cookies makes this disconnected style of operation possible.

Working with Files

These functions encapsulate the meat of file I/O in a file system:

```
op_open              (*open);
op_close             (*close);
op_free_cookie       (*free_cookie);
```

```
op_read          (*read);
op_write         (*write);
op_ioctl         (*ioctl);
op_setflags      (*setflags);
op_rstat         (*rstat);
op_wstat         (*wstat);
op_fsync         (*fsync);
```

The first call, open(), does not take a file name as an argument. As we saw in the discussion of walk(), the walk() routine translates names to vnodes. The open() call is passed a pointer to a node (as created by read_vnode()), the mode with which to open the file, and a pointer to a cookie. If the current thread has permission to access the file in the desired mode, the cookie is allocated, filled in, and success returned. Otherwise, EACCESS is returned, and the open() fails. The cookie allocated in open must at least hold information about the open mode of the file so that the file system can properly implement the O_APPEND file mode. Because the bulk of the work is done elsewhere (notably, walk() and read_vnode()), the open() function is quite small.

Strictly speaking, the vnode layer expects nothing of the close() routine. The close() routine is called once for every open() that happens for a file. Even though the vnode layer expects little of a file system in the close() routine, the multithreaded nature of the BeOS complicates close() in the vnode layer. The problem is that with multiple threads, one thread can call close() on a file descriptor after another thread initiates an I/O on that same file descriptor. If the vnode layer were not careful, the file descriptor would disappear in the middle of the other thread's I/O. For this reason the BeOS vnode layer separates the actions of close()ing a file descriptor from the free_cookie() operation (described next). The file system close() operation should not free any resources that might also be in use by another thread performing I/O.

The free_cookie() function releases any cookie resources allocated in open(). The vnode layer only calls the free_cookie() function when there are no threads performing I/O on the vnode and the open count is zero. The vnode layer guarantees that the free_cookie() function is single threaded for any given cookie (i.e., it is only called once for each open()).

The next two functions, read() and write(), implement the core of file I/O. Both read() and write() accept a few more arguments than specified in the corresponding user-level read() and write() calls. In addition to the data pointer and length of the data to write, the read() and write() calls accept a node pointer (instead of a file descriptor), the file position to perform the I/O at, and the cookie allocated in open(). The semantics of read() and write() are exactly as they are at the user level.

The ioctl() function is a simple hook to perform arbitrary actions on a file that are not covered by the vnode layer API. This function exists in the vnode layer to ensure that a file system that wishes to implement extra functionality has a hook to do so. BFS uses the ioctl() hook to implement a few private features (such as setting a file to be uncached or obtaining the block map of a file). The device file system of the BeOS uses the ioctl() hook to pass through standard user-level ioctl() calls to the underlying device drivers.

A late addition to the vnode layer API, setflags() was added to properly implement the POSIX fcntl() call. The setflags() function is called to change the status of a file's open mode. That is, using fcntl() a programmer can change a file to be in append-only mode or to make it nonblocking with respect to I/O. The setflags() function modifies the mode field that is stored in the cookie that was allocated by open().

The rstat() function is used to fill in a POSIX-style stat structure. The file system should convert from its internal notion of the relevant information and fill in the fields of the stat structure that is passed in. Fields of the stat structure that a file system does not maintain should be set to appropriate values (either zero or some other innocuous value).

If you can read the stat structure, it is also natural to be able to write to it. The wstat() function accepts a stat structure and a mask argument. The mask argument specifies which fields to use from the stat structure to update the node. The fields that can be written are

```
WSTAT_MODE
WSTAT_UID
WSTAT_GID
WSTAT_SIZE
WSTAT_ATIME
WSTAT_MTIME
WSTAT_CRTIME
```

The wstat() function subsumes numerous user-level functions (chown, chmod, ftruncate, utimes, etc.). Being able to modify multiple stat fields in an atomic manner with wstat() is useful. Further, this design avoids having seven different functions in the vnode layer API that all perform very narrow tasks. The file system should only modify the fields of the node as specified by the mask argument (if the bit is set, use the indicated field to modify the node).

The final function in this group of routines is fsync(). The vnode layer expects this call to flush any cached data for this node through to disk. This call cannot return until the data is guaranteed to be on disk. This may involve iterating over all of the blocks of a file.

Create, Delete, and Rename

The create, delete, and rename functions are the core functionality provided by a file system. The vnode layer API to these operations closely resembles the user-level POSIX functions of the same name.

create()

Creating files is perhaps the most important function of a file system; without it, the file system would always be empty. The two primary arguments of create() are the directory in which to create the file, and the name of the file to create. The vnode layer also passes the mode in which the file is being opened, the initial permissions for the file, and pointers to a vnid and a cookie that the file system should fill in.

The create() function should create an empty file that has the name given and that lives in the specified directory. If the file name already exists in the directory, the file system should call get_vnode() to load the vnode associated with the file. Once the vnode is loaded, the mode bits specified may affect the behavior of the open. If O_EXCL is specified in the mode bits, then create() should fail with EEXIST. If the name exists but is a directory, create() should return EISDIR. If the name exists and O_TRUNC is set, then the file must be truncated. If the name exists and all the other criteria are met, the file system can fill in the vnid and allocate the cookie for the existing file and return to the vnode layer.

In the normal case, the name does not exist in the directory, and the file system must do whatever is necessary to create the file. Usually this entails allocating an i-node, initializing the fields of the i-node, and inserting the name and i-node number pair into the directory. Further, if the file system supports indexing, the name should be entered into a name index if one exists.

File systems such as BFS must be careful when inserting the new file name into any indices. This action may cause updates to live queries, which in turn may cause programs to open the new file even before it is completely created. Care must be taken to ensure that the file is not accessed until it is completely created. The method of protection that BFS uses involves marking the i-node as being in a virgin state and blocking in read_vnode() until the virgin bit is clear (the virgin bit is cleared by create() when the file is fully created). The virgin bit is also set and then cleared by the mkdir() and symlink() operations.

The next step in the process of creating a file is for the file system to call new_vnode() to inform the vnode layer of the new vnid and its associated data pointer. The file system should also fill in the vnid pointer passed as an argument to create() as well as allocating a cookie for the file. The final step in the process of creating a file is to inform any interested parties of the new file by calling notify_listener(). Once these steps are complete, the new file is considered complete, and the vnode layer associates the new vnode with a file descriptor for the calling thread.

mkdir()

Similar to create(), the mkdir() operation creates a new directory. The difference at the user level is that creating a directory does not return a file handle; it simply creates the directory. The semantics from the point of view of the vnode layer are quite similar for creating files or directories (such as returning EEXIST if the name already exists in the directory). Unlike a file, mkdir() must ensure that the directory contains entries for "." and ".." if necessary. (The "." and ".." entries refer to the current directory and the parent directory, respectively.)

Unlike create(), the mkdir() function need not call new_vnode() when the directory creation is complete. The vnode layer will load the vnode separately when an opendir() is performed on the directory or when a path name refers to something inside the directory.

Once a directory is successfully created, mkdir() should call notify_listener() to inform any interested parties about the new directory. After calling notify_listener(), mkdir() is complete.

symlink()

The creation of symbolic links shares much in common with creating directories. The setup of creating a symbolic link proceeds in the same manner as creating a directory. If the name of a symbolic link already exists, the symlink() function should return EEXIST (there is no notion of O_TRUNC or O_EXCL for symbolic links). Once the file system creates the i-node and stores the path name being linked to, the symbolic link is effectively complete. As with directories and files, the last action taken by symlink() should be to call notify_listener().

readlink()

Turning away from creating file system entities for a moment, let's consider the readlink() function. The POSIX API defines the readlink() function to read the contents of a symbolic link instead of the item it refers to. The readlink() function accepts a pointer to a node, a buffer, and a length. The path name contained in the link should be copied into the user buffer. It is expected that the file system will avoid overrunning the user's buffer if it is too small to hold the contents of the symbolic link.

link()

The vnode layer API also has support for creating hard links via the link() function. The vnode layer passes a directory, a name, and an existing vnode to the file system. The file system should add the name to the directory and associate the vnid of the existing vnode with the name.

The link() function is not implemented by BFS or any of the other file systems that currently exist on the BeOS. The primary reason for not implementing hard links is that at the time BFS was being written, the C++ user-level file API was not prepared to deal with them. There was no time to modify the C++ API to offer support for them, and so we felt that it would be better not to implement them in the file system (to avoid confusion for programmers). The case is not closed, however, and should the need arise, we can extend the C++ API to better support hard links and modify BFS to implement them.

unlink() and rmdir()

A file system also needs to be able to delete files and directories. The vnode layer API breaks this into three functions. The first two, unlink() and rmdir(), are almost identical except that unlink() only operates on files and rmdir() only operates on directories. Both unlink() and rmdir() accept a directory node pointer and a name to delete. First the name must be found in the directory and the corresponding vnid loaded. The unlink() function must check that the node being removed is a file (or symbolic link). The rmdir() function must ensure that the node being removed is a directory and that the directory is empty. If the criteria are met, the file system should call the vnode layer support routine remove_vnode() on the vnid of the entity being deleted. The next order of business for either routine is to delete the named entry from the directory passed in by the vnode layer. This ensures that no further access will be made to the file other than through already open file descriptors. BFS also sets a flag in the node structure to indicate that the file is deleted so that queries (which load the vnid directly instead of going through path name translation) will not touch the file.

remove_vnode()

The vnode layer support routine remove_vnode() marks a vnode for deletion. When the reference count on the marked vnode reaches zero, the vnode layer calls the file system remove_vnode() function. The file system remove_vnode() function is guaranteed to be single threaded and is only called once for any vnid. The remove_vnode() function takes the place of a call to write_vnode(). The vnode layer expects the file system remove_vnode() function to free up any of the permanent resources associated with the node as well as any in-memory resources. For a disk-based file system such as BFS, the permanent resources associated with a file are the allocated data blocks of the file and extra attributes belonging to the file. The remove_vnode() function of a file system is the last call ever made on a vnid.

rename()

The most difficult of all vnode operations is rename(). The complexity of the rename() function derives from its guarantee of atomicity for a multistep operation. The vnode layer passes four arguments to rename(): the old directory node pointer, the old name, the new directory pointer, and the new name. The vnode layer expects the file system to look up the old name and new name and call get_vnode() for each node.

The simplest and most common rename() case is when the new name does not exist. In this situation the old name is deleted from the old directory and the new name inserted into the new directory. This involves two directory operations but little more (aside from a call to notify_listener()).

The situation becomes more difficult if the new name is already a file (or directory). In that case the new name must be deleted (in the same way that unlink() or rmdir() does). Deleting the entity referred to by the new name is a key feature of the rename() function because it guarantees an atomic swap with an old name and a new name whether or not the new name exists. This is useful for situations when a file must always exist for clients, but a new version must be dropped in place atomically.

After dealing with the new name, the old name should be deleted from the old directory and the new name inserted into the new directory so that it refers to the vnid that was associated with the old name.

The vnode layer expects that the file system will prevent unusual situations such as renaming a parent of the current directory to be a subdirectory of itself (which would effectively break off a branch of the file hierarchy and make it unreachable). Further, should an error occur at any point during the operation, all the other operations must be undone. For a file system such as BFS, this is very difficult.

File systems that support indexing must also update any file name indices that exist to reflect that the old name no longer exists and that the new name exists (or at least has a new vnid). Once all of these steps are complete, the rename() operation can call notify_listener() to update any programs monitoring for changes.

Attributes and Index Operations

The BeOS vnode layer contains attribute and index operations that most existing file systems do not support. A file system may choose not to implement these features, and the vnode layer will accommodate that choice. If a file system does not implement extended functionality, then the vnode layer returns an error when a user program requests an extended operation. The vnode layer makes no attempt to automatically remap extended features in terms of lower-level functionality. Trying to automatically map from an extended operation to a more primitive operation would introduce too much complexity and too much policy into the vnode layer. For this reason the BeOS vnode layer takes a laissez-faire attitude toward unimplemented features and simply returns an error code to user programs that try to use an extended feature on a file system that does not support it.

An application program has two choices when faced with the situation that a user wants to operate on a file that exists on a file system that does not have attributes or indices. The first choice is to simply fail outright, inform the user of the error, and not allow file operations on that volume. A more sophisticated approach is to degrade functionality of the application gracefully. Even though attributes may not be available on a particular volume, an application could still allow file operations but would not support the extra features provided by attributes.

The issue of transferring files between different types of file systems also presents this issue. A file on a BFS volume that has many attributes will lose information if a user copies it to a non-BFS volume. This loss of information is unavoidable but may not be catastrophic. For example, if a user creates a graphical image on the BeOS, that file may have several attributes. If the file is copied to an MS-DOS FAT file system so that a service bureau could print it, the loss of attribute information is irrelevant because the destination system has no knowledge of attributes.

The situation in which a user needs to transfer data between two BeOS machines but must use an intermediate file system that is not attribute- or index-aware is more problematic. We expect that this case is not common. If preserving the attributes is a requirement, then the files needing to be transferred can be archived using an archive format that supports attributes (such as zip).

A file system implementor can alleviate some of these difficulties and also make a file system more Be-like by implementing limited support for attributes and indices. For example, the Macintosh HFS implementation for the BeOS maps HFS type and creator codes to the BeOS file type attribute. The resource fork of files on the HFS volume is also exposed as an attribute, and other information such as the icon of a file and its location in a window are mapped to the corresponding attributes used by the BeOS file manager. Having the file system map attribute or even index operations to features of the underlying file system format enables a more seamless integration of that file system type with the rest of the BeOS.

Attribute Directories

The BeOS vnode layer allows files to have a list of associated attributes. Of course this requires that programs have a way to iterate over the attributes that a particular file may have. The vnode operations to operate on file attributes bear a striking resemblance to the directory operations:

```
op_open_attrdir        (*open_attrdir);
op_close_attrdir       (*close_attrdir);
op_free_cookie         (*free_attrdircookie);
op_rewind_attrdir      (*rewind_attrdir);
op_read_attrdir        (*read_attrdir);
```

The semantics of each of these functions is identical to the normal directory operations. The open_attrdir function initiates access and allocates any necessary cookies. The read_attrdir function returns information about each attribute (primarily a name). The rewind_attrdir function resets the state in the cookie so that the next read_attrdir call will return the first entry. The close_attrdir and free_cookie routines should behave as the corresponding directory routines do. The key difference between these routines and the normal directory routines is that these operate on the list of attributes of a file.

Working with Attributes

Supporting attributes associated with files requires a way to create, read, write, and delete them, and to obtain information about them. The vnode layer supports the following operations on file attributes:

```
op_write_attr           (*write_attr);
op_read_attr            (*read_attr);
op_remove_attr          (*remove_attr);
op_rename_attr          (*rename_attr);
op_stat_attr            (*stat_attr);
```

Notably absent from the list of functions are create_attr() and open_attr(). This absence reflects a decision made during the design of the vnode layer. We decided that attributes should not be treated by the vnode layer in the same way as files. This means that attributes are not entitled to their own file descriptor in the way that files and directories are. There were several reasons for this decision. The most important reason is that making attributes full-fledged file descriptors would make it very difficult to manage regular files. For example, if attributes were file descriptors, it would be possible for a file descriptor to refer to an attribute of a file that has no other open file descriptors. If the file underlying the attribute were to be erased, it becomes very difficult for the vnode layer to know when it is safe to call the remove_vnode function for the file because it would require checking not only the reference count of the file's vnode but also all the attribute vnodes associated with the file. This sort of checking would be extremely complex at the vnode layer, which is why we choose not to implement attributes as file descriptors. Further, naming conventions and identification of attributes complicate matters even more. These issues sealed our decision after several aborted attempts to make attributes work as file descriptors.

This decision dictated that all attribute I/O and informational routines would have to accept two arguments to specify which attribute to operate on. The first argument is an open file descriptor (at the user level), and the second argument is the name of the attribute. In the kernel, the file descriptor argument is replaced with the vnode of the file. All attribute operations must specify these two arguments. Further, the operations that read or write data must also specify the offset to perform the I/O at. Normally a file descriptor encapsulates the file position, but because attributes have no file descriptor, all the information necessary must be specified on each call. Although it may seem that this complicates the user-level API, the calls are still quite straightforward and can be easily wrapped with a user-level attribute file descriptor if desired.

The attribute vnode operations require the file system to handle all serialization necessary. The vnode layer does no locking when calling the file system, and thus it is possible for multiple threads to be operating on the same attribute of a file at the same time. The multithreaded nature of the vnode layer requires the file system to manage its own locking of the i-node. Each of the operations in this section must first lock the i-node they operate on before touching any data. It is important that each attribute call be atomic.

The `write_attr()` call writes data to an attribute. If the named attribute does not exist, the `write_attr()` call must create it. The semantics of the `write_attr()` operation are the same as writing data to a file. One drawback of attributes not being file descriptors is that there is no way to specify that the data be truncated on an `open()` as is often done with files (the `O_TRUNC` option to `open()`). This is generally solved by first deleting an attribute before rewriting the value. When data is written to an attribute, the file system must also update any indices that correspond to the name of the attribute being written.

The `read_attr()` call behaves the same as `read()` does for files. It is possible for `read_attr()` to return an error code indicating that the named attribute does not exist for this file.

The `remove_attr()` call deletes an attribute from a file. Unlike files, there is no separate `unlink` and `remove_vnode` phase. After calling `remove_attr()` on an attribute of a file, the attribute no longer exists. If another thread were reading data from the attribute, the next call to read data after the `remove_attr()` function would return an error. Operations such as this are the reason for the requirement that all attribute actions be atomic.

The `rename_attr()` function should rename an attribute. This function was added for completeness of the API, but BFS does not currently implement it.

The last function, `stat_attr()`, returns stat-structure-like information about an attribute of a file. The size and type of an attribute are the two pieces of information returned. We chose not to require file systems to maintain last modification dates or creation dates for attributes because we wanted them to be very lightweight entities. This decision was partially due to the implementation of attributes in BFS. It is arguable whether this was a wise decision or not. We regard it as a wise decision, however, because it allows a file system API to be used in places where it might not otherwise (such as the BeOS HFS implementation, which maps some Mac resource fork entries to BeOS attributes). If we had required storing extra fields such as creation dates, it might have made it more difficult to implement attributes for other file systems.

Index-Related Operations

Another interesting feature of the BeOS vnode layer is that it supports file systems that have indices to the files on that file system. To find out what indices exist on a file system, the vnode layer has a set of index directory operations:

```
op_open_indexdir        (*open_indexdir);
op_close_indexdir       (*close_indexdir);
op_free_cookie          (*free_indexdircookie);
op_rewind_indexdir      (*rewind_indexdir);
op_read_indexdir        (*read_indexdir);
```

Once again, these operations correspond identically to the normal directory operations except that they operate on the list of indices on a file system. Each read_indexdir call should return the next index on the file system. Currently BFS is the only file system that implements these routines.

Working with Indices

Supporting file systems with indices means that the vnode layer also has to support creating indices. The vnode layer contains the following functions for creating, deleting, renaming, and obtaining information about indices:

```
op_create_index        (*create_index);
op_remove_index        (*remove_index);
op_rename_index        (*rename_index);
op_stat_index          (*stat_index);
```

The create_index operation accepts the name of an index and a type argument. If the index name already exists, this function should return an error. Although there is no way to enforce the connection, the assumption is that the name of the index will match the name of an attribute that is going to be written to files. The type argument specifies the data type of the index. The data type argument should also match the data type of the attribute. The list of supported data types for BFS is string, integer, unsigned integer, 64-bit integer, unsigned 64-bit integer, float, and double. The list of types is not specified or acted on by the vnode layer, and it is possible for another file system to implement indexing of other data types.

The remove_index operation accepts a name argument and should delete the named index. Unlike normal file operations that require a two-phase deletion process (unlink and then remove_vnode), the same is not true of indices. The file system is expected to perform the necessary serialization.

The rename_index operation should rename an index, but currently it is unimplemented in BFS. This has not proven to be a problem. We included the rename_index function for completeness of the vnode layer API, although in retrospect it seems superfluous.

The stat_index function returns information about the index—namely, its size and type. The stat_index function is only used by some informational utilities that print out the name, size, and type of all the indices on the system. The stat_index operation is also useful for a user-level program to detect the presence of an index without having to iterate through the whole index directory.

Query Operations

The last group of vnode operations relates to queries. The vnode layer supports a simple API that allows programs to issue queries about the files on a file system. The result of a query is a list of files that match the query. For a file system to implement queries, it must implement these operations:

```
op_open_query          (*open_query);
op_close_query         (*close_query);
op_free_cookie         (*free_querycookie);
op_read_query          (*read_query);
```

Again, there is a very close resemblance to the normal directory routines, which makes sense since both queries and directories contain a list of files. The rewind function is not present as we felt it added little to the functionality of the API and could potentially be difficult to implement in some file systems.

The open_query() routine accepts a query string that it must parse, and it creates a cookie that it uses to maintain state. The choice to pass a string to open_query() deserves closer examination. By passing a string to a file system routine, file systems wishing to implement the query API need to implement a parser. For example, BFS has a full recursive descent parser and builds a complete parse tree of the query. String manipulation and parse trees are usually the domain of compilers running at the user level, not something typically done in kernel space. The alternative, however, is even less appealing. Instead of passing a string to open_query(), the parsing could have been done in a library at user level, and a complete data structure passed to the kernel. This is even less appealing than passing a string because the kernel would have to validate the entire data structure before touching it (to avoid bad pointers, etc.). Further, a fixed parse tree data structure would require more work to extend and could pose binary compatibility problems if changes were needed. Although it does require a fair amount of code to parse the query language string, the alternatives are even less appealing.

The core of the query routines is read_query(). This function iterates through the results of a query, returning each one in succession. At the vnode layer there is little that differentiates read_query() from a readdir() call, but internally a file system has quite a bit of work to do to complete the call.

10.5 The Node Monitor

The BeOS vnode layer also supports an API to monitor modifications made to files and directories. This API is collectively known as the node monitor

API. The node monitor API allows a program to receive notification when changes are made to a file or directory without having to poll. This is a powerful feature used by many programs in the BeOS. For example, the print server monitors a spool directory for new files, and the desktop file manager watches for changes to files currently being displayed. Beyond that, other programs will monitor for changes made to files they use so that they can automatically pick up the changes without requiring manual action. Node monitoring is not a unique feature of the BeOS; several examples exist of similar APIs in other systems (most notably the Amiga OS and SGI's Irix).

The node monitor API requires close cooperation between the vnode layer and the underlying file systems to ensure that correct and proper notifications are sent to user programs when modifications are made. The file systems must notify the vnode layer whenever changes happen, and the vnode layer manages sending notifications to all interested parties. To enable a file system to send notifications, the vnode layer supports the call

```
int  notify_listener(int event, nspace_id nsid,
                     vnode_id vnida, vnode_id vnidb, vnode_id vnidc,
                     const char *name);
```

A file system should call notify_listener() whenever an event happens in the file system. The types of events supported are

```
B_ENTRY_CREATED
B_ENTRY_REMOVED
B_ENTRY_MOVED
B_STAT_CHANGED
B_ATTR_CHANGED
```

A file system passes one of these constants as the op argument of the notify_listener() call. The vnid arguments are used to identify the file and directories involved in the event. Not all of the vnids must be filled in (in fact, only the B_ENTRY_MOVED notification uses all three vnid slots). The name argument is for the creation of new nodes (files, symbolic links, or directories) and when a file is renamed.

When a file system calls notify_listener(), it does not concern itself with who the notifications are sent to nor how many are sent. The only requirement is that the file system call this when an operation completes successfully. Although it would seem possible for the vnode layer to send the notifications itself, it is not possible because the vnode layer does not always know all the vnids involved in an operation such as rename.

Internally the node monitor API is simple for a file system to implement. It only requires a few calls to notify_listener() to be made in the proper places (create, unlink, rename, close, and write_attr). Implementing this feature in a file system requires no modifications or additions to any data structures, and it can even be used with file systems from other systems that do not support notifications.

At the vnode level, node monitors are managed in two ways. Each `ioctx` has a list of node monitors. The list begins at the `mon` field of the `ioctx` structure. The `mon` list is necessary so that when the `ioctx` is destroyed, the vnode layer can free any node monitors still allocated by a program. In addition, the vnode layer manages a hash table of all node monitors. The hash value is based on the vnid of the node being monitored. This enables efficient lookups when a file system calls `notify_listener()`.

The node monitoring system of the BeOS requires very little extra work on the part of a file system. Even the implemenation at the vnode layer is relatively small. The extra functionality offered by the node monitor makes it well worth the effort.

10.6   Live Queries

In addition to the node monitoring API, the BeOS also supports live queries. A query is a search of the indices maintained by a file system for a set of files that match the query criteria. As an option when opening a query, a program can specify that the query is *live*. A program iterates through a live query the first time just as it would with a static query. The difference is that a live query continues reporting additions and deletions to the set of files that match a query until the live query is closed. In a manner similar to node monitoring, a program will receive updates to a live query as files and directories enter and leave the set of matching files of the query.

Live queries are an extremely powerful mechanism used by the find mechanism of the file manager as well as by other programs. For example, in the BeOS find panel, you can query for all unread email. The find panel uses live queries, and so even after the query is issued, if new mail arrives, the window showing the results of the query (i.e., all new email) will be updated and the new email will appear in the window. Live queries help many parts of the system to work together in sophisticated ways without requiring special APIs for private notifications or updates.

Implementing live queries in a file system is not easy because of the many race conditions and complicated locking scenarios that can arise. Whenever a program issues a live query, the file system must tag all the indices involved in the query so that if a file is created or deleted from the index, the file system can determine if a notification needs to be sent. This requires checking the file against the full query to determine if it matches the query. If the file is entering or leaving the set of files that match the query, the file system must send a notification to any interested threads.

The vnode layer plays a smaller role in live query updates than it does with node monitor notifications. The file system must maintain the information about exactly who to send the notification to and is responsible for calling the vnode layer function:

```
int send_notification(port_id port, long token,
                      ulong what, long op, nspace_id nsida,
                      nspace_id nsidb, vnode_id vnida,
                      vnode_id vnidb, vnode_id vnidc,
                      const char *name);
```

for each update to all live queries. The file system must keep track of the port to send each update to and the token for the message. It is important to keep in mind that changes to a single file may require sending notifications to multiple different live queries.

At first the implementation of live queries seemed a daunting task for BFS, and much effort went into procrastinating on the actual implementation. Although it does seem fraught with race conditions and deadlock problems, implementing live queries did not turn out to be as difficult as initially imagined. The BFS implementation of live queries works by tagging each index used in the query with a callback function. Each index has a list of callbacks, and any modifications made to the index will iterate over the list of callbacks. The index code then calls into the query code with a reference to the file the index is manipulating. The query callback is also passed a pointer to the original query. The file is checked against the query parse tree, and, if appropriate, a notification is sent.

Live queries offer a very significant feature for programmers to take advantage of. They enable programs to receive notification based on sophisticated criteria. The implementation of live queries adds a nontrivial amount of complexity to a file system, but the effort is well worth it for the features it enables.

10.7   Summary

A vnode layer connects the user-level abstraction of a file descriptor with specific file system implementations. In general, a vnode layer allows many different file systems to hook into the file system name space and appear as one seamless unit. The vnode layer defines an API that all file systems must implement. Through this API all file systems appear the same to the vnode layer. The BeOS vnode layer extends the traditional set of functions defined by a vnode layer and offers hooks for monitoring files and submitting queries to a file system. These nontraditional interfaces are necessary to provide the functionality required by the rest of the BeOS. A vnode layer is an important part of any kernel and defines the I/O model of the system.

11

User-Level API

On the BeOS there are two user-level APIs to access files and directories. The BeOS supports the POSIX file I/O API, which provides the standard notions of path names and file descriptors. There are some extensions to this API to allow access to attributes, indices, and queries. We will only discuss the standard POSIX API briefly and spend more time on the extensions. The other API to access files on the BeOS is the C++ Storage Kit. The C++ API is a full-class hierarchy and is intended to make C++ programmers feel at home. We will spend most of this chapter discussing the C++ API. However, this chapter is not intended to be a programming manual. (For more specifics of the functions mentioned in this chapter, refer to the *Be Developer's Guide*.)

11.1 The POSIX API and C Extensions

All the standard POSIX file I/O calls, such as `open()`, `read()`, `write()`, `dup()`, `close()`, `fopen()`, `fprintf()`, and so on, work as expected on the BeOS. The POSIX calls that operate directly on file descriptors (i.e., `open()`, `read()`, etc.) are direct kernel calls. The model of file descriptors provided by the kernel directly supports the POSIX model for file descriptors. Although there were pressures from some BeOS developers to invent new mechanisms for file I/O, we decided not to reinvent the wheel. Even the BeOS C++ API uses file descriptors beneath its C++ veneer. The POSIX model for file I/O works well, and we saw no advantages to be gained by changing that model.

Attribute Functions

The C interface to attributes consists of eight functions. The first four functions provide a way to enumerate the attributes associated with a file. A file can have any number of attributes, and the list of attributes associated with a file is presented as an attribute directory. The API to access the list of attributes associated with a file is nearly identical to the POSIX directory functions (opendir(), readdir(), etc.):

```
DIR            *fs_open_attr_dir(char *path);
struct dirent *fs_read_attr_dir(DIR *dirp);
int            fs_rewind_attr_dir(DIR *dirp);
int            fs_close_attr_dir(DIR *dirp);
```

The similarity of this API to the POSIX directory API makes it immediately usable by any programmer familiar with the POSIX API. Our intent here and elsewhere was to reuse concepts that programmers were already familiar with. Each named entry returned by fs_read_attr_dir() corresponds to an attribute of the file referred to by the path given to fs_open_attr_dir().

The next four functions provide access to individual attributes. Again, we stuck with notions familiar to POSIX programmers. The first routine returns more detailed information about a particular attribute:

```
int            fs_stat_attr(int fd, char *name, struct attr_info *info);
```

The function fills in the attr_info structure with the type and size of the named attribute.

Of note here is the style of API chosen: to identify an attribute of a file, a programmer must specify the file descriptor of the file that the attribute is associated with and the name of the attribute. This is the style for the rest of the attribute functions as well. As noted in Chapter 10, making attributes into full-fledged file descriptors would have made removing files considerably more complex. The decision not to treat attributes as file descriptors reflects itself here in the user-level API where an attribute is always identified by providing a file descriptor and a name.

The next function removes an attribute from a file:

```
int            fs_remove_attr(int fd, char *name);
```

After this call the attribute no longer exists. Further, if the attribute name is indexed, the file is removed from the associated index.

The next two functions provide the I/O interface to reading and writing attributes:

```
ssize_t        fs_read_attr(int fd, char *name, uint32 type,
                            off_t pos, void *buffer, size_t count);
ssize_t        fs_write_attr(int fd, char *name, uint32 type,
                            off_t pos, void *buffer, size_t count);
```

The API follows closely what we've described in the lower levels. Each attribute has a name, a type, and data associated with the name. The file system can use the type code to determine if it is possible to index the attribute. The fs_write_attr() creates the named attribute if it does not exist. These two functions round out the interface to attributes from the POSIX-style API.

Index Functions

The interface to the indexing features is only provided by a simple C language interface. There is no corresponding C++ API to the indexing routines. This is not a reflection on our language preference but rather is a realization that little would have been gained by writing a C++ wrapper for these routines.

The indexing API provides routines to iterate over the list of indices on a volume, and to create and delete indices. The routines to iterate over the list of indices on a volume are

```
DIR             *fs_open_index_dir(dev_t dev);
struct dirent *fs_read_index_dir(DIR *dirp);
int             fs_rewind_index_dir(DIR *dirp);
int             fs_close_index_dir(DIR *dirp);
```

Again, the API is quite similar to the POSIX directory functions. The fs_open_index_dir() accepts a dev_t argument, which is how the vnode layer knows which volume to operate on. The entries returned from fs_read_index_dir() provide the name of each index. To obtain more information about the index, the call is

```
int fs_stat_index(dev_t dev, char *name, struct index_info *info);
```

The fs_stat_index() call returns a stat-like structure about the named index. The type, size, modification time, creation time, and ownership of the index are all part of the index_info structure.

Creating an index is done with

```
int fs_create_index(dev_t dev, char *name, int type, uint flags);
```

This function creates the named index on the volume specified. The flags argument is unused at this time but may specify additional options in the future. The index has the data type indicated by the type argument. The supported types are

- integer (signed/unsigned, 32-/64-bit)
- float
- double
- string

A file system could allow other types, but these are the data types that BFS supports (currently the only file system to support indexing on the BeOS is BFS).

The name of the index should correspond to the name of an attribute that will be added to files. After the file system creates the index, all files that have an attribute added whose name matches the name (and type) of this index will also have the attribute value added to the index.

Deleting an index is almost too easy:

```
int fs_remove_index(dev_t dev, char *name);
```

After calling `fs_remove_index()` the index is deleted and is no more. Deleting an index is a serious operation because once the index is deleted, the information contained in the index cannot be easily re-created. Deleting an index that is still needed can interfere with the correct operation of programs that need the index. There is little that can be done to protect against someone inadvertently deleting an index, so no interface aside from a command-line utility (that calls this function) is provided to delete indices.

Query Functions

A query is an expression about the attributes of files such as `name = foo` or `MAIL:from != pike@research.att.com`. The result of a query is a list of files that match the expression. The obvious style of API for iterating over the list of files that match is the standard directory-style API:

```
DIR             *fs_open_query(dev_t dev, char *query, uint32 flags);
struct dirent *fs_read_query(DIR *dirp);
int             fs_close_query(DIR *dirp);
```

Although the API seems embarrassingly simple, it interfaces to a very powerful mechanism. Using a query, a program can use the file system as a database to locate information on criteria other than its fixed location in a hierarchy.

The `fs_open_query()` argument takes a device argument indicating which volume to perform the query on, a string representing the query, and a (currently unused) `flags` argument. The file system uses the query string to find the list of files that match the expression. Each file that matches is returned by successive calls to `fs_read_query()`. Unfortunately the information returned is not enough to get the full path name of the file. The C API is lacking in this regard and needs a function to convert a `dirent` struct into a full path name. The conversion from a `dirent` to a full path name is possible in the BeOS C++ API, although it is not on most versions of Unix.

The C API for queries also does not support live queries. This is unfortunate, but the mechanism to send updates to live queries is inherently C++ based. Although wrappers could be provided to encapsulate the C++ code, there was not sufficient motivation to do so. The C interface to queries was written to support primitive test applications during the debugging phase (before the C++ API was coded) and to allow access to extended BFS features from C programs. Further work to make the C interface to queries more useful will probably be done in the future.

Volume Functions

This final group of C language interfaces provides a way to find out the device-id of a file, iterate over the list of available device-ids, and obtain information about the volume represented by a device-id. The three functions are

```
dev_t dev_for_path(char *path);
int   fs_stat_dev(dev_t dev, fs_info *info);
dev_t next_dev(int32 *pos);
```

The first function, dev_for_path(), returns the device-id of the volume that contains the file referred to by path. There is nothing special about this call; it is just a convenience call that is a wrapper around the POSIX function stat().

The fs_stat_dev() function returns information about the volume identified by the device-id specified. The information returned is similar to a stat structure but contains fields such as the total number of blocks of the device, how many are used, the type of file system on the volume, and flags indicating what features the file system supports (queries, indices, attributes, etc.). This is the function used to get the information printed by a command-line tool like df.

The next_dev() function allows a program to iterate over all device-ids. The pos argument is a pointer to an integer, which should be initialized to zero before the first call to next_dev(). When there are no more device-ids to return, next_dev() returns an error code. Using this routine, it is easy to iterate over all the mounted volumes, get their device-ids, and then do something for or with that volume (e.g., perform a query, get the volume info of the volume, etc.).

POSIX API and C Summary

The C APIs provided by the BeOS cover all the standard POSIX file I/O, and the extensions have a very POSIX-ish feel to them. The desire to keep the API familiar drove the design of the extension APIs. The functions provided allow C programs to access most of the features provided by the BeOS with a minimum of fuss.

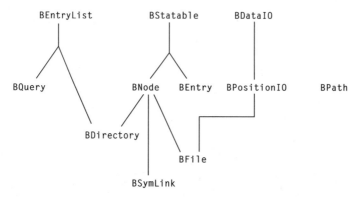

Figure 11-1   The BeOS C++ Storage Kit class hierarchy.

11.2   The C++ API

The BeOS C++ API for manipulating files and performing I/O suffered a trau-
matic birthing process. Many forces drove the design back and forth between the extremes of POSIX-dom and Macintosh-like file handling. The
API changed many times, the class hierarchy mutated just as many times,
and with only two weeks to go before shipping, the API went through one
more spasmodic change. This tumultuous process resulted from trying to
appeal to too many different desires. In the end it seemed that no one was
particularly pleased. Although the API is functional and not overly burden-
some to use, each of the people involved in the design would have done it
slightly differently, and some parts of the API still seem quirky at times. The
difficulties that arose were never in the implementation but rather in the
design: how to structure the classes and what features to provide in each.

This section will discuss the design issues of the class hierarchy and try to
give a flavor for the difficulty of designing a C++ API for file access.

The Class Hierarchy

Figure 11-1 shows the C++ Storage Kit class hierarchy. All three of the base
classes are pure virtual classes. That is, they only define the base level of
features for all of their derived classes, but they do not implement any of the
features. A program would never instantiate any of these classes directly;
it would only instantiate one of the derived classes. The BPath class stands
on its own and can be used in the construction of other objects in the main
hierarchy. Our description of the class hierarchy focuses on the relationships
of the classes and their overall structure instead of the programming details.

The Concepts

The C++ API is grounded in two basic concepts: an *entry* and a *node*. An entry is a handle that refers to a file by its location in the file system hierarchy. An entry is abstract in that it refers to a named entry regardless of whether it is a file or directory. An entry need not actually exist. For example, if an editor is about to save the new file /SomeDisk/file.c, it would create an entry to refer to that file name, but the entry does not exist until the program creates it. An entry can take several forms in the C++ API: a path name, an entry_ref, or a BEntry object. Each of these items has different properties and behaviors.

A node is a handle that refers to the data contained in a file. The concept of a node is, in POSIX terms, a file descriptor. In other words, a node is a handle that allows a program to read and write the data (and attributes) of a named entry in the file system. A node can take several forms in the C++ API, including a BNode, BDirectory, BSymLink, and BFile.

The key distinction between entries and nodes is that entries operate on the file as a whole and data about a file or directory. Nodes operate on the contents of an entry. An entry is a reference to a named object in the file system hierarchy (that may not exist yet), and a node is a handle to the contents of an entry that does exist.

This distinction in functionality may seem unusual. It is natural to ask, Why can't a BEntry object access the data in the file it refers to, and why can't a BFile rename itself? The difference between the name of an object in the file system (an entry) and its contents (a node) is significant, and there can be no union of the two. A program can open a file name, and if it refers to a real file, the file is opened. Immediately after opening that file, the file name is stale. That is, once a file name is created or opened, the file name can change, making the original name stale. Although the name of a file is static most of the time, the connection between the name and the contents is tenuous and can change at any time. If a file descriptor was able to return its name, the name could change immediately, making the information obsolete. Conversely, if a BEntry object could also access the data referred to by its name, the name of the underlying object could change in between writes to the BEntry and that would cause the writes to end up in the contents of two different files. The desire to avoid returning stale information and the headaches that it can cause drove the separation of entries and nodes in the C++ API.

The Entries

There are three entry-type objects: BPath, entry_ref, and BEntry.

BPath

C++ is a great language for encapsulating a simple concept with a nice object. The BPath object is a good example of encapsulating a path name in a C++ object. The BPath object allows a programmer to construct path names without worrying about memory allocation or string manipulation. The BPath object can

- concatenate path names together
- strip off the leaf of a full path name
- return only the leaf
- verify that the path name refers to a valid file

These are not sophisticated operations, but having them in a single convenient object is helpful (even to incorrigible Unix hackers). The BPath object offers convenient methods for dealing with path names that manage the details of memory allocation and string manipulation.

entry_ref

A path name is the most basic way to refer to a file by its location. It is explicit, users understand it, and it can be safely stored on disk. The downside of path names is that they are fragile: if a program stores a path name and any component of the file name changes, the path name will break. Whether or not you like to use path names seems to boil down to whether or not you like programming the Macintosh operating system. POSIX zealots cannot imagine any other mechanism for referring to files, while Macintosh zealots cannot imagine how a program can operate when it cannot find the files it needs.

The typical argument when discussing the use of path names goes something like this:

"If my program stores a full path name and some portion of the path changes, then my program is broken."
"Don't store full path names. Store them relative to the current directory."
"But then how do I communicate a path name to another program that may have a different current directory?"
"Ummmmm ... "

The flip side of this argument goes something like this:

"I have a configuration file that is bad and causes your program to crash. I renamed it to config.bad, but because you don't use path names your program still references the bad config file."
"Then you should throw the file away."
"But I don't want to throw it away. I need to save it because I want to find out what is wrong. How can I make your program stop referencing this file?"
"Ummmmm ... "

In various forms these two arguments repeated themselves far too many times. There was no way that we could devise that would appeal to both camps. Programmers that want to store a direct handle to a file (essentially its i-node number) want nothing to do with path names. Programmers that only understand path names cannot imagine storing something that a user has no knowledge of.

Further technical issues arose as well. One concern that arose was the difficulty of enforcing file security if user programs were allowed to pass i-node numbers directly to the file system. Another more serious problem is that i-node numbers in BFS are simply disk addresses, and allowing user programs to load arbitrary i-node numbers opens a gaping hole that incorrect or malicious programs could use to crash the file system.

Our compromise solution to this thorny problem, the entry_ref structure, is a mixture of both styles. An entry_ref stores the name of a file and the i-node of the directory that contains the file. The name stored in the entry_ref is only the name of the file in the directory, not a full path name. The entry_ref structure solves the first argument because if the directory's location in the file system hierarchy changes, the entry_ref is still valid. It also solves the second argument because the name stored allows users to rename a file to prevent it from being used. There are still problems, of course: If a directory is renamed to prevent using any of the files in it, the entry_ref will still refer to the old files. The other major problem is that entry_refs still require loading arbitrary i-nodes.

The entry_ref feature did not please any of us as being "ideal" or "right." But the need to ship a product made us swallow the bitter pill of compromise. Interestingly the use of entry_refs was almost dropped near the end of the design when the Macintosh-style programmers capitulated and decided that path names would not be so bad. Even more interesting was that the Unix-style programmers also capitulated, and both sides wound up making the exact opposite arguments that they originally made. Fortunately we decided that it was best to leave the design as it stood since it was clear that neither side could be "right."

BEntry

The third entry-type object is a BEntry. A BEntry is a C++ object that is very similar to an entry_ref. A BEntry has access to information about the object (its size, creation time, etc.) and can modify them. A BEntry can also remove itself, rename itself, and move itself to another directory.

A program would use a BEntry if it wanted to perform operations on a file (not the contents of the file, but the entire file). The BEntry is the workhorse of the C++ API for manipulating information about a file.

The Node Object: BNode

Underlying the BNode object is a POSIX-style file descriptor. The BNode object does not actually implement any file I/O functions, but it does implement attribute calls. The reason for this is that both BDirectory and BFile derive from BNode, and a directory cannot be written to as can a file. A BNode only encompasses the functionality that all file descriptors share, regardless of their type.

The BNode object primarily allows access to the attributes of a file. A program can access the contents of the entry using a derived object such as BFile or BDirectory (discussed later). A BNode also allows a program to lock access to a node so that no other modifications are made until the program unlocks the node (or it exits). A BNode is simple, and the derived classes implement most of the functionality.

BEntryList

As we saw in the C API, the set of functions to iterate over a directory, the attributes of a file, and the results of a query are all very similar. The BEntryList object is a pure virtual class that abstracts the process of iterating through a list of entries. The BDirectory and BQuery objects implement the specifics for their respective type of object.

The three interesting methods defined by BEntryList are GetNextEntry, GetNextRef, and GetNextDirents. These routines return the next entry in a directory as a BEntry object, an entry_ref struct, or a dirent struct. Each of these routines performs the same task, but returns the information in different forms. The GetNextDirents() method is but a thin wrapper around the same underlying system call that readdir() uses. The GetNextRef() function returns an entry_ref structure that encapsulates the directory entry. The entry_ref structure is more immediately usable by C++ code, although there is a slight performance penalty to create the structure. GetNextEntry() returns a full-fledged BEntry object, which involves opening a file descriptor for the directory containing the entry and getting information about the file. These tasks make GetNextEntry() the slowest of the three accessor functions.

The abstract BEntryList object defines the mechanism to iterate over a set of files. Derived classes implement concrete functionality for directories and queries. The API defined by BEntryList shares some similarities with the POSIX directory-style functions, although BEntryList is capable of returning more sophisticated (and useful) information about each entry.

BQuery

The first derived class from BEntryList is BQuery. A query in the BeOS is presented as a list of files that match an expression about the attributes of the files. Viewing a query as a list of files makes BQuery a natural descendent of BEntryList that allows iterating over a set of files. BQuery implements the accessor functions so that they return the successive results of a query.

There are two interfaces for specifying the query expression. The first method accepts an expression string using infix notation, much like an expression in C or C++. The other method works with a stack-based postfix notation interface. The infix string name = foo.c can also be expressed as this sequence of postfix operations:

```
push attribute "name"
push string "foo.c"
push operator =
```

The BQuery object internally converts the postfix stack-based operators to an infix string, which is passed to the kernel.

The BQuery object has a method that allows a programmer to specify a port to send update messages to. Setting this port establishes that a query should be live (i.e., updates are sent as the set of files matching a query changes over time). The details of ports are relatively unimportant except that they provide a place for a program to receive messages. In the case of live queries, a file system will send messages to the port informing the program of changes to the query.

BStatable

The next pure virtual base class, BStatable, defines the set of operations that a program can perform on the statistical information about an entry or node in the file system. The methods provided by a BStatable class are

- determine the type of node referred to (file, directory, or symbolic link, etc.)
- get/set a node's owner, group, and permissions
- get/set the node's creation, modification, and access times
- get the size of the node's data (not counting attributes)

The BEntry and BNode objects derive from BStatable and implement the specifics for both entries and nodes. It is important to note that the methods defined by a BStatable object work on both entries and nodes. This may at first seem like a violation of the principles discussed earlier in this section, but it does not violate the tenets we previously set forth because the information that BStatable can get or set always stays with a file regardless of whether the file is moved, renamed, or removed.

BEntry Revisited

Discussed earlier, the BEntry object derives from BStatable. The BEntry object adds to BStatable the ability to rename the entry it refers to, move the entry, and remove the entry. The BEntry object contains a file descriptor for the directory containing a file and the name of the file. BEntry is the primary object used to manipulate files when operating on the file as a whole, such as renaming it.

BNode Revisited

Also discussed earlier, the BNode object has at its core a file descriptor. There are no file I/O methods defined in BNode because of its place in the class hierarchy. The subclass BFile implements the necessary file I/O methods on the file descriptor contained in BNode. BNode implements attribute methods that can

- read an attribute
- write an attribute
- remove an attribute
- iterate over the list of attributes
- get extended information about an attribute

The BNode object can also lock a node so that no other access to it will succeed. BNode can also force the file system to flush any buffered data it may have that belongs to the file. In and of itself, the BNode object is of limited usefulness. If a program only cared to manipulate the attributes of a file, to lock the file, or to flush its data to disk, then a BNode is sufficient; otherwise a derived class is more appropriate.

BDirectory

Derived from both BEntryList and BNode, a BDirectory object uses the iteration functions defined by BEntryList and the file descriptor provided by BNode to allow a program to iterate over the contents of a directory. In addition to its primary function as a way to iterate over the contents of a directory, BDirectory also has methods to

- test for the existence of a name
- create a file
- create a directory
- create a symbolic link

Unlike other BNode-derived objects, a BDirectory object can create a BEntry object from itself. You may question if this breaks the staleness problem discussed previously. The ability for a BDirectory object to create a BEntry for itself depends on the fact that every directory in a file system in the BeOS has entries for "." (the current directory) and ".." (the parent of the current directory). These names are symbolic instead of references to particular names or i-node numbers, which avoids the staleness problem.

BSymLink

The symbolic link object, BSymLink, derives from BNode and allows access to the contents of the symbolic link, *not* the object it points to. In most cases a program would never need to instantiate a BSymLink object because symbolic links are irrelevant to most programs that simply need to read and write data. However, some programs (such as Tracker, the BeOS file browser) need to display something different when an entry turns out to be a symbolic link. The BSymLink class provides methods that allow a program to read the contents of the link (i.e., the path it "points" to) and to modify the path contained in the link. Little else is needed or provided for in BSymLink.

BDataIO/BPositionIO

These two abstract classes are not strictly part of the C++ file hierarchy; instead they come from a support library of general classes used by other Be objects. BDataIO declares only the basic I/O functions Read() and Write(). BPositionIO declares an additional set of functions (ReadAt(), WriteAt(), Seek(), and Position()) for objects that can keep track of the current position in the I/O buffer. These two classes only define the API. They implement nothing. Derived classes implement the specifics of I/O for a particular type of object (file, memory, networking, etc.).

BFile

The last object in our tour of this class hierarchy is the BFile object. BFile derives from BNode and BPositionIO, which means that it can perform real I/O to the contents of a file as well as manipulate some of the statistical information about the file (owner, permissions, etc.). BFile is the object that programs use to perform file I/O.

Although it seems almost anticlimactic for such an important object, there is not much significant to say about BFile. It implements the BDataIO/BPostionIO functions in the context of a file descriptor that refers to a regular file. It also implements the pure virtual methods of BStatable/BNode to allow getting and setting of the statistical information about files. BFile offers no frills and provides straightforward access to performing file I/O on the underlying file descriptor.

Node Monitoring

The final component of the user-level API is known as the node monitor. Although the node monitor is not part of the class hierarchy defined above, it is still part of the C++ API. The node monitor is a service that lets programs ask to receive notification of changes in a file system. You can ask to be told when a change is made to

- the contents of a directory
- the name of an entry
- any properties of an entry (i.e., the stat information)
- any attribute of an entry

Application programs use the node monitor to dynamically respond to changes made by a user. The BeOS Web browser, NetPositive, stores its bookmarks as files in a directory and monitors the directory for changes to update its bookmark menu. Other programs monitor data files so that if changes are made to the data file, the program can refresh the in-memory version being used. Many other uses of the node monitor are possible. These examples just demonstrate two possibilities.

Through a wrapper API around the lower-level node monitor, a program can also receive notifications when

- a volume is mounted
- a volume is unmounted

In the same way that a query sends notifications to a port for live updates, the node monitor sends messages to a port when something interesting happens. An "interesting" event is one that matches the changes a program expresses interest in. For example, a program can ask to only receive notifications of changes to the attributes of a file; if the monitored file were renamed, no notification would be sent.

The node monitor watches a specific file or entry. If a program wishes to receive notifications for changes to any file in a directory, it must issue a node monitor request for all the files in that directory. If a program only wishes to receive notifications for file creations or deletions in a directory, then it only needs to watch the directory.

There are no sophisticated classes built up around the node monitor. Programs access the node monitor through two simple C++ functions, `watch_node()` and `stop_watching()`.

11.3   Using the API

Although our discussion of the BeOS C++ Storage Kit provides a nice high-level overview, it doesn't give a flavor for the details of programming the API.

A concrete example of using the BeOS Storage Kit will help to close the loop and give some immediacy to the API.

In this example, we'll touch upon most of the features of the BeOS Storage Kit to write a program that

- creates a keyword index
- iterates through a directory of files, synthesizing keywords for each file
- writes the keywords as an attribute of the file
- performs a query on the keyword index to find files that contain a certain keyword

Although the example omits a few details (such as how to synthesize a short list of keywords) and some error checking, it does demonstrate a real-life use of the Storage Kit classes.

The Setup

Before generating any keywords or adding attributes, our example program first creates the keyword index. This step is necessary to ensure that all keyword attributes will be indexed. Any program that intends to use an index should always create the index before generating any attributes that need the index.

```
#define INDEX_NAME  "Keyword"

main(int argc, char **argv)
{
    BPath    path(argv[1]);
    dev_t    dev;

    /*
      First we'll get the device handle for the file system
      that this path refers to and then we'll use that to
      create our "Keyword" index.

      Note that no harm is done if the index already exists
      and we create it again.
    */
    dev = dev_for_path(path.Path());
    if (dev < 0)
        exit(5);

    fs_create_index(dev, INDEX_NAME, B_STRING_TYPE, 0);
```

Generating the Attributes

The next phase of the program is to iterate over all the files in the directory referenced by the path. The program does this work in a separate function, generate_keywords(), that main() calls. The main() function passes its BPath object to generate_keywords() to indicate which directory to iterate over.

```
void
generate_keywords(BPath *path)
{
    BDirectory dir;
    entry_ref  ref;

    dir.SetTo(path->Path());
    if (dir.InitCheck() != 0)     /* hmmm, dir doesn't exist? */
        return;

    while(dir.GetNextRef(&ref) == B_NO_ERROR) {
        char *keywords;
        BFile file;

        file.SetTo(&ref, O_RDWR);
        keywords = synthesize_keywords(&file);

        file.WriteAttr(INDEX_NAME,  B_STRING_TYPE, 0,
                       keywords, strlen(keywords)+1);

        free(keywords);
    }
}
```

The first part of the routine initializes the BDirectory object and checks that it refers to a valid directory. The main loop of generate_keywords() iterates on the call to GetNextRef(). Each call to GetNextRef() returns a reference to the next entry in the directory until there are no more entries. The entry_ref object returned by GetNextRef() is used to initialize the BFile object so that the contents of the file can be read.

Next, generate_keywords() calls synthesize_keywords(). Although we omit the details, presumably synthesize_keywords() would read the contents of the file and generate a list of keywords as a string.

After synthesizing the list of keywords, our example program writes those keywords as an attribute of the file using the WriteAttr() function. Writing the keyword attribute also automatically indexes the keywords because the keyword index exists.

One of the nice features of the C++ BFile object is that it will properly dispose of any previous file references each time SetTo() is called, and it automatically cleans up any resources used when it is destroyed. This feature removes the possibility of leaking file descriptors when manipulating many files.

Issuing a Query

The last part of our example shows how to issue a query for files that contain a particular keyword. The setup for issuing the query has few surprises. We construct the predicate for the query, which is a string that contains the expression Keyword = *<word>*. The <word> portion of the query is a string parameter to the function. The use of the asterisks surrounding the query make the expression a substring match.

```
void
do_query(BVolume *vol, char *word)
{
    char     buff[512];
    BQuery   query;
    BEntry   match_entry;
    BPath    path;

    sprintf(buff, "%s = *%s*", INDEX_NAME, word);
    query.SetPredicate(buff);

    query.SetVolume(vol);
    query.Fetch();

    while(query.GetNextEntry(&match_entry) == B_NO_ERROR) {
        match_entry.GetPath(&path);
        printf("%s\n", path.Path());
    }
}
```

The last step to set up the query is to specify what volume to issue the query on using SetPredicate(). To start the query we call Fetch(). Of course, a real program would check for errors from Fetch().

The last phase of the query is to iterate over the results by calling Get-NextEntry(). This is similar to how we iterated over a directory in the generate_keywords() function above. Calling GetNextEntry() instead of GetNextRef() allows us to get at the path of the file that matches the query. For our purposes here, the path is all we are interested in. If the files needed to be opened and read, then calling GetNextRef() might be more appropriate.

The salient point of this example is not the specific case of creating keyword attributes but rather to show the ease with which programs can incorporate these features. With only a few lines of code a program can add attributes and indices, which then gives the ability to issue queries based on those attributes.

11.4   Summary

The two user-level BeOS APIs expose the features supported by the vnode layer of the BeOS and implemented by BFS. The BeOS supports the traditional POSIX file I/O API (with some extensions) and a fully object-oriented C++ API. The C++ API offers access to features such as live queries and node monitoring that cannot be accessed from the traditional C API. The functions accessible only from C are the index functions to iterate over, create, and delete indices.

The design of the C++ API provoked a conflict between those advocating the Macintosh-style approach to dealing with files and those advocating the POSIX style. The compromise solution codified in the BeOS class hierarchy for file I/O is acceptable and works, even if a few parts of the design seem less than ideal.

12

Testing

Often, testing of software is done casually, as an after-thought, and primarily to ensure that there are no glaring bugs. A file system, however, is a critical piece of system software that users must absolutely be able to depend on to safely and reliably store their data. As the primary repository for permanent data on a computer system, a file system must shoulder the heavy burden of 100% reliability. Testing of a file system must be thorough and extremely strenuous. File systems for which testing is done without much thought or care are likely to be unreliable.

It is not possible to issue edicts that dictate exactly how testing should be done, nor is that the point of this chapter. Instead, the aim is to present ways to stress a file system so that as many bugs as possible can be found before shipping the system.

12.1 The Supporting Cast

Before even designing a test plan and writing tests, a file system should be written with the aim that user data should never be corrupted. In practice this means several things:

- Make liberal use of runtime consistency checks. They are inexpensive relative to the cost of disk access and therefore essentially free.
- Verifying correctness of data structures before using them helps detect problems early.
- Halting the system upon detecting corruption is preferable to continuing without checking.

■ Adding useful debugging messages and writing good debugging tools saves lots of time when diagnosing problems.

Runtime checks of data structures are often disabled in a production piece of code for performance reasons. Fortunately in a file system the cost of disk access so heavily outweighs CPU time that it is foolhardy to disable runtime checks, even in a production system. In practice BFS saw a negligible performance difference between running with runtime checks enabled or disabled. The benefit is that even in a production system you can be reasonably assured that if an unforeseen error happens the system will detect it and prevent corruption by halting the system.

Verifying data structures before their use proved to be an invaluable debugging aid in BFS. For example, at every file system entry point any i-node data structure that is passed in is verified before use. The i-node data structure is central to the correct operation of the system. Therefore a simple macro or function call to verify an i-node is extremely useful. For example, in BFS the macro CHECK_INODE() validates the i-node magic number, the size of the file, the i-node size, and an in-memory pointer associated with the i-node. Numerous times during the development of BFS this checking caught and prevented disk corruption due to wild pointers. Halting the system then allowed closer inspection with the debugger to determine what had happened.

12.2   Examples of Data Structure Verification

BFS uses a data structure called a data_stream to enumerate which disk blocks belong to a file. The data_stream structure uses extents to describe runs of blocks that belong to a file. The indirect and double-indirect blocks have slightly different constraints, leading to a great deal of complexity when manipulating the data_stream structure. The data_stream structure is the most critical structure for storing user data. If a data_stream refers to incorrect disk locations or improperly accesses a portion of the disk, then user data will become corrupted. There are numerous checks that the file system performs on the data_stream structure to ensure its correctness:

■ Is the current file position out of range?
■ Is there a valid file block for the current file position?
■ Are there too few blocks allocated for the file size?
■ Are blocks in the middle of the file unexpectedly free?

Each access to a file translates the current file position to a disk block address. Most of the above checks are performed in the routine that does the conversion from file position to disk block address. The double-indirect blocks of a file receive an additional set of consistency checks because of the extra constraints that apply to them (each extent is a fixed size, etc.). Further checking of the data_stream structure is done when changing a file size (either growing or shrinking).

In addition to the above consistency checks, the code that manipulates the data_stream structure must also error-check the results of other BFS functions. For example, when growing a file, the block number returned by the block allocation functions is sanity-checked to ensure that bugs in other parts of the system do not cause damage. This style of defensive programming may seem unnecessary, but cross-checking the correctness of other modules helps to ensure that bugs in one part of the system will not cause another module to crash or write to improper locations on the disk.

BFS also checks for *impossible* conditions in a large number of situations. Impossible conditions are those that should not happen but invariably do. For example, when locating a data block in a file data_stream, it is possible to encounter a block_run that refers to block zero instead of a valid block number. If the file system did not check for this situation (which should of course never happen), it could allow a program to write over the file system superblock and thus destroy crucial file system information. If the check were not done and the superblock overwritten, detecting the error would likely not happen for some time, long after the damage was done. Impossible situations almost always arise while debugging a system, and thus checking for them even when it seems unlikely is always beneficial.

When the file system detects an inconsistent state it is best to simply halt the file system or at least a particular thread of execution. BFS accomplishes this by entering a routine that prints a panic message and then loops infinitely. Halting the system (or at least a particular thread of execution) allows a programmer to enter a debugger and examine the state of the system. In a production environment, it usually renders a locked-up system, and while that is rather unacceptable, it is preferable to a corrupted hard disk.

12.3   Debugging Tools

Early development of a file system can be done at the user level by building a test harness that hooks up the core functionality of the file system to a set of simple API calls that a test program can call. Developing a test environment allows the file system developer to use source-level debugging tools to get basic functionality working and to quickly prototype the design. Working at the user level to debug a file system is much preferable to the typical kernel development cycle, which involves rebooting after a crash and usually does not afford the luxuries of user-level source debugging.

Although the debugging environment of every system has its own peculiarities, there is almost always a base level of functionality. The most basic debugging functionality is the ability to dump memory and to get a stack backtrace that shows which functions were called before the current state.

The debugging environment of the BeOS kernel is based around a primitive kernel monitor that can be entered through a special keystroke or a special non-maskable interrupt (NMI) button. Once in the monitor, a programmer can examine the state of the system and in general poke around. This monitor environment supports dynamically added debugger commands. The file system adds a number of commands to the monitor that print various file system data structures in an easy-to-read format (as opposed to a raw hex dump).

The importance of good debugging tools is impossible to overstate. Many times during the development of BFS an error would occur in testing, and the ability to enter a few commands to examine the state of various structures made finding the error—or at least diagnosing the problem—much easier. Without such tools it would have been necessary to stare at pages of code and try to divine what went wrong (although that still happened, it could have been much worse).

In total the number of file system debugging commands amounted to 18 functions, of which 7 were crucial. The most important commands were

- dump a superblock
- dump an i-node
- dump a `data_stream`
- dump the embedded attributes of an i-node
- find a block in the cache (by memory address or block number)
- list the open file handles of a thread
- find a vnode-id in all open files

This set of tools enabled quick examination of the most important data structures. If an i-node was corrupt, a quick dump of the structure showed which fields were damaged, and usually a few more commands would reveal how the corruption happened.

12.4   Data Structure Design for Debugging

Beyond good tools, several other factors assisted in debugging BFS. Almost all file system data structures contained a magic number that identified the type of data structure. The order of data structure members was chosen to minimize the effects of corruption and to make it easy to detect when corruption did occur. Magic numbers come early in a data structure so that it is easy to detect what a chunk of memory is and to allow a data structure to survive a small overrun of whatever exists in memory before the data structure. For example, if memory contains

String data	I-Node data

and the string overwrites an extra byte or two, the majority of the i-node data will survive, although its magic number will be corrupted. The corrupted magic number is easily detected and the type of corruption usually quite obvious (a zero byte or some ASCII characters). This helps prevent writing damaged data to disk and aids in diagnosing what went wrong (the contents of the string usually finger the guilty party and then the offending code is easily fixed).

A very typical type of file system bug is to confuse blocks of metadata and to write an i-node to a block that belongs to a directory or vice versa. Using magic numbers, these types of corruption are easy to detect. If a block has the magic number of a directory header block, or a B+tree page on disk has the contents of an i-node instead, it becomes much easier to trace back through the code to see how the error occurred.

Designing data structure layout with a modicum of forethought can help debugging and make many types of common errors both easy to detect and easy to correct. Because a file system is a complex piece of software, debugging one is often quite difficult. The errors that do occur only happen after lengthy runtimes and are not easily reproducible. Magic numbers, intelligent layout of data members, and good tools for examining data structures all help considerably in diagnosing and fixing file system bugs.

12.5   Types of Tests

There are three types of tests we can run against a file system: synthetic tests, real-world tests, and end user testing. Synthetic tests are written to expose defects in a particular area (file creation, deletion, etc.) or to test the limits of the system (filling the disk, creating many files in a single directory, etc.). Real-world tests stress the system in different ways than synthetic tests do and offer the closest approximation of real-world use. Finally, end user testing is a matter of using the system in all the unusual ways that a real user might in an attempt to confuse the file system.

Synthetic Tests

Running synthetic tests is attractive because they offer a controlled environment and can be configured to write known data patterns, which facilitates debugging. Each of the synthetic tests generated random patterns of file system traffic. To ensure repeatability, all tests would print the random seed they used and supported a command-line option to specify the random seed. Each test also supported a variety of configurable parameters to enable modifying the way the test program ran. This is important because otherwise running the tests degenerates into repeating a narrow set of access patterns. Writing synthetic tests that support a variety of configurable parameters is extremely important to successful testing.

The synthetic test suite written to stress BFS consisted of the following programs:

- Disk fragmenter
- Muck files
- Big file
- News test
- Rename test
- Random I/O test

The disk fragmenter would create files of either random or fixed size, some number per directory, and when it received an out-of-disk space error it would go back and delete every other file it created. In the case of BFS this perfectly fragmented a disk, and by adjusting the size of the created files to match the file system block size, it was possible to leave the disk with every other disk block allocated. This was a good test to test the block allocation policies. The disk fragmenter had a number of options to specify the depth of the hierarchy it created, the number of files per directory, the ranges of file sizes it created, and the amount of data written per file (either random or fixed). Varying the parameters provided a wide range of I/O patterns.

The muck file program created a directory hierarchy as a workspace and spawned several threads to create, rename, write, and delete files. These threads would ascend and descend through the directory hierarchy, randomly operating on files. As with the disk fragmenter, the number of files per directory, the size of the files, and so on were all configurable parameters. This test is a good way to age a file system artificially.

The big file test would write random or fixed-size chunks to a file, growing it until the disk filled up. This simulated appending to a log file and streaming large amounts of data to disk, depending on the chunk size. This test stressed the data_stream manipulation routines because it was the only test that would reliably write files large enough to require double-indirect blocks. The big file test also wrote a user-specified pattern to the file, which made detecting file corruption easier (if the pattern 0xbf showed up in an i-node it was obvious what happened). This test supported a configurable chunk size for each write, which helped test dribbling data to a file over a long period of time versus fire hosing data to disk as fast as possible.

The news test was a simulation of what an Internet news server would do. The Internet news system is notoriously stressful for a file system, and thus a synthetic program to simulate the effects of a news server is a useful test. The news test is similar in nature to the muck file test but is more focused on the type of activity done by a news server. A configurable number of writer threads create files at random places in a large hierarchy. To delete files, a configurable number of remover threads delete files older than a given age. This test often exposed race conditions in the file system.

The rename test is a simple shell script that creates a hierarchy of directories all initially named aa. In each directory another script is run that renames the subdirectory from aa all the way to zz and then back to aa. This may seem like a trivial test, but in a system such as the BeOS that sends notifications for updates such as renames, this test generated a lot of traffic. In addition, when run in combination with the other tests, it also exposed several race conditions in acquiring access to file system data structures.

The random I/O test was geared at exercising the data_stream structure as well as the rest of the I/O system. The motivation behind it was that most programs perform simple sequential I/O of fixed block sizes, and thus not all possible alignments and boundary cases receive adequate testing. The goal of the random I/O test was to test how well the file system handled programs that would seek to random locations in the file and then perform randomly sized I/O at that position in the file. This tested situations such as reading the last part of the last block in the indirect blocks of a file and then reading a small amount of the first double-indirect block. To verify the correctness of the reads, the file is written as a series of increasing integers whose value is XORed with a seed value. This generates interesting data patterns (i.e., they are easily identifiable) and it allows easy verification of any portion of data in a file simply by knowing its offset and the seed value. This proved invaluable to flushing out bugs in the data_stream code that surfaced only when reading chunks of data at file positions not on a block boundary with a length that was not a multiple of the file system block size. To properly stress the file system it was necessary to run the random I/O test after running the disk fragmenter or in combination with the other tests.

Beyond the above set of tests, several smaller tests were written to examine other corner conditions in the file system. Tests to create large file names, hierarchies that exceed the maximum allowable path name length, and tests that just kept adding attributes to a file until there was no more disk space all helped stress the system in various ways to find its limitations. Tests that ferret out corner conditions are necessary since, even though there may be a well-defined file name length limitation (255 bytes in BFS), a subtle bug in the system may prevent it from working.

Although it was not done with BFS, using file system traces to simulate disk activity is another possibility for testing. Capturing the I/O event log of an active system and then replaying the activity borders between a real-world test and a synthetic test. Replaying the trace may not duplicate all the factors that existed while generating the trace. For example, memory usage may be different, which could affect what is cached and what isn't. Another difficulty with file system traces is that although the disk activity is real, it is only a single data point out of all possible orderings of a set of disk activity. Using a wide variety of traces captured under different scenarios is important if trace playback is used to test a file system.

Real-World Tests

Real-world tests are just that—programs that real users run and that perform real work. The following tasks are common and produce a useful amount of file system activity:

- Handling a full Internet news feed
- Copying large hierarchies
- Archiving a large hierarchy of files
- Unarchiving a large archive
- Compressing files
- Compiling source code
- Capturing audio and/or video to disk
- Reading multiple media streams simultaneously

Of these tests, the most stressful by far is handling an Internet news feed. The volume of traffic of a full Internet news feed is on the order of 2 GB per day spread over several hundred thousand messages (in early 1998). The INN software package stores each message in a separate file and uses the file system hierarchy to manage the news hierarchy. In addition to the large number of files, the news system also uses several large databases stored in files that contain overview and history information about all the active articles in the news system. The amount of activity, the sizes of the files, and the sheer number of files involved make running INN perhaps the most brutal test any file system can endure.

Running the INN software and accepting a full news feed is a significant task. Unfortunately the INN software does not yet run on BeOS, and so this test was not possible (hence the reason for creating the synthetic news test program). A file system able to support the real INN software and to do so without corrupting the disk is a truly mature file system.

The other tests in the list have a varying degree and style of disk activity. Most of the tests are trivial to organize and to execute in a loop with a shell script. To test BFS we created and extracted archives of the BeOS installation, compressed the BeOS installation archives, compiled the entire BeOS source tree, captured video streams to disk, and played back multitrack audio files for real-time mixing. To vary the tests, different source archives were used for the archive tests. In addition we often ran synthetic tests at the same time as real-world tests. Variety is important to ensure that the largest number of disk I/O patterns possible are tested.

End User Testing

Another important but hard-to-quantify component is end user blackbox testing. End user testing for BFS consisted of letting a rabid tester loose on the system to try and corrupt the hard disk using whatever means possible (aside from writing a program to write to the raw hard disk device). This sort of testing usually focused on using the graphical user interface to manipulate files by hand. The by-hand nature of this testing makes it difficult to quantify and reproduce. However, I found that this sort of testing was invaluable to producing a reliable system. Despite the difficulty that there is in reproducing the exact sequence of events, a thorough and diligent tester can provide enough details to piece together events leading up to a crash. Fortunately in testing BFS our end user tester was amazingly devious and found endless clever ways to trash the file system. Surprisingly, most of the errors discovered were during operations that a seasoned Unix veteran would never imagine doing. For example, once I watched our lead tester start copying a large file hierarchy, begin archiving the hierarchy being created while removing it, and at the same time chopping up the archive file into many small files. This particular tester found myriad combinations of ways to run standard Unix tools, such as cp, mv, tar, and chop, that would not perform any useful work except for finding file system bugs. A good testing group that is clever and able to reliably describe what they did leading up to a crash is a big boon to the verification of a file system. BFS would not be nearly as robust as it is today were it not for this type of testing.

12.6   Testing Methodology

To properly test a file system there needs to be a coherent test plan. A detailed test plan document is not necessary, but unless some thought is given to the process, it is likely to degenerate into a random shotgun approach that yields spotty coverage. By describing the testing that BFS underwent, I hope to offer a practical guide to testing. It is by no means the only approach nor necessarily the best—it is simply one that resulted in a stable, shipping file system less than one year after initial coding began.

The implementation of BFS began as a user-level program with a test harness that allowed writing simple tests. No one else used the file system, and testing consisted of making changes and running the test programs until I felt confident of the changes. Two main programs were used during this phase. The first program was an interactive shell that provided a front end to most file system features via simple commands. Some of the commands were the basic file system primitives: create, delete, rename, read, and write. Other commands offered higher-level tests that encapsulated the lower-level primitives. The second test program was a dedicated test that would randomly create and delete files. This program checked the results of its run to guarantee that it ran correctly. These two programs in combination accounted for the first several months of development.

In addition, there were other test harnesses for important data structures so that they could be tested in isolation. The block bitmap allocator and the B+tree code both had separate test harnesses that allowed easy testing separate from the rest of the file system. Changes made to the B+tree code often underwent several days of continuous randomized testing that would insert and delete hundreds of millions of keys. This yielded a much better overall tested system than just testing the file system as a whole.

After the first three months of development it became necessary to enable others to use the BFS, so BFS graduated to become a full-time member of kernel space. At this stage, although it was not feature complete (by far!), BFS had enough functionality for use as a traditional-style file system. As expected, the file system went from a level of apparent stability in my own testing to a devastating number of bugs the minute other people were allowed to use it. With immediate feedback from the testers, the file system often saw three or four fixes per day. After several weeks of continual refinements and close work with the testing group, the file system reached a milestone: it was now possible for other engineers to use it to work on their own part of the operating system without immediate fear of corruption.

At this stage the testing group could still corrupt the file system, but it took a reasonable amount of effort (i.e., more than 15 minutes). Weighing the need for fixing bugs versus implementing new features presented a difficult choice. As needed features lagged, their importance grew until they outweighed the known bugs and work had to shift to implementing new features instead of fixing bugs. Then, as features were finished, work shifted back to fixing bugs. This process iterated many times.

During this period the testing group was busy implementing the tests described above. Sometimes there were multiple versions of tests because there are two file system APIs on the BeOS (the traditional POSIX-style API and an object-oriented C++ API). I encouraged different testers to write similar tests since I felt that it would be good to expose the file system to as many different approaches to I/O as possible.

An additional complexity in testing was to arrange as many I/O configurations as possible. To expose race conditions it is useful to test fast CPUs with slow hard disks, slow CPUs with fast hard disks, as well as the normal combinations (fast CPUs and fast hard disks). Other arrangements with multi-CPU machines and different memory configurations were also constructed. The general motivation was that race conditions often depend on obscure relationships between processor and disk speeds, how much I/O is done (influenced by the amount of memory in the system), and of course how many CPUs there are in the system. Constructing such a large variety of test configurations was difficult but necessary.

Testing the file system in low-disk-space conditions proved to be the most difficult task of all. Running out of disk space is trivial, but encountering the error in all possible code paths is quite difficult. We found that BFS required running heavy stress tests while very low on disk space for many hours to try to explore as many code paths as possible. In practice some bugs only surfaced after running three or four synthetic tests simultaneously for 16 hours or more. The lesson is that simply bumping into a limit may not be adequate testing. It may be necessary to ram head-on into the limit for days on end to properly flush out all the possible bugs.

Before the first release of BFS, the system stabilized to the point where corrupting a hard disk took significant effort and all the real-world tests would run without corruption for 24 hours or more. At first customer ship, the file system had one known problem that we were unable to pinpoint but that would only happen in rare circumstances. By the second release (two months later) several more bugs were fixed, and the third release (another two months later) saw the file system able to withstand several days of serious abuse. That is not to say that no bugs exist in the file system. Even now occasionally an obscure bug appears, but at this point (approximately 16 months after the initial development of the file system), bugs are not common and the system is generally believed to be robust and stable. More importantly, corrupted file systems have been thankfully rare; the bugs that surface are often just debugging checks that halt the system when they detect data structure inconsistencies (before writing them to disk).

12.7 Summary

The real lesson of this chapter is not the specific testing done in the development of BFS, but rather that testing early and often is the surest way to guarantee that a file system becomes robust. Throwing a file system into the gaping jaws of a rabid test group is the only way to shake out the system. Balancing the need to implement features with the need to have a stable base is difficult. The development of BFS saw that iterating between features and bug-fixing worked well. In the bug-fixing phase, rapid response to bugs and good communication between the testing and development group ensures that the system will mature quickly. Testing a wide variety of CPU, memory, and I/O configurations helps expose the system to as many I/O patterns as possible.

Nothing can guarantee the correctness of a file system. The only way to gain any confidence in a file system is to test it until it can survive the harshest batterings afforded by the test environment. Perhaps the best indicator of the quality of a file system is when the author(s) of the file system are willing to store their own data on their file system and use it for day-to-day use.

Appendix

A File System Construction Kit

A.1 Introduction

Writing a file system from scratch is a formidable task. The difficulty involved often prevents people from experimenting with new ideas. Even modifying an existing file system is not easy because it usually requires running in kernel mode, extra disks, and a spare machine for debugging. These barriers prevent all but the most interested people from exploring file systems.

To make it easier to explore and experiment with file systems, we designed a file system construction kit. The kit runs at the user level and creates a file system within a file. With the kit, a user need not have any special privileges to run their own file system, and debugging is easy using regular source-level debuggers. Under the BeOS and Unix, the kit can also operate on a raw disk device if desired (to simulate more closely how it would run if it were "real").

This appendix is not the full documentation for the file system construction kit. It gives an overview of the data structures and the API of the kit but does not provide the full details of how to modify it. The full documentation can be found in the archive containing the file system construction kit. The archive is available at *http://www.mkp.com/giampaolo/fskit.tar.gz* and *ftp://mkp.com/giampaolo/fskit.tar.gz*.

A.2 Overview

The file system construction kit divides the functionality of a file system into numerous components:

- Superblock
- Block allocation

- I-nodes
- Journaling
- Data streams
- Directories
- File operations (create, rename, remove)

The four most interesting components are block allocation, i-node allocation, data stream management, and directory manipulation. The intent is that each of these components is independent of the others. The independence of each component should make it easy to replace one component with a different implementation and to observe how it affects the rest of the system. The journaling component is optional, and the API only need be filled in if desired.

This file system construction kit does not offer hooks for attributes or indexing. Extending the kit to support those operations is not particularly difficult but would complicate the basic API. The intent of this kit is pedagogical, not commercial, so a laundry list of features is not necessary.

In addition to the core file system components, the kit also provides supporting infrastructure that makes the file system usable. The framework wraps around the file system API and presents a more familiar (i.e., POSIX-like) API that is used by a test harness. The test harness is a program that provides a front end to all the structure. In essence the test harness is a shell that lets users issue commands to perform file system operations.

Wildly different ideas about how to store data in a file system may require changes to the overall structure of the kit. The test harness should still remain useful even with a radically different implementation of the core file system concepts.

The file system implementation provided is intentionally simplistic. The goal was to make it easy to understand, which implies easy-to-follow data structures. We hope that by making the implementation easy to understand, it will also be easy to modify.

A.3   The Data Structures

This kit operates on a few basic data structures. The following paragraphs provide a quick introduction to the data types referred to in Section A.4. Understanding these basic data types will help to understand how the kit functions are expected to behave.

All routines accept a pointer to an fs_info structure. This structure contains all the global state information needed by a file system. Usually the fs_info structure will contain a copy of the superblock and references to data structures needed by the other components. Using an fs_info structure, a file system must be able to reach all the state it keeps stored in memory.

The next most important data structure is the disk_addr. A file system can define a disk_addr any way it needs to since it is primarily an internal data structure not seen by the higher levels of the kit. A disk_addr may be as simple as an unsigned integer, or it may be a full data structure with several fields. A disk_addr must be able to address any position on the disk.

Related to the disk_addr is an inode_addr. If a file system uses disk addresses to locate i-nodes (as is done in BFS), then the inode_addr data type is likely to be the same as a disk_addr. If an inode_addr is an index to an i-node table, then it may just be defined as an integer.

Building on these two basic data types, the fs_inode data structure stores all the information needed by an i-node while it is in use in memory. Using the fs_inode structure, the file system must be able to access all of a file's data and all the information about the file. Without the fs_inode structure there is little that a file system can do. The file system kit makes no distinction between fs_inode structures that refer to files or directories. The file system must manage the differences between files and directories itself.

A.4   The API

The API for each of the components of the kit follows several conventions. Each component has some number of the following routines:

- *create*—The create routine should create the on-disk data structure needed by a component. Some components, such as files and directories, can be created at any time. Other components, such as the block map, can only be created when creating a file system for the first time.
- *init*—The init routine should initialize access to the data structure on a previously created file system. After the init routine for a component, the file system should be ready to access the data structure and anything it contains or refers to.
- *shutdown*—The shutdown routine should finish access to the data structure. After the shutdown routine runs, no more access will be made to the data structure.
- *allocate/free*—These routines should allocate a particular instance of a data structure and free it. For example, the i-node management code has routines to allocate and free individual i-nodes.

In addition to this basic style of API, each component implements additional functions necessary for that component. Overall the API bears a close resemblance to the BeOS vnode layer API (as described in Chapter 10).

The following subsections include rough prototypes of the API. Again, this is not meant as an implementation guide but only as a coarse overview of what the API contains. The documentation included with the file system kit archive contains more specific details.

The Superblock

```
fs_info    fs_create_super_block(dev, volname, numblocks, ...);
fs_info    fs_init_super_block(dev);
int        fs_shutdown_super_block(fs_info);
```

Block Allocation

```
int        fs_create_storage_map(fs_info);
int        fs_init_storage_map(fs_info);
void       fs_shutdown_storage_map(fs_info);
disk_addr  fs_allocate_blocks(fs_info, hint_bnum, len, result_lenptr,
                              flags);
int        fs_free_blocks(fs_info, start_block_num, len);
int        fs_check_blocks(fs_info, start_block_num, len, state);
                                              /* debugging */
```

I-Node Management

```
int        fs_create_inodes(fs_info);
int        fs_init_inodes(fs_info);
void       fs_shutdown_inodes(fs_info);
fs_inode   fs_allocate_inode(fs_info, fs_inode parent, mode);
int        fs_free_inode(bfs_info *bfs, inode_addr ia);
fs_inode   fs_read_inode(fs_info, inode_addr ia);
int        fs_write_inode(fs_info, inode_addr, fs_inode);
```

Journaling

```
int        fs_create_journal(fs_info);
int        fs_init_journal(fs_info);
void       fs_shutdown_journal(fs_info);
j_entry    fs_create_journal_entry(fs_info);
int        fs_write_journal_entry(fs_info, j_entry, block_addr, block);
int        fs_end_journal_entry(fs_info, j_entry);
```

Data Streams

```
int        fs_init_data_stream(fs_info, fs_inode);
int        fs_read_data_stream(fs_info, fs_inode, pos, buf, len);
int        fs_write_data_stream(fs_info, fs_inode, pos, buf, len);
int        fs_set_file_size(fs_info, fs_inode, new_size);
int        fs_free_data_stream(fs_info, fs_inode);
```

Directory Operations

```
int      fs_create_root_dir(fs_info);
int      fs_make_dir(fs_info, fs_inode, name, perms);
int      fs_remove_dir(fs_info, fs_inode, name);
int      fs_opendir(fs_info, fs_inode, void **cookie);
int      fs_readdir(fs_info, fs_inode, void *cookie, long *num,
                    struct dirent *buf, bufsize);
int      fs_closedir(fs_info, fs_inode, void *cookie);
int      fs_rewinddir(fs_info, fs_inode, void *cookie);
                    struct dirent *buf, bufsize);
int      fs_free_dircookie(fs_info, fs_inode, void *cookie);
int      fs_dir_lookup(fs_info, fs_inode, name, vnode_id *result);
int      fs_dir_is_empty(fs_info, fs_inode);
```

File Operations

```
int      fs_create(fs_info, fs_inode dir, name, perms,
                    omode, inode_addr *ia);
int      fs_rename(fs_info, fs_inode odir, oname, fs_inode ndir,
                    nname);
int      fs_unlink(fs_info, fs_inode dir, name);
```

Bibliography

General

Be Development Team. *The Be Developer's Guide*. Sebastopol, CA: O'Reilly, 1997.

Comer, Douglas. The ubiquitous B-tree. *Computing Surveys* 11(2), June 1979.

Folk, Michael, Bill Zoellick, and Greg Riccardi. *File Structures*. Reading, MA: Addison-Wesley, 1998.

Kleiman, S. Vnodes: An architecture for multiple file system types in Sun Unix. In *Proceedings of the 1986 Summer Usenix Conference*, 1986.

McKusick, M., K. Bostic, et al. *The Design and Implementation of the 4.4 BSD Operating System*. Reading, MA: Addison-Wesley, 1996.

Stallings, William. *Operating Systems: Internals and Design Principles, Third Edition*. Upper Saddle River, NJ: Prentice Hall, 1998.

Other File Systems

Apple Computer. *Inside Macintosh: Files*. Cupertino, CA: Apple Computer.

Custer, Helen. *Inside the Windows NT File System*. Redmond, WA: Microsoft Press, 1994.

Sweeney, Adam, et al. Scalability in the XFS file system. In *Proceedings of the USENIX 1996 Annual Technical Conference*, January 1996.

File System Organization and Performance

Chen, Peter. A new approach to I/O performance evaluation—self-scaling I/O benchmarks, predicted I/O performance. In *ACM SIGMETRICS, Conference on Measurement and Modeling of Computer Systems*, 1993.

Ganger, Greg, and M. Frans Kaashoek. Embedded inodes and explicit grouping: Exploiting disk bandwidth for small files. In *Proceedings of the Usenix Technical Conference*, pages 1–17, January 1997.

Ganger, Gregory R., and Yale N. Patt. Metadata update performance in file systems. In *Usenix Symposium on Operating System Design and Implementation*, pages 49–60, November 1994.

McKusick, M. K. A fast file system for UNIX. *ACM Transactions on Computer Systems* 2(3):181–197, August 1984.

McVoy, L. W., and S. R. Kleiman. Extent-like performance from a UNIX file system. In *Usenix Conference Proceedings*, winter 1991.

McVoy, Larry, and Carl Staelin. lmbench: Portable tools for performance analysis. In *Proceedings of the 1996 Usenix Technical Conference*, pages 279–295, January 1996. Also available via *http://www.eecs.harvard.edu/~vino/fs-perf/*.

Seltzer, Margo, et al. File system logging versus clustering: A performance comparison. In *Proceedings of the Usenix Technical Conference*, pages 249–264, January 1995.

Smith, Keith A., and Margo Seltzer. A comparison of FFS disk allocation policies. In *Proceedings of the Usenix Technical Conference*, January 1996.

Smith, Keith, and Margo Seltzer. *File Layout and File System Performance*. Technical report TR-35-94. Cambridge, MA: Harvard University. Also available via *http://www.eecs.harvard.edu/~vino/fs-perf/*.

Journaling

Chutani, et al. The Episode file system. In *Usenix Conference Proceedings*, pages 43–60, winter 1992.

Haerder, Theo. Principles of transaction-oriented database recovery. *ACM Computing Surveys* 15(4), December 1983.

Hagmann, Robert. Reimplementing the Cedar file system using logging and group commit. In *Proceedings of the 11th Symposium on Operating Systems Principles*, November 1987.

Hisgen, Andy, et al. *New-Value Logging in the Echo Replicated File System*. Technical report. Palo Alto, CA: DEC Systems Research Center, June 1993.

Rosenblum, Mendel, and John K. Ousterhout. The design and implementation of a log-structured file system. *ACM Transactions on Computer Systems* 10(1):26–52, February 1992.

Attributes, Indexing, and Queries

Giampaolo, Dominic. *CAT-FS: A Content Addressable, Typed File System* (Master's thesis). Worcester, MA: Worcester Polytechnic Institute, May 1993.

Gifford, David K., et al. Semantic file systems. *Operating Systems Review*, pages 15–25, October 1991.

Mackovitch, Mike. *Organization and Extension of an Attribute-Based Naming System* (Master's thesis). Worcester, MA: Worcester Polytechnic Institute, May 1994.

Mogul, Jeffrey. *Representing Information about Files* (PhD thesis). Stanford, CA: Stanford University, September 1983. Technical Report 86-1103.

Sechrest, Stuart. *Attribute-Based Naming of Files*. Technical report CSE-TR-78-91. Ann Arbor, MI: University of Michigan Department of Electrical Engineering and Computer Science, January 1991.

Sechrest, Stuart, and Michael McClennen. Blending hierarchical and attribute-based file naming. In *Proceedings of the 12th International Conference on Distributed Systems*, pages 572–580, 1992.

Index